EDUGORILLA
PUBLICATION

JAIIB

Principles and Practices of Banking

Latest Edition
Practice Kit

05 Tests
05 Mock Test

Based On Real Exam Pattern

✓ Thoroughly Revised and Updated

✓ Detailed Analysis of all MCQs

<table>
<tr><td>Title</td><td>: JAIIB Principles and Practices of Banking</td></tr>
<tr><td>Author Name</td><td>: Mr. Rohit Manglik</td></tr>
<tr><td>Published By</td><td>: EduGorilla Community Pvt. Ltd.</td></tr>
<tr><td>Publishers Address</td><td>: 12/651, First Floor Opp. Arvindo Park, Near Jama Masjid,
Indira Nagar, Lucknow, Uttar Pradesh-226016, India</td></tr>
</table>

Copyright EduGorilla

Disclaimer EduGorilla

Compiled and created by EduGorilla Community Pvt. Ltd

Printed By EduGorilla Community Pvt. Ltd.

ROHIT MANGLIK
CEO, EduGorilla

Dear Applicants,

People say *"Success comes to those who work hard."* But I've seen people working hard for their exams day in and day out for marginal success. While others succeed in their examinations by putting in just half the work. So are they God Gifted? No! I believe that it's because they work *smart* and not just *hard*. Similarly, for your exams, you should strategize your preparation so as to increase the likelihood of success. Well with EduGorilla get ready to increase your *chances of selection* in your exam by *16x*.

EduGorilla helps you in not only working *hard* but also working in a *smart and strategic* manner. With EduGorilla's preparation package, you get a chance to make your exam preparation easy, and a fun learning path towards selection. Finding the right path to your preparations can be difficult if you don't know in which direction to head. Don't worry, we have you covered! EduGorilla will be your guide to success in your journey. With our Preparation Package, you can prepare strategically and beat the exam in just one attempt.

EduGorilla's Preparation Package includes-

• **Test Series**   • **Books**

Our preparation package is handcrafted as per the latest changes, expert opinions, and students' discretion. Thus, enabling you to get through each stage of the selection process for your exam.

Our Books are designed by the teachers and experts of the respective exam with a combined 150+ years of experience; to provide you with easy, efficient, and effective learning. Our books are smart, in the sense that not only do they give you the answers to the questions but also provide similar questions for practice.

EduGorilla's competent Test Series gives you real-time experience and confidence through which you can clear your offline or online exam in just one attempt. We currently host 83,000+ mock tests for 1,440+ competitive and academic exams.

Thus, EduGorilla misses no chance to assist you in your preparation and covers all stages of the exam, so that you don't have to look anywhere else.

We provide complete preparation packages for defense, banking, teaching, and other National & State-Level exams. Hence, it doesn't matter which exam you aspire to because you will reach your success.

ALL THE BEST !
Let EduGorilla be your Guide to Success.

Rohit Manglik,
Founder and CEO, EduGorilla

INTRODUCTION

EduGorilla focuses on guiding students to succeed in their examinations. With that in mind, our book, titled "JAIIB : Principles and Practices of Banking", has been drafted through the collective efforts of our distinguished experts with 150+ years of combined experience. This book consists of questions that are created following the latest changes in the syllabus and exam pattern. We compiled the book on the basis of questions that are most likely to appear in the JAIIB Exam. Through EduGorilla's "JAIIB : Principles and Practices of Banking" your chances of success will increase 16x.

EduGorilla does this through our Complete Preparation Package. This package consists of well-conceptualized and structured content in the form of questions that are tailor-made according to your needs and will help you practice for exams in a smart way by pinpointing all the necessary information. It also provides hints and solutions, along with a smart answer sheet for your self-evaluation. You can assess your shortcomings and work accordingly on areas that may require more of your attention.

EduGorilla promises to help you succeed in your examination and accomplish your dream goals. We believe in our aspirants and see them at the top of the merit list. And the first step towards the top is to start preparing with us. EduGorilla's "JAIIB : Principles and Practices of Banking" includes the following attributes.

➤ Well-Researched Content

➤ Top-Notch Quality

➤ Detailed Answers and Analysis

➤ Smart Answer Sheet

➤ Exam Relevant Questions

Therefore, EduGorilla fortifies your preparation and makes it durable enough to help you stand tall and beat the examination.

JAIIB Exam

Scan QR code for Eligibility, Exam Pattern, Syllabus and more.

Book ID: 0706

TABLE OF CONTENTS

Q.1 The main function of an Asset Management Company is to:

A. Hold the securities of various schemes

B. Manage the funds by making investments in various types of securities

C. Hold its property for the benefit of the unit holders

D. Act on behalf of SEBI

Q.2 Account payee crossing is a direction to ________.

A. Collecting Bank

B. Paying Bank

C. Drawer Bank

D. None of the above

Q.3 Currency notes and coins are called as:

A. Flat money

B. Legal tenders

C. Fiat money

D. Both (B) and (C)

Q.4 Can a locker be rent to a minor?

A. Yes

B. No

C. Varies from bank to bank

D. Depends on the mangers authority

Q.5 Every about (above 18 years) of our country should have a bank account as recommended by Nachiket Mor Committee. This account will be known as:

A. Universal transfer Bank Account

B. Universal Electronic Bank Account

C. Universal credit Bank Account

D. Universal saving Bank Account

Q.6 What is the full form of BBPS?

A. Bharat Bill Payment Secure

B. Bharat Board Payment System

C. Bharat Bill Permanent System

D. Bharat Bill Payment System

Q.7 Which among the following is an unsecured money market instrument issued in the form of a promissory note?

A. Treasury Bill

B. Commercial Paper

C. Government Security

D. Participatory Note

Q.8 The institution that accepts deposits for lending purposes is known as:

A. Commercial Bank

B. Central Bank

C. Insurer

D. Company

Q.9 Under the new provision a new domestic company incorporated on or after 1 October 2019 making fresh investment in manufacturing and commences their production on or before 31 March, 2023, will have to pay income tax at rate of only?

A. 22%   **B.** 25.17%   **C.** 15%   **D.** 25%

Q.10 When an unlisted company issues fresh securities (in primary market) for the first time, it is called:

A. Initial Public Offering

B. Rights issue

C. Follow-on public offering

D. Bonus shares

Q.11 The data/information provided by a credit information company to member banks is called

A. Credit Information Report (CIR)

B. Credit Report

C. Confidential Report

D. Confidential Credit Report (CCR)

Q.12 What is the cost of credit expressed as a percentage on a yearly basis called?

A. APR

B. APY

C. WPI

D. None of these

Q.13 Recently RBI has altered in the name of "IDFC Bank Limited" in the Second Schedule to the Reserve Bank of India Act, 1934. What is the new name of IDFC Bank Limited?

A. IDFC INDIA Bank Limited

B. IDFC LAST Bank Limited

C. IDFC FIRST Bank Limited

D. IDFC Bank

Q.14 Which of the following option/s is/ are correct about the PM-KISAN Scheme?

A. PM KISAN is a Central Sector Scheme with 100% funding from Government of India.

B. Under the scheme an income support of Rs.6000/- per year in three equal instalments.

C. Schemes comes under the Ministry of Agriculture & Farmers Welfare.

D. All of the above

Q.15 In Pradhan Mantri Jan-Dhan Yojana (PMJDY), What is the revised age limit for availing of OD facility?

A. 18-60 years

B. 18-65 years

C. 21-60 years

D. 21-65 years

Q.16 What is the main theme of expanded coverage of PMJDY 2.0?

A. Every Household to Every Unbanked Adult

B. Every household to every individual

C. Every household to every person

D. Every person to every adult

Q.17 Which of the following statements is/are correct Basic Savings Bank Deposit Account (BSBDA)?

A. Deposit of cash at bank branch as well as ATMs/CDMs

B. This account shall not have the requirement of any minimum balance

C. No charge will be levied for non-operation/activation of in-operative 'Basic Savings Bank Deposit Account'

D. All of the above

Q.18 The Financial Stability Reports are published by the __________.

A. SEBI

B. RBI

C. IRDAI

D. Ministry of finance

Q.19 What is the new cash withdrawal limit at Points of Sale (PoS) devices?

A. Cash withdrawal to ₹ 500/- per day in Tier I and II centers and ₹ 1,000/- per day in Tier III to VI centers

B. Cash withdrawal to ₹ 1000/- per day in Tier I and II centers and ₹ 2,000/- per day in Tier III to VI centers

C. Cash withdrawal to ₹ 2000/- per day in Tier I and II centers and ₹ 5,000/- per day in Tier III to VI centers

D. Cash withdrawal to ₹ 5000/- per day in Tier I and II centres and ₹ 10,000/- per day in Tier III to VI centres

Q.20 A loan account is required to be classified as special mention account – 2 (SMA-2) where the principal or interest is overdue for a period ___ as per RBI guidelines on Framework for revitalizing distressed assets.

A. up to 30 days

B. between 31st to 60th day

C. between 61st to 90 day

D. 91st day onwards

Q.21 Government's approval to extend the benefits of Interest Subvention at 2% and Prompt Repayment Incentive (PRI) at __________ to fisheries and animal husbandry farmers to meet their working capital needs under the KCC scheme.

A. 2%

B. 3%

C. 5%

D. 7%

Q.22 Which of the following e-banking service is based in voice processing facility?

A. Tele banking

B. Any where banking

C. Any time banking

D. Universal banking

Q.23 POA (Power of attorney) is a stamped document and it is executed in the presence of__________.

A. a gazetted officer.

B. magistrate of the court.

C. notary of the public.

D. All of the above.

Q.24 The payment of foreign trade is related with__________.

A. The merits of import

B. The merits of export

C. The multiplier of foreign trade

D. Balance of payment

Q.25 Monetary control is exercised through __________.

A. cash reserve ratio

B. statutory liquidity ratio

C. Both (A) and (B)

D. None of these

Q.26 Which of the following option is correct about that most of the companies begin the process of establishing organizational ethics programs by developing?

A. Ethics training programs by company

B. Codes of conduct

C. Ethics enforcement mechanisms

D. Hidden agendas of a company

Q.27 When the banker received deposits from the customer, then the banker becomes __________ of the customer.

A. Debtor

B. Creditor

C. Bailee

D. Trustee

Q.28 How much court fees is charged in Lok Adalats?

A. Rs. 10000

B. Rs. 1000 per 1 Lakh

C. Rs. 100 per 1 Lakh

D. No court fees charged

Q.29 A bailment of goods as a security for payment of a debt or performance of a promise is known as___.

A. pledge

B. hypothecation

C. assignment

D. mortgage

Q.30 Which of the following is done on movable property?

A. Assignment

B. Hypothecation

C. Mortgage

D. None of the above

Q.31 Primary dealers mainly deal in __________.

A. government securities

B. shares and mutual fund units

C. private securities

D. None of these

Q.32 Transfer of an interest in a specific immovable property, for the purpose of securing an existing or future debt, is known as:

A. Pledge

B. Hypothecation

C. Mortgage

D. Assignment

Q.33 In the Public Provident Fund account, How many nominees can be?

A. 1

B. 2

C. 4

D. 1 or more than 1

Q.34 What is the total priority sector (PSL) target for small finance bank?

A. 75% of Adjusted Net Bank Credit

B. 75% of total outstanding

C. 40% of Adjusted Net Bank Credit

D. 40% of total outstanding

Q.35 What is the foreclosure charges/pre-payment penalties on any floating rate term loan sanctioned for purposes other than business, to individual borrowers by banks?

A. 1% of total due interest amount

B. 2% of due interest amount

C. 1% of total outstanding amount

D. No any charge or penalty imposed

Q.36 In corporate Hedging, which of the following types of risks can be covered?

A. Liquidity risk

B. Currency risk

C. Credit risk

D. Transaction risk

Q.37 Financial institutions can be categorized under which one of the following?

A. Banking Institutions

B. Non-Banking Financial Institutions

C. Both (A) and (B)

D. None of the above

Q.38 The monthly pension would be available to the subscriber, and after him to his spouse and after their death, the pension corpus, as accumulated at _______ of the subscriber, would be returned to the nominee of the subscriber.

A. 40 years   **B.** 55 years   **C.** 60 years   **D.** 65 years

Q.39 Issue and servicing of government debt is managed by __________ .

A. RBI   **B.** Commercial banks

C. E- banking   **D.** None of these

Q.40 What is the full form of CGTMSE?

A. Credit Guarantee Fund Trust for Micro and Small Enterprises

B. Credit Guarantee Fund Trust for Medium and Small Enterprises

C. Card Guarantee Fund Trust for Micro and Small Enterprises

D. Credit Guarantee Fund Trust for Micro, Small and Medium Enterprises

Q.41 The interest rate of on saving bank accounts has been decided by:

A. RBI

B. Government of India

C. Ministry of finance

D. Bank themselves

Q.42 A saving account as well as current account, there are no transactions in the account for over a period of two years, it is treated as

A. freeze account.

B. dormant account.

C. unclaimed deposit account.

D. partially freeze account.

Q.43 How much amount will be provided by NITI Aayog to every district to encourage a digital payment system?

A. Rs 1 lakh   **B.** Rs 2 lakh

C. Rs 5 lakh   **D.** Rs 10 lakh

Q.44 What is the limitation period for lodging the complaint from the date of cause of action in the Consumer Protection Act, 1986?

A. 2 years   **B.** 3 years

C. 12 months   **D.** 30 days

Q.45 Credit Guarantee Fund Trust for Micro and Small Enterprises (CGTMSE) set up by

A. Government of India.

B. RBI & SIDBI.

C. Government of India and SIDBI.

D. Ministry of finance.

Q.46 The complainant should accept the award within how many days of receipt of the copy of the award?

A. 15 days   **B.** 30 days   **C.** 45 days   **D.** 60 days

Q.47 Urban Cooperative Banks are controlled by:

A. RBI   **B.** State Governments

C. Both the above   **D.** None of these

Q.48 The major suppliers of trading instruments in capital markets are_______.

A. Individuals

B. Instrumental Corporations

C. Manufacturing Corporations

D. Government and Corporations

Q.49 Subscriber of Atal Pension Yojana (APY) would receive the fixed pension of:

A. Rs. 1000 per month   **B.** Rs. 2000 per month

C. Rs. 5000 per month   **D.** All of the above

Q.50 Reserve Bank of India has framed which of the following scheme to the utilization of the unclaimed deposit amount received by the banks and financial institutions?

A. Depositor Education and Awareness Fund (DEAF)

B. Financial inclusion fund scheme

C. Investor Education and Protection Fund (IEPF)

D. There is no any scheme about it, RBI transfer it to GOI

Q.51 If an account is a red-flagged account, it will indicate:

A. Potential Non-Performing Assets

B. Willful defaulter

C. Fraud prone

D. Loss account

Q.52 Lahiri Committee Recommendation relates to which of the following?

A. Issue of units by Mutual Funds

B. Issue of Depository Receipts

C. Issue of Participation Certificates by Banks

D. Issue of Participatory notes by FIIs

Q.53 Banks have over a long period of time, been using electronic and telecommunication networks for delivering a wide range of value-added products and services. The delivery channels are used for anytime banking, anywhere bank home banking, internet banking, mobile banking, e-commerce, ATMs, easy access to the World Wide Web (WWW). The increasing attractiveness of internet banking can be attributed to several factors. E-banking delivers new services through additional capabilities, but these services themselves carry new risks. These risks can be characterized by the velocity of innovation in technological change and attendant customer service. Read the case let and answer-

Which type of risk a bank is Prone to, through Internet Banking?

A. The major driving force behind the rapid spread of e-banking is its acceptance as an extremely cost-effective delivery channel. The channel has also brought about a new orientation to risks viz., operational risk (transactional risk) security risk/ reputational risk (negative public

opinion)/legal risk [money laundering risk/cross border risk/ strategic risk and other risks like credit-liquidity-interest rate-market risks.

E-banking removes the traditional geographical barriers through the internet. However, the internet is not an unmixed blessing to the banking sector. The various limited number of risks are inaccurate processing of transactions / crackers-hackers /infringing customer's privacy/risk of customer's account accessibility.

B.

E-banking has enabled banks and other financial institutions to increase the use of internet banking for the receipt and delivery of their products and services. The only and main risk is exposure to money laundering resulting in legal punishments for non-compliance with Know Your Customer (KYC) rules of RBI.

C.

D. None of the above

Q.54 CGTMSE shall cover credit facilities (Fund based and/or Nonfund based) extended by Regional Rural Banks (RRBs) to a single eligible borrower in the Micro and Small Enterprises sector for a credit facility:

A. Not exceeding ₹50 lakh

B. Not exceeding ₹100 lakh

C. Not exceeding ₹200 lakh

D. Not exceeding ₹10 lakh

Q.55 The system of marketing information is ______ that pertains to marketing.

A. the structure of people, equipment and procedures for generation and processing of information

B. the software used for collection of information

C. the computer hardware which is used for handling database

D. the set of inputs to collate the information

Q.56 Foreign exchange control in India is administered by:

A. FEDAI **B.** RBI

C. EXIM Bank **D.** IBA

Q.57 Mutual Funds are regulated in India by ______.

A. IRDA **B.** AMFI

C. NABARD **D.** SEBI

Q.58 A cheque payable to Mr. William is endorsed by him in blank and delivered to Mr. Jhon. adds the following above the blank endorsement made by Mr. William "pay Saji Sharma or order" and handed over the cheque to Saji Sharma. Which of the following statement is correct about it?

A. The cheque is rendered invalid as there is a material alteration.

B. Mr. Jhon is only liable if the cheque is dishonored.

C. All the parties are liable because it is misrepresentation.

D. The cheque is valid and Mr. Jhon incurs no liability as an endorser.

Q.59 The rate of interest payable by banks to the depositors/claimants on the unclaimed interest bearing deposit amount transferred to the fund shall be

A. 4% simple interest per annum.

B. 3.5% simple interest per annum.

C. 6% interest per annum.

D. 4% compound interest per annum.

Q.60 Authorized dealers in India maintain foreign currency accounts with their correspondent banks abroad. In their mutual communication Ads in India call these accounts as:

A. Vostro **B.** Nostro **C.** Loro **D.** Forex

Q.61 Assured return or guaranteed monthly income plans are essential in:

A. Hybrid funds **B.** Growth Funds

C. Debt/Income funds **D.** Sector funds

Q.62 Risk on account of possible default by the borrower in meeting his commitment. It is known as:

A. Market Risk **B.** Legal Risk

C. Credit Risk **D.** Operational Risk

Q.63 Which of the following is designed to ensure that banks build up capital buffer during the normal times which can be used if losses are incurred during a stress period?

A. Capital Adequacy Ratio

B. Market Discipline

C. Supervisory Review Process

D. Capital Conservation Buffer

Q.64 In which of the following owner (Buyer) has the right to purchase and the seller has the obligation to sell, a specified number of instruments at a specified rate during the time prior to the expiry date?

A. Forward contract **B.** Future contract

C. Put option **D.** Call option

Q.65 Who among the following announces EXIM policy in India?

A. RBI

B. FEDAI

C. Ministry of Commerce

D. Ministry of Finance

Q.66 In case of default in maintenance of CRR requirement on a daily basis which is currently 95 percent of the total CRR requirement, penal interest will be recovered for that day at the rate of:

A. 2 percent per annum

B. 3 percent per annum

C. 4 percent per annum

D. 5 percent per annum

Q.67 Which of the following statement is/are correct about the P-Notes?

I. An instrument issued by a registered foreign institutional investor (FII) to an overseas investor who wishes to invest in Indian stock markets without registering themselves with the market regulator.

II. SEBI permitted foreign institutional investors to register and participate in the Indian stock market.

A. Only I **B.** Only II

C. Both I and II **D.** None of the above

Q.68 What are the minimum and maximum maturity period of government dated securities?

A. 7 days to 364 days
B. 7 days to 10 years
C. 1 year to 20 years
D. 91 days to less than one year

Q.69 Who is the regulator of commodity exchange in India?
A. FMC   **B.** RBI   **C.** IRDAI   **D.** SEBI

Q.70 Multi Commodity Exchange of India Limited (MCX), India's first listed exchange is dealing with the:
A. Equity shares
B. Equity future contract
C. Commodity future contract
D. Commodity forward contract

Q.71 _________ is when a company buys a debt or invoice from another company.
A. Securitization   **B.** Factoring
C. Forfeiting   **D.** Take out finance

Q.72 In which type of banking, electronic financial transactions are done?
A. E-Banking   **B.** POS Banking
C. M-Banking   **D.** Universal Banking

Q.73 What is the limitation period for filing complaint with the banking ombudsman from the date of the receipt of reply from the bank?
A. Six months from the date of receipt of reply.
B. One year from the date of receipt of reply
C. One year six months from the date of receipt of reply.
D. 2 years from the date of receipt of the reply.

Q.74 As per the Reserve Bank guideline, the working hour for non-cash transactions is to be extended up to hours(s) before the closing hours of the bank.
A. 1   **B.** 2
C. half an hour   **D.** one and half hour

Q.75 The form of ethics that endeavors to help professionals decide what to do when they are confronted with a case or situation that raises an ethical question or moral problem is referred to as
A. business ethics.
B. organizational ethics
C. professional ethics
D. code of conduct

Q.76 Which of the following insurance cover any loss or damage to goods in transit by rail, sea, road, air or post?
A. Travel Insurance
B. Property Insurance
C. General Insurance
D. Marine Cargo Insurance

Q.77 Mutual Funds Units of___________ must be listed on the stock exchange.
A. sector funds   **B.** arbitrage funds
C. close ended funds   **D.** liquid funds

Q.78 Risk on account of trading in securities is known as:

A. Credit Risk   **B.** Market Risk
C. Operational Risk   **D.** Legal Risk

Q.79 What is the first stage of Idea Screening?
A. New product development
B. Product pricing
C. Product modification
D. Product promotion

Q.80 A customer wants to subscribe to a magazine published in London. The exchange rate for the draft will be______.
A. TT buying   **B.** TT selling
C. Bills buying   **D.** Bills selling

Q.81 Which of the following is a form of trade finance involving discounting of export bills receivables such as drafts drawn under LC, bills of exchange, promissory notes, or other instruments on without recourse basis?
A. Forfaiting
B. Letter of Undertaking
C. Bill of lading
D. Factoring

Q.82 A cash credit account will become NPA if it _______.
A. remains out of order for more than 90 days
B. stock statement not submitted for 60 days
C. account not reviewed for 3 months
D. All of the above

Q.83 RBI has the sole right to issue Bank Note as per_______.
A. Section 22 of the RBI Act 1934
B. Section 21 of the RBI Act 1934
C. Section 20 of the RBI Act 1934
D. Section 19 of the RBI Act 1934

Q.84 Leasing, hire purchase and bill discounting are the domain of
A. Commercial banks.
B. Mutual funds.
C. Non-Banking Finance Companies.
D. None of the above

Q.85 The principal regulator for Stock Exchanges in India is:
A. RBI   **B.** SEBI
C. HDFC   **D.** None of these

Q.86 Which of the following is not a pillar in Basel –II?
A. Minimum Capital Requirement
B. Supervisory Review Process
C. Market Discipline
D. Risk-Weighted Asset

Q.87 According to BCBS, Basel norms are-
A. mandatory in nature.
B. voluntary in nature.
C. at the discretion of the central bank.
D. Neither (A) nor (B)

Q.88 In the USA and UK, the banking regulators is/are_____
A. Federal Reserve Board.

B. Bank of England.

C. Both (A) and (B)

D. None of these

Q.89 Which of the following foreign exchange transaction is a capital account transaction?

A. Encashment of TC by a foreign tourist.

B. Issuance of a foreign TC to a person in India for visit abroad.

C. Payment of import or export bills relating to merchandise.

D. Subscription of share capital by a foreign institution in an Indian company.

Q.90 The Central Board of Directors of RBI comprises______

A. One Governor.

B. Four Deputy Governors.

C. Fifteen Directors.

D. All of the above

Q.91 Nowadays due to increased competition, the businesses became _______ driven.
(i) Customer
(ii) Market
(iii) Money

A. (i) and (ii)

B. (i) and (iii)

C. (ii) and (iii)

D. (i), (ii) and (iii)

Q.92 A document which reads as follows: "I acknowledge receipt of Rs. 2000 from Raman. This amount will be paid on demand" is a ___

A. bill of exchange.

B. promissory note.

C. cheque.

D. ambiguous instrument.

Q.93 The system which is used for electronically paying dividends to the company to a large no. of its shareholders including the small amounts?

A. ECS - Debit

B. ECS - Credit

C. ECS - Automatic

D. ECS - Suspense

Q.94 What will happen if a cheque is written in different handwritings and different inks?

A. Shall be Paid

B. Shall be not Paid

C. As per different bank policies

D. None of these

Q.95 Mr. A has invested in ABC bank share since the IPO issue. He and his family members have 4000 shares of ABC bank whose present market value is Rs. 3 Lakh (approx). As the share price is low he does not want to dispose the shares and instead he has approached in ABC bank for availing loan against the shares. What will be course of action of ABC bank?

A. Sanction loan after getting permission from SEBI.

B. Advances against ABC bank's own shares is restricted as per Banking Regulation Act.

C. Sanction loan after getting permission from RBI.

D. ABC bank can sanction loan against its own shares after a haircut.

Q.96 Sanjay draws a cheque payable to Suresh or bearer which is lost by Suresh. It is found by Satish. The holder of cheque is______.

A. Satish

B. Suresh

C. Any bearer

D. There cannot be any holder in a lost cheque

Q.97 The third pillar of BASEL-II Accord is known as ______.

A. Market Discipline

B. Stare Decisis

C. Exchange Control

D. Blue Sky Law

Q.98 New and reissuable notes are stored in ________ maintained by banks as of RBI.

A. currency chests

B. agents

C. Both the above

D. None of these

Q.99 Cash Reserve Ratio (CRR) refers to:

A. The ratio of cash holding to reserves of banks

B. The share of Net Demand and time liabilities (NDTL) that banks have to hold as liquid assets

C. The share of Net Demand and time liabilities (NDTL) that banks have to hold as part of their cash reserves

D. The share of Net Demand and time liabilities (NDTL) that banks have to hold as balances with the RBI

Q.100 What does justice as an ethical principle aims for?

A. Guides to do what is good.

B. Ethical decisions should be consistent with ethical theory.

C. Allow people to reign over themselves.

D. A person should choose to do the least harm.

Q.101 A thief steals a cheque & transfers it to a shopkeeper who accepts it towards payment of goods sold to him, without having any reason to believe that it was a stolen cheque. The shopkeeper gets a title to the cheque while the thief was not having the same. This is based on the principle

A. a thief cannot have a title.

B. consideration is a contract.

C. negotiability of a cheque.

D. None of the above

Q.102 Where a suspicion of fraudulent activity is thrown up by the presence of one or more Early Warning Signals in a loan account, it is called

A. willful default account.

B. red-flagged account.

C. non-cooperative borrower account.

D. special mention account.

Q.103 Which body notifies place of deposit of the title deed for the purpose of creation of equitable mortgage?

A. Central Government

B. Munincipality

C. State Government

D. None of these

Q.104 Mr. Raghu draws a cheque in favor of Damodar. However, before he could hand over it to Damodar, he died in a car accident. Who is the holder of the cheque?

A. Mr. Raghu **B.** Raghu's legal heirs
C. Damodar **D.** None of the above

Q.105 The color of dynamism, an organization, responsive to market conditions and customer needs:

A. Orange **B.** Blue **C.** Grey **D.** White

Q.106 Which of the following is known as the bank wire?

A. It is used primarily for transferring reserves account balances of the depository institution and government securities high-value domestic deposit, bank to bank, and third party transfer such as interbank overnight funds sales and purchase.

B. It is the pioneer private sector electronic telecommunication network owned by an association of banks in the USA.

C. It is used at retailer's sites for making direct payments by customer electronically.

D. It is the pioneer private sector electronic telecommunication network owned by an association of banks in London.

Q.107 The MD of a Pvt Ltd company endorses a cheque payable to the company in his favour & wants you to collect the same in his personal account. You will

A. allow after verifying the genuineness of endorsement.

B. allow only after verifying the genuineness of the transaction.

C. not allowed as the Bank may be liable for conversion.

D. not allowed as cheque favouring a company cannot be endorsed.

Q.108 Direction: For the given term which statement is true?

Ethics of duty – categorical imperatives

(i) Universality - I ought never to act except in such a way as I can also will that my maxim should become a universal law Human Dignity - Act in such a way that you always treat humanity. Never simply as a means, but always at the same time as an end.

(ii) Universality – I ought to always act in a way that will allow me to act within the universal law of Human Dignity – Act in such a way that you never treat humanity's means as an end.

A. Only (i) **B.** Only (ii)
C. Either (i) or (ii) **D.** Both (i) and (ii)

Q.109 When did insurance begin in Babylon?

A. 1750 BC **B.** 1907 BC
C. 1971 BC **D.** 2000 BC

Q.110 In a gilt fund, the mutual funds make an investment in

A. Government Securities.
B. Corporate Securities.
C. Corporate Debt.
D. Government and Corporate Debt.

Q.111 Who is the regulator of money market in India?

A. RBI **B.** SEBI **C.** IRDAI **D.** PFRDA

Q.112 To calculate Net NPA, which of the following is required to be deducted from Gross NPA?

(i) Balance held in no lien account.

(ii) DICGC/ECGC claims received and held, pending adjustment.

(iii) Part payment received and kept in no lien account.

(iv) Total provisions held (excluding amount of technical write off and provision on standard assets)

A. i and ii **B.** i, ii and iii only
C. ii, iii and iv only **D.** ii and iv only

Q.113 ABC Bank as a collecting banker represented cheques through clearing to XYZ bank and the cheque bears a special crossing of two banks, In this case, what will you do?

A. Paying bank will pay the bank whose name first in special crossing
B. Payment in due course, pay either ABC bank or XYZ bank
C. Check is invalid
D. Return the cheque with remarks that crossed to two banks

Q.114 An establishment having its shop just opposite the New Delhi railway station is authorized by RBI to purchase & sell foreign traveler cheques & foreign currency notes from/to the foreign tourist. This is known as________.

A. Authorized Dealer
B. Authorized Money Changer
C. Authorized Authority
D. Money Changer

Q.115 Funds and securities pay-in and pay-out are settled on

A. T+5 day. **B.** T+1 day.
C. T+2 day. **D.** T+7 day.

Q.116 The process of maintenance of account books, discounting of bills, and collection of bills on due date by a person other than the seller is called

A. securitization. **B.** factoring.
C. forfeiting. **D.** take out finance.

Q.117 Mr. ABC an employee of your branch colluded with customer A and defrauded the bank for Rs.9000/- which came to light when the original customer B reported non-withdrawal of the same. what action will be taken?

A. Ask Mr. ABC to make good the loss of Rs. 9000/- to Mr.B.
B. Advise B to make a complaint at police station.
C. Request B to co-operate with the enquiry and report the matter in details with your observation and recommendation to higher authority .
D. You conclude it as fraud and lodge FIR in local police station.

Q.118 In Mutual Fund, Investment objective is closely linked to ________.

A. scheme **B.** option **C.** plan **D.** SIP

Q.119 The assets of the mutual fund are held by _____.
A. AMC **B.** Trustees
C. Custodian **D.** Registrar

Q.120 Investors' KYC details are stored in the server of ____.
A. AMC **B.** AMFI **C.** SEBI **D.** KRA

// Smart Answer Sheet //

Correct   Indicates percentage of students who answered questions correctly.

Skipped   Indicates percentage of students who skipped questions.

Q.	Ans.	Correct	Skipped	Q.	Ans.	Correct	Skipped	Q.	Ans.	Correct	Skipped	Q.	Ans.	Correct	Skipped	Q.	Ans.	Correct	Skipped
1	B	61.46 %	4.41 %	17	D	64.81 %	16.91 %	33	D	41.58 %	16.7 %	49	D	56.73 %	21.96 %	65	C	26.64 %	24.7 %
2	A	28.6 %	10.08 %	18	B	49.43 %	17.78 %	34	A	27.6 %	19.22 %	50	A	54.8 %	22.16 %	66	B	22.85 %	25.01 %
3	D	36.86 %	11.33 %	19	B	20.78 %	13.56 %	35	D	24.35 %	20.29 %	51	C	27.24 %	20.77 %	67	C	43.84 %	25.73 %
4	B	71.18 %	12.31 %	20	C	40.6 %	14.58 %	36	A	19.7 %	19.64 %	52	D	22.92 %	20.55 %	68	C	11.0 %	25.48 %
5	B	32.91 %	13.61 %	21	B	39.79 %	15.62 %	37	C	37.97 %	21.01 %	53	A	22.02 %	23.1 %	69	A	21.38 %	25.42 %
6	D	45.0 %	13.63 %	22	A	61.68 %	17.69 %	38	C	54.86 %	21.38 %	54	A	24.3 %	23.04 %	70	C	29.46 %	25.94 %
7	B	44.38 %	14.28 %	23	D	43.62 %	15.15 %	39	A	64.45 %	21.33 %	55	A	47.49 %	22.19 %	71	B	29.78 %	22.65 %
8	A	59.88 %	14.68 %	24	D	46.63 %	17.49 %	40	A	48.93 %	21.42 %	56	B	36.15 %	23.03 %	72	A	48.21 %	23.32 %
9	C	34.29 %	16.02 %	25	C	69.34 %	19.16 %	41	D	53.35 %	19.38 %	57	D	45.94 %	24.01 %	73	B	28.58 %	25.31 %
10	A	67.63 %	15.5 %	26	B	40.84 %	19.7 %	42	B	67.26 %	20.57 %	58	D	38.26 %	23.82 %	74	A	35.51 %	25.89 %
11	A	59.8 %	15.69 %	27	A	46.41 %	17.27 %	43	C	39.41 %	20.29 %	59	B	34.37 %	23.09 %	75	A	16.82 %	26.44 %
12	A	44.99 %	15.96 %	28	D	48.67 %	18.71 %	44	A	13.63 %	21.23 %	60	B	34.08 %	22.09 %	76	D	25.26 %	25.48 %
13	C	58.7 %	15.05 %	29	A	43.26 %	17.92 %	45	C	35.96 %	20.03 %	61	C	28.31 %	23.77 %	77	C	21.38 %	26.2 %
14	D	69.1 %	15.96 %	30	B	62.61 %	18.56 %	46	A	22.83 %	21.24 %	62	C	48.75 %	24.34 %	78	B	51.6 %	26.04 %
15	B	40.5 %	16.17 %	31	A	57.05 %	19.04 %	47	C	51.64 %	21.19 %	63	D	23.74 %	24.05 %	79	A	48.85 %	23.46 %
16	A	26.77 %	15.81 %	32	C	54.7 %	18.61 %	48	D	37.26 %	21.87 %	64	D	15.98 %	24.98 %	80	B	17.33 %	24.22 %

Q.	Ans.	Correct		Q.	Ans.	Correct		Q.	Ans.	Correct		Q.	Ans.	Correct		Q.	Ans.	Correct
		Skipped				Skipped				Skipped				Skipped				Skipped
81	A	21.6 %		89	D	27.08 %		97	A	44.05 %		105	A	25.59 %		113	D	29.98 %
		23.99 %				27.54 %				26.91 %				27.69 %				25.37 %
82	A	35.43 %		90	D	59.95 %		98	C	21.48 %		106	B	13.2 %		114	B	22.21 %
		25.49 %				26.9 %				27.07 %				28.39 %				26.69 %
83	A	58.59 %		91	A	23.65 %		99	D	29.4 %		107	C	12.74 %		115	C	32.26 %
		26.37 %				26.88 %				26.35 %				26.26 %				27.17 %
84	C	36.94 %		92	B	44.02 %		100	B	36.78 %		108	A	10.37 %		116	B	30.66 %
		26.16 %				26.9 %				26.27 %				28.18 %				27.68 %
85	B	63.23 %		93	B	35.34 %		101	C	39.38 %		109	A	26.3 %		117	C	37.85 %
		26.37 %				25.25 %				26.83 %				26.11 %				25.06 %
86	D	30.12 %		94	A	36.62 %		102	B	39.56 %		110	A	33.74 %		118	A	25.12 %
		26.73 %				25.88 %				27.54 %				26.71 %				26.22 %
87	B	11.01 %		95	B	40.73 %		103	C	31.13 %		111	A	47.14 %		119	C	16.66 %
		26.79 %				26.74 %				27.44 %				24.43 %				25.31 %
88	C	54.38 %		96	B	16.25 %		104	B	20.56 %		112	D	17.65 %		120	D	23.75 %
		26.99 %				26.07 %				26.83 %				27.1 %				23.54 %

Performance Analysis

Avg. Score (%)	37.0%
Toppers Score (%)	100.0%
Your Score	

//Hints and Solutions//

1. The main function of an Asset Management Company is to manage the funds by making investments in various types of securities.

Asset management is a systematic process of deploying, operating, maintaining, upgrading, and disposing of assets cost-effectively. The term is most commonly used in the financial world to describe people and companies that manage investments on behalf of others.

Hence, the correct option is (B).

2. Account payee crossing is a direction to Collecting Bank. Any bank, other than the remitting bank, that is involved in processing a collection. In collection terminology, the remitting bank is the bank to which the drawer has entrusted the handling of a collection, usually the Drawer's bank of account. The bank that collects money from the account of the writer of a cheque on behalf of the person who has deposited the cheque into the bank. The Collecting bank asked the drawee if the cheque was paid by telephone.

Hence, the correct option is (A).

3. Currency notes and coins are called fiat money. They are also called legal tenders as they cannot be refused by any citizen of the country for payment/discharge of debt.

Currency = Notes + Coins

A fiat currency is a national currency that is not pegged to the price of a commodity such as gold or silver. The value of fiat money is largely based on the public's faith in the currency's issuer, which is normally that country's government or central bank.

Hence, the correct option is (D).

4. There is a nominal annual rent (payable in advance), which depends upon the size of the locker and the center at which the branch is located. However, Lockers are not leased out to minors. At the time of hiring the locker, the bank will obtain a minimum security deposit in the form of FDR from the lessee which will be decided by the bank from time to time.
Hence, the correct option is (B).

5. Every about (above 18 years) of our country should have a bank account as recommended by Nachiket Mor Committee. This account will be known as Universal Electronic Bank Account.

The "Committee on Comprehensive Financial Services for Small Businesses and Low-Income Households" was set up by the RBI in Sep 2013 under the chairmanship of Nachiket Mor, an RBI board member. the Nachiket committee recommends that every adult Indian (18 years and above) resident should be given a universal electronic bank account (UEBA) by Jan 1, 2016.

Hence, the correct answer is (B).

6. The full form of BBPS is Bharat Bill Payment System.

Bharat Bill Payment System (BBPS) is an integrated bill payment system that will enable payment services online or through an offline network. Payment can be made through multiple modes and the users will get instant confirmation.

It offers bill payment services to consumers through the network of agents/retail shops/bank branches and digital channels like - Internet banking of banks, Mobile app of banks, etc. allowing multiple payment modes like Card, UPI, AePS, Wallet, Cash and provides instant confirmation. It will facilitate a less-cash society through the migration of bill payments from cash to electronic channels.

Hence, the correct option is (D).

7. Commercial Paper is an unsecured money market instrument issued in the form of a promissory note.

Commercial Paper:

- It is an unsecured money market instrument issued in the form of a promissory note.

- Corporates, primary dealers (PDs) and the All-India Financial Institutions (FIs) are eligible to issue commercial paper.

- It was introduced in India in 1990 with a view to enabling highly rated corporate borrowers to diversify their sources of short-term borrowings and to provide an additional instrument to investors.

- Yes, all eligible participants shall obtain the credit rating for issuance of Commercial Paper either from Credit Rating Information Services of India Ltd. (CRISI) or the Investment Information and Credit Rating Agency of India Ltd.

Hence, the correct option is (B).

8. The institution that accepts deposits for lending purposes is known as a commercial bank.

The term commercial bank refers to a financial institution that accepts deposits, offers checking account services, makes various loans, and offers basic financial products like certificates of deposit (CDs) and savings accounts to individuals and small businesses.

Hence, the correct option is (A).

9. In order to attract fresh investment in manufacturing and thereby provide a boost to the 'Make-in-India' initiative of the Government, another new provision has been inserted in the Income-tax Act with effect from FY 2019-20 which allows any new domestic company incorporated on or after 1st October 2019 making fresh investment in manufacturing, an option to pay income-tax at the rate of 15%.
Hence, the correct option is (C).

10. The company issues securities for the first time in the primary market, this process is known as an Initial Public Offering (IPO).

The Initial Public Offering is the process by which a private company can go public by sale of its stocks to the general public. After IPO, the company's shares are traded in an open market. Those shares can be further sold by investors through secondary market trading.

Hence, the correct option is (A).

11. A Credit Information Report (CIR) is a report on past repayment performance as reported by various member banks and financial institutions about an individual. It is important that you monitor your Credit Information Report (CIR) from time to time. There are a number of things you can do to improve your credit profile: It provides information on prompt payment, as well as defaulted payments. The Credit Information Report (CIR) additionally has a list of inquiries made on your account by various member banks/financial institutions/NBFCs for the purpose of approving a credit facility.

Hence, the correct option is (A).

12. The term "annual percentage rate (APR)" refers to the annual rate of interest charged to borrowers and paid to investors. APR is expressed as a percentage that represents the actual yearly cost of funds over the term of a loan or income earned on an investment. This includes any fees or additional costs associated with the transaction, but it does not take compounding into account. The APR provides consumers with a bottom-line number they can easily compare with rates from other lenders.

Hence, the correct option is (A).

13. The name of " IDFC Bank Limited " has been changed to "IDFC FIRST Bank Limited" in the Second Schedule to the Reserve Bank of India Act, 1934 with effect from January 12, 2019, by virtue of 'Certificate of Incorporation pursuant to a change of name' issued by the Registrar of Companies, Chennai," it said in a BSE filing. IDFC Bank and non-banking financial company Capital First had announced the completion of their merger on December 18, creating a combined loan asset book of Rs 1.03 lakh crore for the merged entity.
Hence, the correct option is (C).

14. The Pradhan Mantri Kisan Samman Nidhi (PM-KISAN) Scheme, launched by PM Narendra Modi in 2019, aims to provide income support to all landholder farmer families across the country with cultivable land, subject to certain exclusions. Under the Scheme, an amount of Rs 6000 per year is released in three 4-monthly installments of Rs 2000 each directly into the bank accounts of the beneficiaries. All landholding farmers' families, which have cultivable landholding in their names are eligible to get benefits under the scheme.
Hence, the correct option is (D).

15. Pradhan Mantri Jan-Dhan Yojana (PMJDY) is National Mission for Financial Inclusion to ensure access to financial services, namely, basic savings & deposit accounts, remittance, credit, insurance, pension in an affordable manner. Under the scheme, a basic savings bank deposit (BSBD) account can be opened in any bank branch or Business Correspondent (Bank Mitra) outlet, by persons not having any other account.
The age limit for availing of overdraft facility on Jan Dhan accounts has been revised to 18-65 years. A bank account under the financial inclusion scheme Pradhan Mantri Jan Dhan Yojana (PMJDY) can be opened in any bank branch or business correspondent outlet.
Hence, the correct option is (B).

16. In 2018, the government launched PMJDY 2.0 with enhanced features and benefits. Under the new version, the government decided to shift focus from **'Every Household' to 'Every**

Unbanked Adult' and free accidental insurance cover on RuPay cards doubled to Rs 2 lakh for PMJDY accounts opened after August 28, 2018.

Hence, the correct option is (A).

17. -The 'Basic Savings Bank Deposit Account' should be considered a normal banking service available to all.

-This account shall not have the requirement of any minimum balance.

-The following basic minimum facilities will be offered in the BSBD Account, free of charge, without any requirement of minimum balance.

a) The deposit of cash at bank branch as well as ATMs/CDMs.

b) Receipt/ credit of money through any electronic channel or by means of deposit /collection of cheques drawn by Central/State Government agencies and departments.

c) No limit on the number and value of deposits that can be made in a month.

d) Minimum of four withdrawals in a month, including ATM withdrawals.

e) ATM Card or ATM-cum-Debit Card.

- No charge will be levied for non-operation/activation of in-operative 'Basic Savings Bank Deposit Account'.

Hence, the correct option is (D).

18.

- The Financial Stability Reports are bi-annual reports published by the Reserve Bank of India(RBI).
- The report is the collective assessment of the Sub-Committee of the Financial Stability and Development Council (FSDC) on risks to financial stability.
- It reviews the nature, magnitude, and implications of risks that may have a bearing on the macroeconomic environment, financial institutions, markets, and infrastructure.

Hence, the correct option is (B).

19. A reference is invited to the cash withdrawal at PoS devices enabled for all debit cards/open-loop prepaid cards issued by banks. The instructions outlined therein, limit –
• Cash withdrawal to ₹ 1000/- per day in Tier I and II centers and ₹ 2,000/- per day in Tier III to VI centers.
• Customer charges, if any, on such cash withdrawals to not more than 1% of the transaction amount.
Hence, the correct option is (B).

20. A loan account is required to be classified as special mention account – 2 (SMA-2) where the principal or interest is overdue for a period between 61st to 90 days as per RBI guidelines on Framework for revitalizing distressed assets:

SMA Sub-category	Basis for classification
SMA-NF	Non-financial (NF) signals of incipients stress.
SMA-1	The principal or interest payment overdue

	between 31-60 days.
SMA-2	The principal or interest payment overdue between 61-90 days.

Hence, the correct option is (C).

21. The Government has approved to extend the benefits of Interest Subvention at 2% and Prompt Repayment Incentive (PRI) at 3% to fisheries and animal husbandry farmers to meet their working capital needs up to ₹ 2 lakh under the KCC scheme. This also implies that the farmers repaying promptly as above would get short term loans 4% per annum during the years 2018-19 and 2019-20.
Hence, the correct option is (B).

22. The function of telebanking services is based on the voice processing facility available with the bank computers.
Most telephone banking services use an automated phone answering system with phone keypad response or voice recognition capability.
Hence, the correct option is (A).

23. A POA creates a special power of agency that entitles the holder to use the principal's name in the transaction entered. Registration of this document is not compulsory. Power of attorney attracts stamp duty which varies from State to State. It has to be executed in the presence of certain designated officers notary public, a court, consul or vice-consul, or a representative of the Central Government, A gazetted officer, Magistrate of court.

Hence, the correct option is (D).

24. The payment of foreign trade is related to the Balance of payment.

Balance of Payment (BOP) of a country can be defined as a systematic statement of all economic transactions of a country with the rest of the world during a specific period usually one year. The balance of payments includes both the current account and capital account. The current account includes a nation's net trade in goods and services, its net earnings on cross-border investments, and its net transfer payments. The capital account consists of a nation's transactions in financial instruments and central bank reserves. The balance of payments (BOP) summarizes all transactions that a country's individuals, companies, and government bodies complete with individuals, companies, and government bodies outside the country. These transactions consist of imports and exports of goods, services, and capital, as well as transfer payments, such as foreign aid and remittances.

Hence, the correct option is (D).

25. The RBI is the main body that controls the monetary policy in India. They control the flow of money into the market through various instruments of monetary policy. This helps RBI control inflation and liquidity in the economy. **1. Cash Reserve Ratio (CRR):** The Cash Reserve Ratio in India is decided by RBI's Monetary Policy Committee in the periodic Monetary and Credit Policy. The Reserve Bank of India takes stock of the CRR in every monetary policy review, which, at present, is conducted every six weeks. CRR is one of the major weapons in the RBI's arsenal that allows it to maintain a desired level of inflation, control the money supply, and also liquidity in the economy.

2. Statutory Liquidity Ratio

Every bank must have a particular portion of their Net Demand and Time Liabilities (NDTL) in the form of cash, gold, or other liquid assets by the end of the day. The ratio of these liquid assets to the demand and time liabilities is called the Statutory Liquidity Ratio (SLR). The Reserve Bank of India (RBI) has the authority to increase this ratio by up to 40%. An increase in the ratio constricts the ability of the bank to inject money into the economy.

Hence, the correct option is (C).

26. A code of conduct defines how a company's employees should act on a day-to-day basis. It reflects the organization's daily operations, core values, and overall company culture. Yet many companies struggle with how to write a great code of conduct and, as a result, their codes fall short.
Hence, the correct option is (B).

27. When the banker received deposits from the customer, then the banker becomes the debtor of the customer.

The banker accepts money as a deposit from the customer. So, the banker becomes the debtor and the customer becomes the creditor. The only responsibility is to return the amount deposited with the particular interest on demand. The banker can deal with the amount the way he wishes to.

Hence, the correct option is (A).

28. There is no court fee payable when a matter is filed in a Lok Adalat. If a matter pending in the court of law is referred to the Lok Adalat and is settled subsequently, the court fee originally paid in the court on the complaints/petition is also refunded back to the parties. The persons deciding the cases in the Lok Adalats are called the Members of the Lok Adalats, they have the role of statutory conciliators only and do not have any judicial role; therefore they can only persuade the parties to come to a conclusion for settling the dispute outside the court in the Lok Adalat and shall not pressurize or coerce any of the parties to compromise or settle cases or matters either directly or indirectly.
Hence, the correct option is (D).

29. Section 172 states the bailment of goods as security for payment of a debt or performance of a promise is called 'pledge'. The bailor is in this case called the 'pawnor'. The bailee is called 'pawnee'.

Hence, the correct option is (A).

30. 1. Hypothecation is defined under the Securitisation and Reconstruction of Financial Assets and Enforcement of Security Interest Act, 2002 as a charge in or upon any movable property, existing or future, created by a borrower in favor of a secured creditor without delivery of possession.

2. Assignment is a legal term used in the context of the law of contract and of property. In both instances, the assignment is the process whereby a person, the assignor, transfers rights, or benefits to another, the assignee.

3. A mortgage loan or simply mortgage is a loan used either by purchasers of real property to raise funds to buy real estate, or alternatively by existing property owners to raise funds for any purpose while putting a lien on the property being mortgaged.

Hence, the correct option is (B).

31. Primary dealers in the U.S. are a system of banks and broker-dealers authorized by the Federal Reserve System to deal directly in government bonds. Primary government securities dealers must meet specific liquidity and quality requirements. They also provide a valuable flow of information to central banks about the state of worldwide markets.
Hence, the correct option is (A).

32. Transfer of an interest in a specific immovable property, for the purpose of securing an existing or future debt, is known as mortgage.

A mortgage is the transfer of an interest in specific immovable property for the purpose of securing the payment of money advanced or to be advanced by way of loan, an existing or future debt, or the performance of an engagement that may give rise to a pecuniary liability.

Hence, the correct option is (C).

33. Public Provident Fund allows you to nominate more than one person. You can nominate one or more nominees to your Public Provident Fund account if you so wish. The Public Provident Fund account holder has to mention the percentage of share in case the nominee is more than one person. But do remember nomination is not allowed to an account opened on behalf of minors. You can change or cancel the nomination at any point of time during the Public Provident Fund account period, but do note that you cannot nominate a trust to your Public Provident Fund account. But being the nominee does not mean you will be allowed to continue the account. All the nominee gets is the right of ownership in terms of an authority to collect the money on the death of the subscriber and retain the money as a trustee for the benefit of the persons who are entitled to it under the law.

Hence, the correct option is (D).

34. In view of the objective for which a small finance bank will be set up, it will be required to extend 75% of its Adjusted Net Bank Credit (ANBC) to the sectors eligible for classification as priority sector lending (PSL) by RBI. For regional rural banks (RRBs) and small finance banks (SFBs), the PSL target is 75%. The overall PSL target of only urban co-operative banks will go up in a phased manner from the existing target of 40% to 75% by March-end 2024.
Hence, the correct option is (A).

35. It is clarified BY RBI that banks shall not charge foreclosure charges/ pre-payment penalties on any floating rate term loan sanctioned, for purposes other than business, to individual borrowers with or without co-obligant(s).

Hence, the correct option is (D).

36. In corporate Hedging, Liquidity risk can be covered.

Liquidity risk occurs when an individual investor, business, or financial institution cannot meet its short-term debt obligations. Corporate hedging can increase shareholder value in the presence of capital market imperfections such as direct and indirect costs of financial distress.

Hence, the correct answer is (A).

37. Financial institutions can be classified into two categories.

Financial institutions are the intermediaries who facilitate the smooth functioning of the financial system by making investors and borrowers meet. They mobilize savings of the surplus units and allocate them in productive activities promising a better rate of return. Financial institutions can be classified into two categories:

- Banking Institutions: The RBI as the apex institution organizes, runs, supervises, regulates, and develops the monetary system and the financial system of the country.

- Non-Banking Financial Institutions: They help in the overall development of the economy by providing a fillip to transportation, employment generation, wealth creation, bank credit in rural areas, and by supporting the financially weaker sections of the society.

Hence, the correct option is (C).

38. APY provides a guaranteed pension of Rs 1,000 to Rs 5,000 (as explained above) to the subscribers. The scheme also allows a subscriber to decrease or increase pension amount during the course of the accumulation phase, once a year.
In case of death of the subscriber, the spouse of the subscriber shall be entitled to the same amount of pension till his or her death. And after the demise of both spouse and subscriber, the nominee will be entitled to receive the pension money that the subscriber had accumulated till 60 years of age. However, if the subscriber dies before 60 years, the spouse will have the choice to either exit the scheme and claim the accumulated amount or continue maintaining the account under the subscriber's name for the remaining vested years. The spouse of the subscriber shall be entitled to receive the same pension amount as the subscriber until the death of the spouse in the latter case.
Hence, the correct option is (C).

39. The Reserve Bank of India Act, 1934 requires the Central Government to entrust the Reserve Bank with all its money, remittance, exchange, and banking transactions in India and the management of its public debt. The Government also deposits its cash balances with the Reserve Bank. The Reserve Bank may also, by agreement, act as the banker and debt manager to State Governments. The Reserve Bank has well-defined obligations and provides several banking services to the governments. The Reserve Bank acts as an adviser to Government, whenever called upon to do so, on monetary and banking-related matters. The Central Government and State Governments may make rules for the receipt, custody, and disbursement of money from the consolidated fund, contingency fund, and public account. These rules are legally binding on the Reserve Bank as accounts for these funds are with the Reserve Bank.
Hence, the correct option is (A).

40. The Credit Guarantee Fund Trust for Micro and Small Enterprises (CGTMSE) is a trust launched by the Ministry of Micro, Small and Medium Enterprises, Government of India, and the Small Industries Development Bank of India (SIDBI). Launched on 30 August 2000, the primary objective of the CGTMSE scheme is to give credit guarantees to financial institutions that provide

loans to SMEs and MSMEs.
Hence, the correct option is (A).

41. In the past, before RBI had deregulated the savings bank interest rate regime, all banks were offering the same interest rate, which was 4% per annum. Every individual has a Savings Bank account but pays little attention to the interest earned on the balance in this account.

Hence, the correct option is (D).

42. 1. Savings, as well as current accounts, should be treated as **inoperative/dormant** if there are no transactions in the account for over a period of two years. The accounts which have not been operated upon over a period of two years should be segregated and maintained in separate ledgers.

2. An account freeze is an action taken by a bank or brokerage that prevents some transactions from occurring in the account. Typically, any open transactions will be canceled, and checks presented on a frozen account will not be honored. However, the account holder can still deposit money into the account.

3. Unclaimed deposits are deposits where the proceeds/maturity amount has not been claimed for 10 years or more. In other words, term deposits are deemed unclaimed if they are inactive/inoperative for more than 10 years. The same holds good for accounts too.

4. "If the accounts are still KYC non-compliant after six months of imposing initial **'partial freezing'** banks may disallow all debits and credits from/to the accounts, rendering them inoperative," it said. Further, it would "always be open to the bank to close" the account of such customers, the RBI added.

Hence, the correct option is (B).

43. NITI Aayog will provide Rs. 5 lakh for every district in India to encourage a digital payment system. For availing the incentive, the district collector, commissioner or magistrates would have ensured that individuals transiting to digital payment mode should do at least two successful transactions by any of the five methods. These five modes are – unified payment interface (UPI), Unstructured Supplementary Service Data (USSD), Aadhaar Enabled Payments, e-wallets, and Rupay debit/credit/prepaid cards. The top ten best performing districts of India will be awarded the Digital Payment Champions of India Award by NITI Aayog/Government of India. Similarly, the 50 Panchayats which go cashless will be awarded the Digital Payment Award of Honour.

Hence, the correct option is (C).

44. The District Forum has failed to consider the fact that as per Section 24-A of the Consumer Protection Act, 1986 period of limitation to file a complaint is 2 years from the date of cause of action. The District Forum has failed to appreciate the fact that no reason was stated by the respondent for not filing the complaint within the period of limitation.
Hence, the correct option is (A).

45. Availability of bank credit without the hassles of collaterals / third party guarantees would be a major source of support to the first generation entrepreneurs to realise their dream of setting up a unit of their own Micro and Small Enterprise (MSE). Keeping this objective in view, Ministry of Micro, Small & Medium Enterprises (MSME), Government of India launched Credit Guarantee Scheme (CGS) so as to strengthen credit delivery system and facilitate flow of credit to the MSE sector. To operationalise the scheme, Government of India and SIDBI set up the Credit Guarantee Fund Trust for Micro and Small Enterprises (CGTMSE).

Hence, the correct option is (C).

46. An award shall not be binding on a bank against which it is passed unless the complainant furnishes to it, within a period of 15 days from the date of receipt of a copy of the award, a letter of acceptance of the award in full and final settlement of his claim in the matter.
Hence, the correct option is (A).

47. The move by the cabinet to grant greater powers to the Reserve Bank of India over the jurisdiction of cooperative banks will provide additional teeth to the central bank in dealing with the cooperative banks that are not exactly registered as bank entities but as cooperative societies. So far, the urban and multi-state cooperative banks are registered and governed by the state governments under the respective Co-operative Societies Act of the concerned states. They also come under RBI jurisdiction under the Banking Regulation Act, 1949.
Hence, the correct option is (C).

48. The major suppliers of trading instruments in capital markets are government and corporations.

Capital markets refer to the places where savings and investments are moved between suppliers of capital and those who are in need of capital. Capital markets consist of the primary market, where new securities are issued and sold, and the secondary market, where already-issued securities are traded between investors.

Hence, the correct option is (D).

49. Subscriber of Atal Pension Yojana (APY) would receive the fixed minimum pension of Rs. 1000 per month, Rs. 2000 per month, Rs. 3000 per month, Rs. 4000 per month, Rs. 5000 per month, at the age of 60 years.

- Atal Pension Yojana (APY), a pension scheme for citizens of India is focused on the unorganized sector workers. Atal Pension Yojana is open to all bank account holders.

- The scheme is available to any citizen of India with Age 18-40 Years.

- Under APY, the monthly pension would be available to the subscriber, and after him to his spouse and after their death, the pension corpus, as accumulated at age 60 of the subscriber, would be returned to the nominee of the subscriber.

Hence, the correct option is (D).

50. Depositor Education and Awareness Fund Scheme (DEAF) was established in 2014 and was inserted in the Banking Regulation Act, 1949 empowering the central bank. All banks are required to transfer money lying in accounts that have been inoperative for at least 10 years to the Depositor Education and Awareness Fund

Scheme (DEAF) according to specific guidelines.
Hence, the correct option is (A).

51. If an account is a red-flagged account, it will indicate fraud prone.

1. A red flag(Fraud prone) is a warning or indicator, suggesting that there is a potential problem or threat with a company's stock, financial statements, or news reports. A red If an account is a red-flagged account, it will indicate:flag for one investor may not be one for another.

2. Potential Non-Performing Assets are those accounts showing overdue and irregularities persist beyond 30 days. These are also known as Borderline Performing Assets.

3. The RBI defines a borrower as a 'wilful defaulter' if the company has not met repayment obligations despite having the capacity to do so. While a 'Wilful default' tag does not necessarily imply wrongdoing on the part of the promoters, the classification is also used while referring to loan fraud cases, where the borrower has diverted the loan for purposes other than those initially stated.

4. A Loss account shows a company's expenses over a particular period, typically either one month or consolidated months over a year. These figures show whether your business has made a loss over that period.

Hence, the correct option is (C).

52. Lahiri Committee Recommendation relates to the Issue of Participatory notes by FIIs. During the UPA government's tenure, a committee headed by the then Chief Economic Advisor, Ashok Lahiri, released a report in November 2005 on encouraging FII flows and checking the vulnerability of capital markets to speculative flows. On recommendation from Lahiri Committee, in 2004, it passed a regulation that derivative instruments like PNs against underlying Indian securities can be issued only to regulated entities, and further transfers, if any, can also be to other regulated entities only.

Hence, the correct option is (D).

53. Despite the rising virtual presence of traditional banks, online-only competitors still offer some clear advantages for consumers.
The lack of significant infrastructure and overhead costs allow direct banks to pay higher interest rates or annual percentage yields (APYs) on savings. The most generous of them offer as much as 1% to 2% more than you'll earn on accounts at a traditional bank—a gap that can really add up with a high balance. While some direct banks with especially generous APYs offer only savings accounts, most of them offer other options including high-yield savings accounts, certificates of deposit (CDs), and no-penalty CDs for early withdrawal.
You're less likely to be dinged with a wide range of fees at a direct bank including those associated with keeping an account open with a low balance, making direct deposits, or paying by check or debit card. Accounts at direct banks are more likely to carry no minimum balance or service fees
Hence, the correct option is (A).

54. The Trust shall cover credit facilities (Fund based and/or Non-fund based) extended by select RRB(s) to a single eligible borrower in the Micro and Small Enterprises sector for credit facility not exceeding 50 lakh by way of term loan and/or working capital facilities on or after entering into an agreement with the Trust, without any collateral security and/or third-party guarantees.

Hence, the correct option is (A).

55. "A marketing information system is a continuing and interacting structure of people, equipment and procedures to gather, sort, analyse, evaluate, and distribute pertinent, timely and accurate information for use by marketing decision makers to improve their marketing planning, implementation, and control".
Hence, the correct option is (A).

56. 1. The RBI sets India's exchange-control policy and administers foreign exchange regulations in consultation with the GOI. The Reserve Bank of India is India's central bank, responsible for the issue and supply of the Indian rupee and the regulation of the Indian banking system. It also manages the country's main payment systems and works to promote its economic development.

2. Foreign Exchange Dealer's Association of India (FEDAI) was set up in 1958 as an Association of banks dealing in foreign exchange in India (typically called Authorised Dealers - ADs) as a self-regulatory body and is incorporated under Section 25 of The Companies Act, 1956. Its major activities include framing of rules governing the conduct of inter-bank foreign exchange business among banks public and liaison with RBI for reforms and development of the forex market.

3. Export-Import Bank of India (EXIM Bank) is a specialized financial institution, wholly owned by the Government of India, set up in 1982, for financing, facilitating, and promoting foreign trade of India. Including the share capital of ` 1,300 crores received during the year from the Government of India, the paid-up capital as of March 31, 2015, stood at ` 5,059 crores and the Net Worth stood at ` 9,902 crores. Profit after tax of the Bank for the year 2014-15 amounted to ` 726 crores.

4. Indian Banks' Association, formed on 26 September 1946 as a representative body of management of banking in India operating in India - an association of Indian banks and financial institutions based in Mumbai

Hence, the correct option is (B).

57. Mutual Funds are regulated in India by SEBI.

Securities and Exchange Board of India (SEBI) is a legal body that regulates the Indian capital markets including mutual funds. SEBI supervises and controls the securities market, but most importantly, it protects your interests as an investor by enforcing firm rules and regulations.

Hence, the correct option is (D).

58. The cheque is valid and Mr. Jhon incurs no liability as an endorser.

The endorser of a negotiable instrument may, by express words in the endorsement, exclude his own liability thereon, or make such liability or the right of the endorsee to receive the amount due thereon depend upon the happening of a specified event,

although such event may never happen.
Hence, the correct option is (D).

59. The rate of interest has since been reviewed and it has been decided that the rate of interest payable by banks to the depositors/claimants on the unclaimed interest bearing deposit amount transferred to the Fund shall be 3.5% simple interest per annum with effect from July 01, 2018.
Hence, the correct option is (B).

60. A **Nostro** account refers to an account that a bank holds in a foreign currency in another bank. Nostros, a term derived from the Latin word for "ours," are frequently used to facilitate foreign exchange and trade transactions. Nostro account is a mechanism that banks use to keep track of all funds being held in other banks in the currency of the country where the funds are held.

Hence, the correct option is (B).

61. Assured return or guaranteed monthly income plans are essential in debt/income funds.

Debt/income funds are a class of debt mutual funds that invest in corporate bonds, government bonds and money market instruments. The portfolio is managed based on interest rates movements keeping in mind the creditworthiness. They are investment graded with credit quality, assuring capital preservation. Debt funds have lower transaction fees compared to equity and other mutual funds.

Hence, the correct option is (C).

62. 1. Credit risk is most simply defined as the potential that a bank borrower or counterparty will fail to meet its obligations in accordance with agreed terms. The goal of credit risk management is to maximize a bank's risk-adjusted rate of return by maintaining credit risk exposure within acceptable parameters. Banks need to manage the credit risk inherent in the entire portfolio as well as the risk in individual credits or transactions.

2. Market risk is the possibility of an investor experiencing losses due to factors that affect the overall performance of the financial markets in which he or she is involved.

3. Basel II classified **legal risk** as a subset of operational risk in 2003. This conception is based on a business perspective, recognizing that there are threats entailed in the business operating environment.

4. Operational risk is "the risk of a change in value caused by the fact that actual losses, incurred for inadequate or failed internal processes, people and systems, or from external events, differ from the expected losses".

Hence, the correct option is (C).

63. The capital conservation buffer (CCB) is a capital buffer of 2.5% of a bank's total exposures that need to be met with an additional amount of Common Equity Tier-1 capital. The buffer sits on top of the 4.5% minimum requirement for Common Equity Tier-1 capital. Its objective is to conserve a bank's capital.
Hence, the correct option is (D).

64. 1. A call option, often simply labeled a "call", is a contract, between the buyer and the seller of the call option, to exchange security at a set price. In the call option owner (Buyer) has the

right to purchase and the seller has the obligation to sell, a specified number of instruments at a specified rate during the time prior to the expiry date.

2. In finance, a **forward contract** or simply a forward is a non-standardized contract between two parties to buy or sell an asset at a specified future time at a price agreed on at the time of conclusion of the contract, making it a type of derivative instrument.

3. A futures contract is a legal agreement to buy or sell a particular commodity asset, or security at a predetermined price at a specified time in the future. Futures contracts are standardized for quality and quantity to facilitate trading on a futures exchange.

4. In finance, a put or **put option** is a financial market derivative instrument that gives the holder the right to sell an asset, at a specified price, by a specified date to the writer of the put. The purchase of a put option is interpreted as a negative sentiment about the future value of the underlying stock.

Hence, the correct option is (D).

65. The Government of India, Ministry of Commerce and Industry announced New Foreign Trade Policy on 01st April 2015 for the period 2015-2020, earlier this policy known as Export-Import (Exim) Policy.

Hence, the correct option is (C).

66. In case of default in maintenance of CRR requirement on a daily basis which is currently 95 percent of the total CRR requirement, penal interest will be recovered for that day at the rate of 3 percent per annum above the Bank Rate on the amount by which the amount actually maintained falls short of the prescribed minimum on that day and if the shortfall continues on the next succeeding day/s, penal interest will be recovered at the rate of five percent per annum above the Bank Rate.

Hence, the correct option is (B).

67. A participatory note, commonly known as a P-note or PN, is an instrument issued by a registered Foreign Institutional Investor (FII) to an overseas investor who wishes to invest in Indian stock markets without registering themselves with the market regulator, the Securities and Exchange Board of India (SEBI).
Hence, the correct option is (C).

68. Normally the dated Government Securities, have a period of 1 year to 20 years. Government Securities when issued in physical form are normally issued in the form of Stock Certificates. Such Government Securities when are required to be traded in the physical form are delivered by the transferor to transfer along with a special transfer form designed under the Public Debt Act 1944.
Hence, the correct option is (C).

69. 1. The **Forward Markets Commission (FMC)** was the chief regulator of commodity futures markets in India. As of July 2014, it regulated Rs 17 trillion worth of commodity trades in India. It is headquartered in Mumbai and this financial regulatory agency is overseen by the Ministry of Finance**2.** The **Reserve Bank of India** is India's central bank, responsible for the issue and supply of the Indian rupee and the regulation of the Indian banking system. It

also manages the country's main payment systems and works to promote its economic development.**3.** The **Insurance Regulatory and Development Authority of India** is an autonomous, statutory body tasked with regulating and promoting the insurance and re-insurance industries in India.**4.** The **Securities and Exchange Board of India** is the regulator of the securities and commodity market in India owned by the Government of India. It was established on 12 April 1988 and given Statutory Powers on 30 January 1992 through the SEBI Act, 1992.
Hence, the correct option is (A).

70. 1. The Multi Commodity Exchange of India Limited (MCX),- India's first listed exchange, is a state-of-the-art, commodity derivatives exchange that facilitates online trading of commodity derivatives transactions, thereby providing a platform for price discovery and risk management.

2. Equity shares are long-term financing sources for any company. These shares are issued to the general public and are non-redeemable. Investors in such shares hold the right to vote, share profits, and claim assets of a company.

3. A future contract that facilitates the purchase or sale of an underlier at a fixed price on a future date.

4. Forward contracts are non-standardized agreements between two parties, concerning the future delivery of a commodity for a presently set price. Their customizable variables are commodity type, delivery date, and amount. Commodity forwards can be settled in cash or through actual delivery of the contracted commodity.

Hence, the correct option is (C).

71. Factoring is a financial transaction and a type of debtor finance in which a seller sells its accounts receivable to a third party in which the whole responsibility passes to the factor. In a typical factoring arrangement, the client (you) makes a sale, delivers the product or service, and generates an invoice. The factor (the funding source) buys the right to collect on that invoice by agreeing to pay you the invoice's face value less a discount typically 2 to 6 percent. The factor pays 75 percent to 80 percent of the face value immediately and forwards the remainder (less the discount) when your customer pays.

Hence, the correct option is (B).

72. E-banking, use of computers and telecommunications to enable banking transactions to be done by telephone or computer rather than through human interaction. Its features include electronic funds transfer for retail purchases, automatic teller machines (ATMs), and automatic payroll deposits and bill payments.

Hence, the correct option is (A).

73. Complaints can be made when: The complaint was made to the bank and the bank had rejected it OR no reply was received within a period of one month OR the complainant is not satisfied with the reply given by the bank;
A period of more than one year has not elapsed after receipt of the bank reply.
The complaint is not for issues already settled/dealt with Ombudsman OR for which proceedings before a court, tribunal or arbitrator or any other forum is pending or a decree or award

or order has been passed;
The complaint is within the limitation period under the Indian Limitation Act 1963.
Hence, the correct option is (B).

74. Banks should extend business hours for banking transactions other than cash, up to one hour before the close of the working hours.

The following non-cash transactions should be undertaken by banks during the extended hours, i.e., up to one hour before the close of working hours:

(a) Non-voucher generating transactions :

- Issue of passbooks/statement of accounts.
- Issue of checkbooks.
- Delivery of term deposit receipts/drafts.
- Acceptance of share application forms.
- Acceptance of clearing cheques.
- Acceptance of bills for collection.

(b) Voucher generating transactions:

- Issue of term deposit receipts.
- Acceptance of cheques for locker rent due.
- Issue of traveler's cheques.
- Issue of gift cheques.
- Acceptance of individual cheques for transfer credit.

Such non-cash transactions to be done during the extended business hours should be notified adequately for information of the customers.
Hence, the correct option is (A).

75. 1. Business ethics refers to implementing appropriate business policies and practices with regard to arguably controversial subjects. Some issues that come up in a discussion of ethics include corporate governance, insider trading, bribery, discrimination, social responsibility, and fiduciary responsibilities.
2. Organizational ethics are the principles and standards by which businesses operate, according to Reference for Business. They are best demonstrated through acts of fairness, compassion, integrity, honor, and responsibility.
3. Professional ethics encompass the personal and corporate standards of behavior expected by professionals. The word professionalism originally applied to vows of a religious order.
4. A code of conduct is a set of rules outlining the norms, rules, and responsibilities or proper practices of an individual party or an organization.
Hence, the correct option is (A).

76. 1. Marine cargo insurance is a class of property insurance that insures property while in transit against loss or damage arising from perils associated with the navigation of the sea or air and subsequent land and inland waterways.

2. Travel insurance is a type of insurance that covers the costs and losses associated with traveling. It is useful protection for those traveling domestically or abroad.

3. Property insurance protects against most risks to property, such as fire, theft, and some weather damage. This includes specialized forms of insurance such as fire insurance, flood insurance, earthquake insurance, home insurance, or boiler insurance.

4. Still, perplexed at how does a **general insurance** policy comes into play? Consider that your mother suffered a heart attack suddenly and she needs a transplant. At the same time, your daughter's college fee was due. It definitely is a huge expense to be made at the same time and none can be preferred over the other. In this time of stress, the family's health insurance policy can save your burden and the fees can be paid from the savings. A General Insurance Policy here works to save your burden for money.

Hence, the correct option is (D).

77. 1. A closed-end fund is a portfolio of pooled assets that raises a fixed amount of capital through an initial public offering (IPO) and then lists shares for trade on a stock exchange. Like a mutual fund, a closed-end fund has a professional manager overseeing the portfolio and actively buying and selling holding assets.

2. A sector fund is an investment fund that invests solely in businesses that operate in a particular industry or sector of the economy. Sector funds are commonly structured as mutual funds or exchange-traded funds (ETFs).

3. Arbitrage funds work by exploiting the price differential between assets that should theoretically have the same price. One of the most important types of arbitrage takes place between the cash and futures markets. A typical fund purchases stocks with the hope of selling them later after the price has gone up.

Mutual Funds Units' of Close-ended funds must be listed on the stock exchange.

4. Liquid funds are a category of debt mutual funds that primarily invest in financial instruments like treasury bills, commercial papers, fixed deposits, and any other form of debt securities. The most defining feature of these funds is that they are short-term investments and come with a maturity period of 91 days.

Hence, the correct option is (C).

78. 1. Risk on account of trading in securities is known as **Market Risk**. Market risk is the possibility of an investor experiencing losses due to factors that affect the overall performance of the financial markets in which he or she is involved. Market risk, also called "systematic risk," cannot be eliminated through diversification, though it can be hedged against in other ways.

2. Credit risk is most simply defined as the potential that a bank borrower or counterparty will fail to meet its obligations in accordance with agreed terms. The goal of credit risk management is to maximize a bank's risk-adjusted rate of return by maintaining credit risk exposure within acceptable parameters. Banks need to manage the credit risk inherent in the entire portfolio as well as the risk in individual credits or transactions.

3. Operational risk is "the risk of a change in value caused by the fact that actual losses, incurred for inadequate or failed internal

processes, people and systems, or from external events, differ from the expected losses"

4. Basel II classified **legal risk** as a subset of operational risk in 2003. This conception is based on a business perspective, recognizing that there are threats entailed in the business operating environment.

Hence, the correct option is (B).

79. It involves the criteria for selecting the best idea, creating a strategic plan, and implementing the idea into practice. Here are some steps for idea generation in new product development that will assist you to stay on the curve and rule the market. Hence, the correct option is (A).

80. 1. TT Selling rate indicates the rate at which the bank sends an outward remittance through telegraphic transfer.

2. TT (Telegraphic Transfer) buying rate indicates the rate at which banks convert foreign inward remittances to INR. TT Selling rate indicates the rate at which the bank sends an outward remittance through telegraphic transfer.

3. Bills are export-import proceeds. Bills buying rate is nothing but inward remittances, bill selling rate nothing but outward remittances. Foreign currency converted into domestic currency through bill buying rate; domestic currency converted into foreign currency through bill selling rate. Here bills are export-import bill, and any other kind of foreign, foreign currency-denominated instruments.

4. TT Buying/Selling Rate & Bills Buying/Selling Rate is rather called a Merchant exchange rate. Merchant rates are lower than the spot rate definitely and somewhat around the interbank rate which is one of the lowest rates in the market. At merchant rate, high volume export-import transaction takes place, because the volume of transaction of the exporter importers maybe millions of dollar and they get a comparable rate generally favorable to them

Hence, the correct option is (B).

81. The term forfaiting refers to a form of trade finance involving discounting of export bills receivables such as drafts drawn under LC, bills of exchange, promissory notes, or other instruments on without recourse basis. The export of capital goods involves account receivables of medium and long-term maturities. It is a general practice that the exporter sells the claim of trade receivable on capital goods to an intermediary called forfeiture and gets an immediate payment of money for future receivable without recourse against him. It means that the exporter has no further interest in the transaction. It is the forfeiture who collects the future payments due from the importer and it is the forfeiture who runs all the risks of non-payment, as he cannot claim the payment back from the exporter. This type of relinquishing the right by an exporter to a forfeiture over trade receivables is called forfaiting.

Hence, the correct option is (A).

82. A cash credit account will become NPA if it remains out of order for more than 90 days.

NPA stands for Non-Performing Asset. It is an asset when it ceases to generate income for the bank and becomes overdue for more than 90 days. It places a financial burden on the lender.

NPA is categorized into 3 categories:

- Sub-standard assets: For less than 12 months.
- Doubtful assets: For more than 12 months.
- Loss assets: The one that needs to be fully written off.

'Project Sashakt India AMC' has been implemented by the government to tackle the problem of NPAs. The project is recommended by Sunil Mehta Committee. SBI has the highest NPA in India with over Rs. 1.86 lakh crore followed by Punjab National Bank and Bank of India.

Hence, the correct option is (A).

83. RBI has the sole right to issue bank notes as per Section 22 of the RBI Act 1934.

Section 22 of the RBI Act 1934 makes provided that RBI has the sole right to issue Banknotes of all denominations. Thus, Reserve Bank is responsible for the design, production, and overall management of the nation's currency, with the goal of ensuring an adequate supply of clean and genuine notes. At present, paper currency notes in India are issued in the denomination of Rs. 5, Rs. 10, Rs. 20, Rs. 50, Rs. 100, Rs. 500 and Rs. 2,000.

Hence, the correct option is (A).

84. A Non-Banking Financial Company (NBFC) is a company registered under the Companies Act, 1956 engaged in the business of loans and advances, acquisition of shares/stocks/bonds/debentures /securities issued by Government or local authority or other marketable securities of a like nature, leasing, hire-purchase, insurance business, chit business but does not include any institution whose principal business is that of agriculture activity, industrial activity, purchase or sale of any goods (other than securities) or providing any services and sale/purchase/construction of the immovable property.
Hence, the correct option is (C).

85. The Securities and Exchange Board of India (SEBI) is the regulatory authority established under the SEBI Act 1992 and is the principal regulator for Stock Exchanges in India. SEBI's primary functions include protecting investor interests, promoting and regulating the Indian securities markets. All financial intermediaries permitted by their respective regulators to participate in the Indian securities markets are governed by SEBI regulations, whether domestic or foreign. Foreign Portfolio Investors are required to register with DDPs in order to participate in the Indian securities markets.
Hence, the correct option is (B).

86. Risk-weighted assets are used to determine the minimum amount of capital that must be held by banks and other financial institutions in order to reduce the risk of insolvency. The capital requirement is based on a risk assessment for each type of bank asset.
For example, a loan that is secured by a letter of credit is considered to be riskier and, thus, requires more capital than a

mortgage loan that is secured with collateral.
Hence, the correct option is (D).

87. Basel guidelines refer to broad supervisory standards formulated by this group of central banks called the Basel Committee on Banking Supervision (BCBS). The set of the agreement by the BCBS, which mainly focuses on risks to banks and the financial system is called the Basel accord. Voluntary, spontaneous agree in applying to something that is a natural outgrowth of natural expression arising from circumstances and conditions. Voluntary implies having given previous consideration or having exercised judgment a voluntary confession a voluntary movement. The offer was a voluntary one.
Hence, the correct option is (B).

88. 1. The **Federal Reserve System** is the central banking system of the United States of America. It was created on December 23, 1913, with the enactment of the Federal Reserve Act.

2. The **Bank of England** is the central bank of the United Kingdom and the model on which most modern central banks have been based. Established in 1694 to act as the English Government's banker, and still one of the bankers for the Government of the United Kingdom, it is the world's eighth-oldest bank.
Hence, the correct option is (C).

89. A foreign exchange transaction is a type of currency transaction that involves two countries. Generally, a foreign exchange transaction involves the conversion of the currency of one country with that of another.

Hence, the correct option is (D).

90. At present, the Central Board has 18 members, including five official directors governors, and four deputy governors. Besides, the present Economic Affairs Secretary and Financial Services Secretary are the government nominees. Also, there are four other directors representing the Local Boards (one for each region) and seven more directors appointed by the government. These non-official part-time directors were appointed between March 2016 and August 2018. They enjoy a term of four years. The RBI Act allows for a five-year term for the Governor and the deputy governors, but it can also be less.
Hence, the correct option is (D).

91. The customer decides what's valuable and worth paying for, not the business. By focusing on delivering solutions that help customers be successful, business results follow. This simple principle is critical to business success.

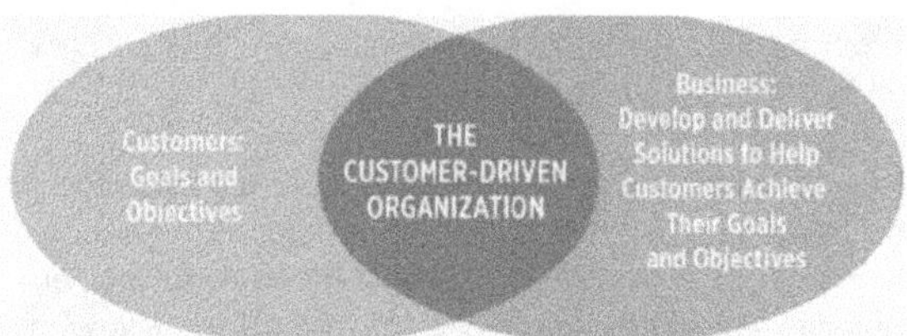

Hence, the correct option is (A).

92. 1. A promissory note is a financial instrument that contains a written promise by one party (the note's issuer or maker) to pay another party (the note's payee) a definite sum of money, either on-demand or at a specified future date.

2. A bill of exchange is a written order used primarily in international trade that binds one party to pay a fixed sum of money to another party on demand or at a predetermined date.

A document which reads as follows: "I acknowledge receipt of Rs. 2000 from Raman . This amount will be paid on demand" is a Promissory Note.

3. A cheque, or check, is a document that orders a bank to pay a specific amount of money from a person's account to the person in whose name the cheque has been issued.

4. An ambiguous instrument is basically one that may be either a bill or a note for its holder. Such situations arise in peculiar circumstances only.

Hence, the correct option is (B).

93. The system which is used for electronically paying a dividend to by the company to a large no. of its shareholders including the small amounts is ECS-Credit. ECS (Credit) is used for affording credit to a large number of beneficiaries by raising a single debit to an account, such as dividend, interest, or salary payment.

Hence, the correct option is (B).

94. Since there is nothing contained in the Negotiable Instruments Act or the Banking Regulation Act or the RBI Guidelines for not passing a cheque if it is filled in two different inks. But mind it, if you do your signatures in two different inks, your cheque is tended to be rejected as most of the banks do not consider it to be appropriate (i.e., many people have long signatures including their names).

So if you fill your check details in two different inks, it's ok, your cheque will be surely passed, even if the details handwritings do not match (many times people draw a cheque in favor of some person i.e., Mr. X and then Mr. X is told to fill in the details of the amount by himself when he will present the cheque for clearing on a specific date. Here Mr. X's handwriting of amount details and the drawer's handwriting of Mr. X's name detail will be different, but still the cheque will be passed.)

You just need to ensure that your/drawer's signature is done in continuation and with a single ink. If two separate inks are used or even a pen for signatures, your cheque might not be passed. Hence, the correct option is (A).

95. Section 20 in BANKING REGULATION ACT,1949
Restrictions on loans and advances.-
(a) grant any loans or advances on the security of its own shares, or-
(b) enter into any commitment for granting any loan or advance to or on behalf of-
(i) any of its directors,
(ii) any firm in which any of its directors is interested as partner, manager, employee or guarantor, or
(iii) any company not being a subsidiary of the banking company or a company registered under section 25 of the Companies Act, $1956(1$ of 1956), or a Government company of which ^{108} or the subsidiary or the holding company of which any of the directors of the banking company is a director, managing agent, manager, employee or guarantor or in which he holds substantial interest, or

(iv) any individual in respect of whom any of its directors is a partner or guarantor.
Hence, the correct option is (B).

96. The holder of the cheque will be Suresh.

An order cheque is one that can only be paid to a particular payee, who can only pass the cheque to another person by signing his or her name behind it. The bearer cheque does not require you not to cancel the printed words 'bearer' on the cheque, just to fill the amount you want to be withdrawn.

Hence, the correct option is (B).

97. The third pillar of the BASEL-II Accord is known as market discipline.

Market discipline is based on enhanced disclosure of risk. This may be an important pillar due to the complexity of Basel. Under Basel II, banks may use their own internal models (and gain lower capital requirements) but the price of this is transparency.

Hence, the correct option is (A).

98. Currency requirements of other centers are met through currency chests, which are receptacles in which stocks of new and reissuable notes are stored along with Re coins, maintained by Bank with

(i) Its agencies namely SBI and its associates and nationalized banks and some private sector commercial banks.

(ii) Currency chests are fed by periodical remittances of new and reissuable notes and balances in the chests are property of RBI. Currency chests cover all the centers in the countries.
Hence, the correct option is (C).

99. Cash Reserve Ratio (CRR) refers to the share of Net Demand and time liabilities (NDTL) that banks have to hold as balances with the RBI.

Cash Reserve Ratio is a specific part of the total deposit that is held as a reserve by the commercial banks and is maintained by the reserve bank of India. CRR ensures that the banks do not run out of money. CRR in India is decided by the Monitory Policy Committee. If the CRR is low the liquidity with banks increases, which in turn goes into investment and lending. Higher CRR creates a negative impact on the economy and also lowers the availability of loanable funds.

Significance of CRR:

- It regulates the money supply and level of inflation.
- CRR ensures the security of the preserved amount.
- It also has a major role to play during high inflation.

Hence, the correct option is (D).

100. The principle of justice states that there should be an element of fairness in all medical decisions fairness in decisions that burden and benefit, as well as equal distribution of scarce resources and new treatments, and for medical practitioners to uphold applicable laws and legislation when making choices. Hence, the correct option is (B).

101. If it is negotiating a cheque for example you are referring to a negotiable instrument. These guarantee the payment of a specific amount of money, either on-demand or after a set time, without conditions in addition to payment imposed on the payer.

Hence, the correct option is (C).

102. 1. A Red Flagged Account (RFA) is one where a suspicion of fraudulent activity is thrown up by the presence of one or more Early Warning Signals (EWS). These signals in a loan account should immediately put the bank on alert regarding a weakness or wrong doing which may ultimately turn out to be fraudulent.

2. A wilful defaulter is an entity or a person that has not paid the loan back despite the ability to repay it. The minister was replying to a question whether the cases of wilful defaulters of banks have increased during the last five years.

3. RBI has defined a **non-cooperative borrower** as "one who does not engage constructively with his lender by defaulting in timely repayment of dues while having the ability to pay, thwarting lenders' efforts for recovery of their dues by not providing necessary information sought, denying access to assets financed or collateral securities, obstructing the sale of securities".

4. Special Mention Accounts are those assets/accounts that show symptoms of bad asset quality in the first 90 days itself or before it is identified as NPA.

Hence, the correct option is (B).

103. 1. Where a person in any of the following towns, namely, the towns of Calcutta, Madras, and Bombay and in any other town which the **State Government** concerned may by notification in the Official Gazette, specify in this behalf, delivers to a creditor or his agent documents of title to immovable property, with intent to create a security thereon, the transaction is called a mortgage by deposit of title deeds.

2. A central government is a government that is a controlling power over a unitary state. Always equivalent in a federation is the federal government, which may have distinct powers at various levels authorized or delegated to it by its federated states, though the adjective 'central' is sometimes also used to describe it.

3. A municipality is usually a single administrative division having corporate status and powers of self-government or jurisdiction as granted by national and regional laws to which it is subordinate.

All mortgages other than a mortgage by deposit of title deeds can be effected by a registered instrument signed by a mortgagor and attested by at least two witnesses.

Hence, the correct option is (C).

104. Raghu's legal heirs is the holder of the cheque.

If the payee of the cheque is dead, the legal heirs can request the issuer (drawer)to issue a fresh cheque in favor of the legal heir/s. This new cheque can be encashed. Merely because a legal heir receives the amount of the cheque in his name or encashes the same, it does not become the exclusive property of the payee. This amount is received by him in "TRUST" and the money, so received has to be shared by the legal heirs who are entitled to the same.

All other rules for payment of cheque will apply, like date, the amount in figures and words, Signature must match with the specimen.

Hence, the correct option is (B).

105. The color orange mainly means creativity and dynamism. It's similar to red, but orange gives a more youthful and fun tone. It can also represent communication and open-mindedness. In the world of design, orange is used in logos for its playfulness and optimistic side.

Hence, the correct option is (A).

106. A bank wire is an electronic message system, which allows major banks to communicate various actions or occurrences regarding client accounts. The wire represents a secure computerized messaging system that sends account information, notifications, and transaction requests between banks.

It is the pioneer private sector electronic telecommunication network owned by an association of banks in the USA.

Hence, the correct option is (B).

107. The correct answer is- " not allowed as the Bank may be liable for conversion". This issue could come up when you receive documents from sources. For example, if a bank employee gives you checking account records for bank customers, you may both be liable for conversion because the employee likely does not have permission from his or her employer to turn over a customer's records.

Hence, the correct option is (C).

108. Duty-based ethics are usually what people are talking about when they refer to 'the principle of the thing'. Duty-based ethics teaches that some acts are right or wrong because of the sorts of things they are, and people have a duty to act accordingly, regardless of the good or bad consequences that may be produced.

Universality - I ought never to act except in such a way as I can also will that my maxim should become a universal law Human Dignity - Act in such a way that you always treat humanity. Never simply as a means, but always at the same time as an end. Hence, the correct option is (A).

109. The first methods of transferring or distributing risk in a monetary economy were practiced by Chinese and Babylonian traders in the 3rd and 2nd millennia BC, respectively. Chinese merchants traveling treacherous river rapids would redistribute their wares across many vessels to limit the loss due to any single vessel's capsizing. The Babylonians developed a system that was recorded in the famous Code of Hammurabi, 1750 BC, and practiced by early Mediterranean sailing merchants. If a merchant received a loan to fund his shipment, he would pay the lender an additional sum in exchange for the lender's guarantee to cancel the loan should the shipment be stolen or lost at sea. Hence, the correct option is (A).

110. Gilt mutual funds are considered ideal for long-term debt mutual fund investors with an aggressive risk profile. However, these schemes are extremely sensitive to the interest rate environment. The government has a funding requirement, it borrows from the Reserve Bank of India (RBI). To meet the government's funding needs, RBI collects the required amount from the banks and insurance companies and routes it to the government. In exchange for such funding received from various institutions, RBI issues g-secs of fixed tenure on behalf of the government. Gilt funds subscribe to these securities. At maturity, gilt funds return g-secs and receive a payout in return.

Hence, the correct option is (A).

111. RBI governs and regulates the money market instruments under sections $45\,K, 45\,L,$ and $45\,W$ of the RBI Act, 1934. The Reserve Bank of India issues guidelines to regulate the money market instruments by addressing the eligible market participants accounting for Certificate of Deposits, Treasury bills, call or notice money market, commercial paper and non-convertible debentures with a maturity of up to 1 year.

Hence, the correct option is (A).

112. Banks should deduct the following items from the Gross Advances and Gross NPAs to arrive at the Net advances and Net NPAs respectively:

i) Balance in Interest Suspense Account

ii) DICGC/ECGC claims received and held, pending adjustment

iii) Part payment received and kept in suspense account

iv) Total provisions held (excluding amount of technical write off and provision on standard assets)

For the purpose, the amount of gross advances should exclude the amount of Technical Write off but would include all outstanding loans and advances; including the advances for which refinance has been availed but excluding the amount of rediscounted bills. The level of gross and net NPAs will be arrived at in percentage terms by dividing the amount of gross and net NPAs by gross and net advances, computed as above, respectively.

Hence, the correct option is (D).

113. A cheque is a negotiable instrument. It can either be open or crossed. An open cheque is the bearer's cheque. It is payable over the counter on presentment by the payee to the paying banker. While a crossed cheque is not payable over the counter but shall be collected only through a banker. The amount payable for the crossed cheque is transferred to the bank account of the payee. Types of cheque crossing are General Crossing, Special Crossing, and Restrictive Crossing. Let us learn about cheque crossing in more detail.

Hence, the correct option is (D).

114. Authorized Money Changers/ AMCs are entities that are authorized by the Reserve Bank of India as per Section 10 of the Foreign Exchange Management Act of 1999. Accordingly, an AMC may either be a Restricted Money Changer (RMC) or a Full Fledged Money Changer (FFMC). As defined by the Act, an Authorised Person essentially means an authorized dealer, money changer, off-shore banking unit, or any other individual for the time being authorized under sub-section (1) of Section 10 to involve in foreign securities or foreign exchange. A license is required by FFMCs to purchase foreign exchange from residents and non-residents visiting India and to sell foreign exchange for

specifically approved purposes.
Hence, the correct option is (B).

115. Payout day is the day when the exchange makes payment or delivery securities to the broker. The settlement cycle is on a T+2 rolling settlement basis w.e.f. April 01, 2003. The exchanges have to ensure that the payout of funds and securities to the clients is done by the broker within 24 hours of the payout.
The securities obligations of members are downloaded to members by clearing corporation after the trading period is over. The current settlement cycle in India is T+2. The members make available the required securities in the pool accounts with the depository participants. Members are required to open accounts with depository participants of both the depositories, NSDL and CDSL
Hence, the correct option is (C).

116. We can define factoring as the sale of book debts by a firm to a financial intermediary called the factor on theunderstanding that the factor will pay for the debts as and when they are collectedor on a guaranteed payment date. Usually the factor makes a part paymentimmediately after the debts are purchased thereby providing immediate liquidity tothe client.

Hence, the correct option is (B).

117. 5 simple steps to locking down the threat of employee fraud collusion:

Step 1: Monitoring user behavior

Step 2: Understand the context of employee behavior

Step 3: Correlate activities across the organization

Step 4: Detecting commonalities in employee actions

Step 5: Connect all the dots
Hence, the correct option is (C).

118. An investment objective is the planning of investment by an individual which is based on certain goals. The objectives are what drives the person to invest in schemes for determining the strategies that they have set for attaining their goals.

Once the person has decided to invest thereafter they try to identify the best scheme and options that are available for them that would give them suitable returns and gains. Every scheme has its set objectives and time period that is attached to them for attaining the end targets.

Hence, the correct option is (A).

119. 1. A custodian or custodian bank is a financial institution that holds customers' securities for safekeeping to prevent them from being stolen or lost. Since they are responsible for the safety of assets and securities worth hundreds of millions or even billions of dollars, custodians tend to be large and reputable firms.

2. The full form of AMS is the Annual Maintenance Contract. It is also recognized as the annual fee for repairs. It is provided after shipment by all manufacturers. It is the term that applies to the manufacturers and the customers. The manufacturer gives its buyers maintenance services for their high – value products. As

per the agreement, this type of maintenance may be fee-based or free of cost.

3. Trustee is a legal term which, in its broadest sense, is a synonym for anyone in a position of trust and so can refer to any person who holds property, authority, or a position of trust or responsibility

4. A registrar is an official in an institution, often a bank or trust company, responsible for keeping records of bondholders and shareholders after an issuer offers securities to the public.

Hence, the correct option is (C).

120. Investors' KYC details are stored in the server of KRA.

KRA or KYC Registration Agency is a SEBI registered agency, that maintains the KYC records of the investors centrally, on behalf of capital market institutions complying with SEBI. KRA is registered with SEBI under the KYC Regulations Act of 2011. KRA allows the investors to invest in multiple Mutual Fund schemes of different Asset Management Companies (AMCs) without repeating the same KYC process for each AMC. It can be accessed by other intermediaries in the market and KYC registration agencies. Also, any changes that might occur in the future are also updated on a central server.

Hence, the correct option is (D).

Q.1 Cheques returned due to wanting of funds will be returned with the reason_____.
- **A.** insufficiency of funds
- **B.** refer to drawer
- **C.** not arranged for
- **D.** None of the above

Q.2 All pensioners are required to submit a life certificate in the month _______ every year.
- **A.** October
- **B.** November
- **C.** December
- **D.** January

Q.3 Whether non-residents can open accounts under the PPF scheme?
- **A.** Yes
- **B.** No
- **C.** No such guidelines
- **D.** After 15th July 2003 non-residents are permitted to open an account

Q.4 What is the minimum and maximum amount that can be deposited in the PPF account in a financial year?
- **A.** Rs. 500 and Rs. 60,000
- **B.** Rs. 1,000 and Rs. 70,000
- **C.** Rs. 500 and Rs. 1,50,000
- **D.** Rs. 500 and Rs. 1,00,000

Q.5 The lump-sum amount received towards maturity proceeds of the PPF account is taxed at the rate of
- **A.** 10%
- **B.** 30%
- **C.** 11.25%
- **D.** No tax is levied

Q.6 The organization which provides the facility to hold share in demat form are called
- **A.** banks.
- **B.** depository.
- **C.** SEBI.
- **D.** None of the above

Q.7 The system of marketing information is _____ that pertains to marketing.
- **A.** the structure of people, equipment, and procedures for the generation and processing of information
- **B.** the software used for the collection of information
- **C.** the computer hardware which is used for handling database
- **D.** the set of inputs to collate the information

Q.8 The standard messaging system used by the RTGS is called
- **A.** SMS.
- **B.** FSMS.
- **C.** SFMS.
- **D.** MFSS.

Q.9 At a Railway station, you withdraw cash from the ATM of Punjab National Bank. PNB is a______.
- **A.** paying banker
- **B.** collecting banker
- **C.** advising banker
- **D.** issuing banker

Q.10 Financial statements in India refer to
- **A.** cash flow statements only.
- **B.** profit and loss account only.
- **C.** balance sheet.
- **D.** All of the above

Q.11 ______ is a set of values, beliefs, goals, norms, and ways of solving problems by the members of the organization.
(i) Corporate culture
(ii) Organizational culture
- **A.** Only (i)
- **B.** Only (ii)
- **C.** Either (i) or (ii)
- **D.** Both (i) and (ii)

Q.12 In Garnishee Order, Subsequent proceedings of a court are called
- **A.** subsequent proceedings.
- **B.** garnishee absolute.
- **C.** garnishee Order.
- **D.** None of the above

Q.13 Risk category is reviewed under KYC has to be undertaken by banks in:
- **A.** Not less than 5 years
- **B.** Not less than 1 year
- **C.** Not less than 6 months
- **D.** Not less than 3 months

Q.14 The Paid-up value of shares is defined as______.
- **A.** the amount which the company has received against its issued shares
- **B.** the value which the company is liable to pay to the stakeholders
- **C.** total no. of shares multiplied by the share price
- **D.** company has paid against buyback of shares

Q.15 'Cache Memory" is a
- **A.** volatile memory.
- **B.** permanent memory.
- **C.** absolute memory.
- **D.** waste memory.

Q.16 Which of the following is correct about ethics?
- **A.** It is general guidelines framed by society like respect your elders
- **B.** They are prescribed by society, culture, or religion
- **C.** Moral principles that govern a person's behavior or the conducting of an activity
- **D.** It is broadly pertinent in the business as business ethics

Q.17 The process under Process Risk Management that prioritizes risks for further analysis or action by assessing and combining their probability of occurrence and impact is called
- **A.** Perform Qualitative Risks Analysis.
- **B.** Perform a Quantitative Risk Analysis.
- **C.** Plan Risk Management.
- **D.** Plan Risk Responses.

Q.18 "Microsoft Excel 2007" is a/an _______ .

A. Operating System
B. Application Software
C. System Software
D. Middleware

Q.19 Which of the following does the term Corporate Social Responsibility relate to?
(i) Ethical conduct
(ii) Environmental practice
(iii) Human rights and employee relations

A. Only (i) and (ii)
B. Only (i) and (iii)
C. Only (ii) and (iii)
D. (i), (ii) and (iii)

Q.20 A Joint savings (Non-Resident) account in the names of R and S, with instructions of "former or survivor" is in a bank where garnishee order is received in the name of R only. What can the bank do?

A. Return the order with the remark "No such account in the name of R
B. Attach the account, with the garnishee amount, since R is the exclusive owner of the account, during his lifetime
C. Inform the authorities the account is in two names and the bank can attach the account only on assent by S only
D. Cannot be attached since it is a non-resident account, return with these remarks to authorities

Q.21 A saving bank customer of Modern Bank issues a cheque of Rs.1500 in favor of M/s swastica Enterprises or order. The cheque is paid by the bank on presentation through clearing with an endorsement from the payee as 'Svastika Enterprises'. The endorsement is also confirmed by the collecting bank. The drawer claims that the payment has not been made in due course and claims a refund of the amount

A. this is a payment on the guarantee by the collecting bank due to which the paying bank's position is safe.
B. the cheque is of a small amount,. Hence the bank should refund the money.
C. if a customer is valuable, the customer's request should be accepted.
D. the endorsement is irregular due to which the paying bank is not protected under the provisions of Section 85 of the NI Act.

Q.22 The inputs used in the process of Perform Qualitative Risk Analysis includes all except
A. Scope Baseline.
B. Risk Register.
C. Quality Management Plan.
D. Risk Management Plan.

Q.23 Mr. X is maintaining a few accounts with Popular bank with its Trichur branch. The bank branch receives an attachment order.
Which of the following accounts, will be attached by the order?

A. Overdraft limit of Rs. 0.30 lakh, in which there is a nominal debit balance
B. Overdraft limit against shares of a company, where there is some unavailed balance available
C. Amount of term deposit of Rs. 1 lakh minus the balance including interest in the overdraft li limit of Rs. 0.50 lakh against this Term Deposit

D. Overdraft limit of Rs. 0.40 lakh against Gold ornaments

Q.24 In international Factoring, the number of factors that are involved in the factoring process is____.
A. one
B. two
C. three
D. depends upon the transaction

Q.25 Which of the following is part of off-site supervision of banks by RBI?
(A) Analysis of statements called by banks
(B) Analysis of the balance sheet of the bank
(C) Meeting with the management periodically
(D) Rating reports of rating agencies

A. (A) to (D) all
B. (A), (B) and (C)
C. (A), (C) and (D)
D. (B), (C) and (D)

Q.26 A common port for all devices is known as
A. Universal Serial Bus.
B. Parallel port.
C. Smart port.
D. Serial port.

Q.27 Out of incremental export credit over corresponding year, how much amount, the domestic banks can classify under priority sector?
A. 2% of ANBC or CEOBE
B. 2.5% of ANBC or CEOBE
C. 2.5% of priority sector loans
D. 2.5% of total bank credit

Q.28 Function of a distribution channel does not include________.
A. risk taking
B. matching
C. product synchronization
D. negotiation

Q.29 "Phishing" is
A. novel way of catching fishes.
B. an internet game.
C. online fraud to get personal data.
D. a networking device to connect a PC to a remote desktop.

Q.30 The locker room should be fully checked before locking the room and this is the responsibility of the ________.
A. custodian of the locker room key
B. branch
C. no need of checking
D. any person

Q.31 Define the main objectives of computerization at the branch level.
A. Improvement in customer service and quality of housekeeping
B. Generation of data for better management control
C. Improvement in productivity and profitability
D. Both (A) and (B)

Q.32 An asset will be classified Doubtful if it has remained in the substandard category for more than______months.

A. 24 **B.** 18 **C.** 12 **D.** 6

Q.33 Risk and Reward has________.

A. positive correlation **B.** negative correlation
C. strong correlation **D.** no correlaton

Q.34 Which is correct in the case of BCSBI?

A. BCSBI Registered under the Societies Registration Act 1860
B. BCSBI is not part of RBI
C. Option (A) is correct
D. Both the options (A) and (B) correct

Q.35 Regional Rural Banks are sponsored by

A. Syndicate Bank. **B.** RBI.
C. SBI. **D.** GOI.

Q.36 What does 'Kite Flying' refers to in the banking terminology?

A. When overdraft is allowed by the Bank.
B. When an additional loan is allowed by the bank to cover the amount of irregularity.
C. Permitting drawls against uncleared cheques.
D. When the loan is allowed for low amount transaction.

Q.37 Which of the following is the apex institution to handle finance for agriculture and rural development in India?

A. RBI **B.** SIDBI
C. NABARD **D.** AMFI

Q.38 On the death of an account holder of the nominated jointly operated account to whom the payment will be made?

A. Survivor
B. Survivor and nominee
C. Nominee
D. Legal heirs of deceased and survivor

Q.39 ________specifies methods for reporting violations, disciplinary action for violations and the structure of the due process to be followed.
(i) Business ethics
(ii) Code of ethics

A. Only (i) **B.** Only (ii)
C. Either (i) or (ii) **D.** Both (i) and (ii)

Q.40 A note which is washed, shrunk, altered, or partially obliterated is called a_____ note.

A. soiled **B.** mutilated
C. imperfect **D.** obliterated

Q.41 The advantages of Local Area Network to banks are

A. sharing of expensive resources by several users.
B. availability of stored information to all users.
C. all the terminals are intelligent terminals; the processing load is shared by computers in LAN.
D. Both (A) and (B)

Q.42 The Banking Ombudsman is appointed by
A. the central government under the banking regulation act.

B. the Reserve bank as required by the RBI act.
C. committee of supreme court judges.
D. The Reserve bank in terms of the scheme framed under the Banking Regulation Act.

Q.43 Which type of loans are lent on teaser rate?

A. Personal Loan **B.** Car Loan
C. House Loan **D.** Business Loan

Q.44 An NRE-RA account can be opened as

A. current, saving RD only.
B. saving, RD and FD only.
C. saving, current, RD, and FD only.
D. FD and saving only.

Q.45 The monetary policy committee is under which body?

A. SEBI **B.** RBI **C.** GOI **D.** SBI

Q.46 In a computer monitor, "LCD" stands for

A. liquid cathode display.
B. local crystal display.
C. low-calorie display.
D. liquid crystal display.

Q.47 Among the following, which type of banking system works on the principles of 'sharia'?

A. Corporate banking system
B. Shadow banking
C. Islamic banking
D. Payments bank system

Q.48 SEBI Act was enacted in________.

A. 1992 **B.** 1995 **C.** 1959 **D.** 1982

Q.49 ASBA stands for

A. Application Supported by Bank Accounts.
B. Application Supported by Beneficiary Account.
C. Application Supported by Blocked Amount.
D. Application Submitted by Agents.

Q.50 Hindi Day is celebrated on ________ every year.

A. 14th September **B.** 14th November
C. 17th September **D.** 17th November

Q.51 CVV is a term used for

A. Customer Verification Value.
B. Card Verification Value.
C. Credit Verification Value.
D. Customer Value Verification.

Q.52 Which type of letter of credit is used for mostly Inter-Trade transactions?

A. Revocable Letter of Credit
B. Irrevocable Letter of Credit
C. Revolving Letter of Credit
D. None of the above

Q.53 The average life span for a strategic alliance is about

A. 10 years. **B.** 9 years. **C.** 8 years. **D.** 7 years.

Q.54 An investor is allowed to invest in the equity market of the foreign countries through which instrument?

A.   Depository Receipt

B.   American Depository Receipt

C.   Global Depository Receipt

D.   Promissory Note

Q.55 A minor of 15 years is having an SB account wants to make a nomination in favor of his sister

A.   cannot be allowed to do so.

B.   nomination can be done by his mother.

C.   minor himself can nominate at the age of 10.

D.   can do if the nominee belongs to same family.

Q.56 Features of channels for banking services are

A.   intangibility/inseparability from the seller variability in customer experiences.

B.   perishability and non storability/personal contacts with clients.

C.   banking services have no physical and personal channels of distribution.

D.   Both (A) and (B)

Q.57 Up to what percentage the scheduled commercial banks are permitted to borrow to the extent of their capital funds in the Call/Money Market?

A. 100%   B. 75%   C. 125%   D. 80%

Q.58 A loan becomes a Non-Performing Asset (NPA) when the interest or principal becomes overdue for a period of:

A. 5 years   B. 90 days   C. 180 days   D. 365 days

Q.59 What is the current Repo Rate and Statutory Liquidity Ratio Rate respectively?

A. 5.50% and 20.50%   B.   4.00% and 18.00%

C. 6.50% and 21.20%   D. 5.50% and 18.50%

Q.60 "ISDN "stands for

A.   international society for digital networks.

B.   international subscribers distance networking.

C.   integrated system for day and night.

D.   integrated services digital network.

Q.61 2nd Pillar in Basel II relates to

A. minimum capital.   B. supervisory review.

C. market discipline.   D. risk management.

Q.62 A customer deposits certain valuable items, documents, and billions with the banks for the safety of the valuables. In this transaction customer and bank developed a relationship, which is______.

A.   Bailee (Bank) and customer (Bailor)

B.   Lessor (Bank) and customer (lessee)

C.   Trustee (Bank) and customer (Beneficiary)

D.   Pawner (Bank) and customer (pawnee)

Q.63 The functions of collecting and assembling data, it's processing, analyzing, storage, and dissemination of information is called

A.   mechanised information system.

B.   marketing information system.

C.   master processing strategy.

D.   computerization of clerical work.

Q.64 The case can be filed in DRT against the borrower having an outstanding ledger balance of Rs. ______lacs and above in the NPA/Written-off account.

A. 5   B. 10   C. 20   D. 25

Q.65 12 of PMLA, 2002 Cash transaction report consisting aggregate value of transaction more than __________ will be submitted to the director of Financial Intelligence Unit-India (FIU-IND).

A.   25 lakhs   B.   10 lakhs

C.   15 lakhs   D.   20 lakhs

Q.66 In the address portion of a website, what prefix indicates your communications are being encrypted during transit?

A. Htp   B. Https   C. Ftp   D. Tcp

Q.67 A person can obtain high interest rate from ______ .

A. time deposit   B. demand deposit

C. current deposit   D. deferred deposit

Q.68 Cash Management services eliminate which of the following service?

A.   DD Drawing Cheque/DD Drawing Arrangement

B.   Receivables Management Cheque Collections

C.   Auto Sweeping Facility

D.   Business Risk Management

Q.69 Facilities for the exchange of soiled and mutilated currency notes are available in ______ branches.

A.   branches having currency chests

B.   selected branches

C.   authorised barnches

D.   all Branches

Q.70 'CDMA' stands for

A.   Code Division Multiple Access.

B.   Combined Division for Mobile Access.

C.   Company Designed Mobile Accessories.

D.   Code Distribution for Mobile Activation.

Q.71 In PPF, the minimum period of deposit under this scheme is ______ financial years extendable by ______ financial years at a time.

A.   5 and 5   B.   5 and 10

C.   10 and 5   D.   15 and 5

Q.72 Core Banking is computerization in which branches are connected to a central host server and its advantages are

A.   reliable centralized data repository.

B.   provision of online ATM, tele-banking, internet banking.

C.   quick adoption of software changes and relief from data backup, 24 X 7 service to customer.

D.   Both (A) and (B)

Q.73 "LINUX" is

A.   Operating System.

B. another version of Microsoft Office.
C. a high-speed processor from IBM.
D. None of these

Q.74 'Windows' applications run on______.
A. CUI   **B.** GUI   **C.** MUI   **D.** RUI

Q.75 Consortium funding is an example of

A. the loan provided by few banks and the bank with maximum credit extending acts as the main bank.

B. the loan provided by a single bank to different companies under one group of businesses.

C. funds available with different banks.

D. credit extended by different banks to different companies under one group.

Q.76 Need for Marketing Information System is due to

A. better understanding of the market ups and downs.

B. better knowledge of customer behaviour and expectations.

C. information explosion, and avoidance of communication gap and to take prompt decisions and to face non-price competition.

D. competition in the modern market, like branding, packaging, and advertising only.

Q.77 FATF stands for

A. Foreign Account Taxation Force.
B. Financial Action Task Force.
C. Financial Account Trade Force.
D. None of the above

Q.78 A flexible limit of __________ is provided to Marginal farmer as Flexi KCC based on landholding and crops grown including post-harvest warehouse storage-related credit needs and other farm expenses.

A. Rs. 10,000 to 1,00,000
B. Rs. 10,000 to 50,000
C. Rs. 50,000 to 1,00,000
D. above Rs. 50,000

Q.79 "Skimmer" is a device to

A. skim milk from the cream.
B. copy the data from magnetic strip of cards.
C. capture the image of card holder.
D. add the value of the credit cards.

Q.80 A Government bill is

A. a quasi negotiable instrument.
B. not a negotiable instrument.
C. negotiable instrument.
D. None of the above

Q.81 In a ________, there is the transfer of an interest in the property to the creditor but in ________ there is only an obligation to repay the money and no transfer of interest.

A. mortgage, hypothecation
B. pledge, mortgage
C. Both (A) and (B) above
D. None of the above

Q.82 Businesses becomes customer-centric and industry-driven due to________.

A. profitability   **B.** technology
C. competition   **D.** consumption

Q.83 'Straight through the process' (STP) is used for

A. RTGS.   **B.** OLTAS.   **C.** ECS.   **D.** CTS.

Q.84 Which of the following two duties should not be clubbed with respect to the banking software system?

A. Security administration and security audit
B. Security administration and network administration
C. Systems development and maintenance
D. All of the above

Q.85 Which among the following is not a feature of Saving Accounts?

A. Preferred by individuals savers
B. Usually low scale transactions
C. Earns interest
D. Overdraft Facility

Q.86 Monetary and Credit policy is issued by RBI each year ______ times.

A. 2   **B.** 3   **C.** 4   **D.** 5

Q.87 Which is an example of book debts?

A. Account receivable
B. Cash and bank balance written in books
C. Debt taken by company and reported in books
D. Inventory

Q.88 NPA/Written-off accounts can be settled in Lok Adalat having outstanding ledger balance up to Rs________.

A. 5 lakhs   **B.** 10 lakhs   **C.** 20 lakhs   **D.** 25 lakhs

Q.89 Where principal or interest payment becomes overdue between 31 to 60 days?

A. SMA-0   **B.** SMA-1   **C.** SMA-2   **D.** SMA-3

Q.90 When a cheque is drawn on a bank, the bank is called the

A. payee.   **B.** drawee.
C. drawer.   **D.** None of these

Q.91 __________ are the features of Mobile Banking.

A. Encryption with 128 bit
B. Open internet technology
C. Dependent on any specific service provider
D. Both (A) and (B)

Q.92 '________' is a center promoted by RBI for research in banking technology.

A. N I B M   **B.** C A B
C. CERT-IN   **D.** IDRBT

Q.93 In the Indian Banking System, _____ acts as the banker's bank and also as lender of the last resort.

A. RBI   **B.** SEBI
C. NABARD   **D.** None of these

Q.94 Information Technology Bill was enacted on___.

A. 2002   **B.** 2000   **C.** 1998   **D.** 2005

Q.95 Which of the following schemes has been launched specifically for helping Senior Citizens to avail of loan by mortgage of the residential property?
A. English mortgage scheme
B. Senior capital loan scheme
C. Reverse mortgage loan scheme
D. DEMAT account scheme

Q.96 Which statements are true about HUF?
A. Karta has an implied authority to avail of a loan, however, documents should be signed by all adult male members.
B. Karta has the power to transfer an asset.
C. Name of male minor coparceners should be kept on record and their guardians must sign the documents on his behalf.
D. All of the above

Q.97 An asset will be straightway classified as Doubtful if the erosion in the value of the security is_______ than the value assessed by the bank or accepted by RBI at the time of the last inspection.
A. 50 percent   **B.** 25 percent
C. 20 percent   **D.** 10 percent

Q.98 Considering u/s 141 of the NI Act, offences by companies - which of the following statements satisfy the legal act of above act?

I) If the person who has committed an offence is a company, then every person responsible for such offence, as well as the company itself, shall be deemed to be guilty of the offence

II) A person nominated as a director by virtue of his holding any office or employment in the Central or State government, he/she shall not be liable for prosecution

III) Magistrate issuing summons to an accused or a witness may direct a copy of the summons to be served by speed post or by such courier services as are approved by a court of session

(IV) Evidence of complaint may be given by him on affidavit and may subject to all just exceptions be read in evidence in any enquiry, trial

A. (I),(III) and (IV)   **B.** (I) and (II)
C. (II) and (III)   **D.** (I), (II) and (III)

Q.99 Any Bank/NBFC is obliged to provide redressal of grievances within how many days before a customer exercises his option to approach the banking ombudsman?
A. 30 days   **B.** 45 Days   **C.** 15 days   **D.** 60 days

Q.100 Which bank has signed an MoU with NIIF in a pact for funding infrastructure projects?
A. HDFC   **B.** SBI   **C.** Axis   **D.** Yes

Q.101 MCLR replaced which of the following existing rate?
A. Base Rate
B. BPLR
C. External Benchmark Rate
D. Policy Rate

Q.102 Minimum Support Scheme was started by GOI to safeguard the interest of_____.
A. traders   **B.** farmers
C. industries   **D.** commission agents

Q.103 Contingent liabilities including guarantee obligation, while examining audited financials can be studied through
A. balance sheet.
B. profit & Loss of A/c.
C. auditor's notes to the account.
D. director's report.

Q.104 Which of the following statements about Central Bank is incorrect?
A. Central Bank regulates currency in accordance with the requirements of business and the general public
B. Central Banks performs general banking and agency service for the state
C. Central Bank generally deals with the public and tries to encourage saving habits among people
D. None

Q.105 Under National Agriculture Insurance Scheme (NAIS) risk insurance will not cover_______.
A. fire caused by natural disaster and lightning
B. drought, dry spells
C. losses arising out of war & nuclear risks
D. pests/diseases

Q.106 RBI has been playing its role of supervision, control, and development of the monetary and banking system in the country through its following functions (state what is not true)?
A. Development of the banking system
B. Development of financial institutions
C. Development of backward areas
D. Banker to the General public

Q.107 Which of the following is not true with reference to capital budgeting?
A. Capital budgeting is related to asset replacement decisions
B. Cost of capital is equal to the minimum required return
C. Existing investment in a project is not treated as a sunk cost
D. Timing of cash flows is relevant

Q.108 "IMEI "stands for
A. International Mobile Equipment Identity.
B. International Mobile Enforcement Institute.
C. Indian Mobile Equipment Institute.
D. International Market for Equipment Implants.

Q.109 The methods of data transmission for communication can be
A. simplex, capable of transmitting data in one direction.
B. half-duplex, data movement in both directions.
C. full-duplex, simultaneous two-way transmission.
D. Both (A) and (B)

Q.110 Under the scheme of Liberation and Rehabilitation of Scavengers (SLRS), the loan can be given to scavengers_______.

A. up to Rs. 50,000 (break up of 50,000 would be a subsidy of Rs. 10,000, Rs. 7,500 margin money from the State Scheduled Caste Development Corporations and Rs. 32,500 loan from the banks

B. up to Rs. 1,00,000 (break up of 1,00,000 would be subsidy of Rs. 25,000, Rs. 17,500 margin money from the State Scheduled Caste Development Corporations and Rs. 57,500 loan from the banks

C. up to Rs. 10,000 (break up of 10,000 would be a subsidy of Rs. 2,000, Rs. 1,250 margin money from the State Scheduled Caste Development Corporations and Rs. 6,750 loans from the banks

D. None of the above

Q.111 Which of the following risks are covered by Pradhan Mantri Fasal Bima Yojana (PMFBY) for Short Term Production Credit under United Kisan Credit Card?

A. Prevented Sowing/ Plantation risk

B. Standing Crop risk

C. Post-harvest Losses & Localized Calamities

D. All of the above

Q.112 Which of the following is not a salient feature of SHG?

A. Group of homogenous people from similar economic backgrounds

B. Focus on work

C. Focus on Children's

D. Saving first, credit later

Q.113 When given a loan for buying a car, the nature of charge created is______.

A. hypothecation

B. mortgage

C. pledge

D. general Lien

Q.114 To make the computer work faster, increase the

A. ROM.

B. Hard disk storage capacity.

C. RAM.

D. USB.

Q.115 Which of the following applications are possible on VSAT Network for banks?

A. Anywhere/Anytime banking/Electronic Fund Transfer

B. Plastic cards implementation/Treasury Management

C. Inter-branch Reconciliation or transfer like DD/TT/MT advice, accounting, and transfer, e-mail, the circulars- corporate website for employees MIS for credit risk management

D. Both (A) and (B)

Q.116 ______are the principles, which govern and guide business people to perform business functions.
(i) Business ethics
(ii) Code of conduct

A. Only (i)

B. Only (ii)

C. Either (i) or (ii)

D. Both (i) and (ii)

Q.117 Mr. Hilton has approached Corporation bank to take a car loan. The bank considering the reputation of Mr. Hilton, a loan was provided of Rs. 50 Lakh. later after reviewing the behavior of the loan bank has concluded that the loan has been classified as SMA-0. After few days of classification, Mr.

Hilton again approached the Corporation bank to deposit Rs. 5 lakh into his savings account to pay the amount of the cheque issued by Mr. Hilton to Gillette India Ltd. and states that this money is used only to pay the amount to Gillette India Ltd. And should not be used towards his car loan account. Now u/s 59 of Indian Contract act what are the possible options Corporation bank has toward recover the loan amount given against car?

A. Corporation bank has the right to set off the amount towards the car loan account and reduce the credit balance in his own books

B. the bank can recover the loan from Gillette India Ltd

C. Bank has no right to appropriate the funds except to meet the cheque amount as stated by Mr. Hilton

D. Bank can put pressure on Mr. Hilton to firstly pay the loan amount and after that, the cheque will be honored

Q.118 "Software as a Service' (SAS) works on

A. CUI model.

B. GPS Model.

C. Cloud Computing Model.

D. None of these

Q.119 A________ is a set of rules outlining the norms, rules, and responsibilities or proper practices of an individual party or an organization.
(i) business ethics
(ii) code of conduct

A. Only (i)

B. Only (ii)

C. Either (i) or (ii)

D. Both (i) and (ii)

Q.120 What is attachable under Garnishee Orders?

A. The specified amount in the garnishee order

B. If the amount is unspecified, then the account is frozen and no payment is allowed

C. Any amount payable on demand or time deposits

D. Both (A) and (B)

// Smart Answer Sheet //

Correct — Indicates percentage of students who answered questions correctly.

Skipped — Indicates percentage of students who skipped questions.

Q.	Ans.	Correct / Skipped
1	A	70.13 % / 11.81 %
2	B	51.26 % / 21.49 %
3	B	36.33 % / 18.97 %
4	C	61.96 % / 23.11 %
5	D	58.83 % / 22.8 %
6	B	52.67 % / 21.5 %
7	A	56.21 % / 23.81 %
8	C	40.97 % / 23.31 %
9	A	52.77 % / 23.62 %
10	D	46.22 % / 22.2 %
11	A	17.05 % / 20.39 %
12	B	41.37 % / 22.61 %
13	C	27.95 % / 17.56 %
14	A	37.34 % / 23.31 %
15	A	55.5 % / 18.97 %
16	C	57.21 % / 19.38 %
17	A	35.82 % / 23.92 %
18	B	52.47 % / 23.01 %
19	D	48.03 % / 9.69 %
20	B	51.46 % / 17.16 %
21	D	44.4 % / 18.26 %
22	C	27.45 % / 23.0 %
23	C	49.24 % / 15.24 %
24	B	27.04 % / 23.62 %
25	A	36.73 % / 24.12 %
26	A	55.3 % / 23.11 %
27	A	23.31 % / 17.66 %
28	C	21.09 % / 23.81 %
29	C	73.56 % / 18.06 %
30	A	69.73 % / 21.39 %
31	D	64.58 % / 20.38 %
32	C	50.55 % / 19.08 %
33	A	44.2 % / 16.24 %
34	D	43.79 % / 22.81 %
35	D	48.34 % / 19.17 %
36	C	23.21 % / 20.69 %
37	C	70.94 % / 23.31 %
38	D	27.55 % / 22.0 %
39	B	32.39 % / 23.82 %
40	C	12.41 % / 23.11 %
41	D	60.34 % / 17.56 %
42	D	48.64 % / 23.11 %
43	C	32.19 % / 19.88 %
44	C	38.35 % / 23.51 %
45	B	71.75 % / 18.26 %
46	D	60.24 % / 22.91 %
47	C	59.84 % / 21.09 %
48	A	48.64 % / 23.11 %
49	C	45.51 % / 23.61 %
50	A	53.88 % / 22.41 %
51	B	66.3 % / 19.07 %
52	B	28.36 % / 18.16 %
53	D	20.59 % / 23.91 %
54	A	28.36 % / 21.59 %
55	A	44.6 % / 19.98 %
56	D	56.61 % / 23.91 %
57	C	34.51 % / 24.12 %
58	B	28.46 % / 22.4 %
59	B	50.86 % / 20.58 %
60	D	53.58 % / 18.37 %
61	B	42.38 % / 23.41 %
62	A	34.01 % / 22.2 %
63	B	38.65 % / 20.08 %
64	C	42.08 % / 23.21 %
65	B	53.08 % / 21.69 %
66	B	65.79 % / 21.7 %
67	A	62.46 % / 22.91 %
68	D	29.77 % / 24.11 %
69	D	45.71 % / 23.21 %
70	A	46.32 % / 23.51 %
71	D	44.2 % / 15.44 %
72	D	65.39 % / 17.96 %
73	A	64.58 % / 23.61 %
74	B	47.12 % / 22.1 %
75	A	37.84 % / 24.22 %
76	C	36.13 % / 21.59 %
77	B	56.0 % / 23.31 %
78	B	30.27 % / 22.61 %
79	B	65.39 % / 16.75 %
80	B	28.25 % / 18.87 %

Q.	Ans.	Correct / Skipped	Q.	Ans.	Correct / Skipped	Q.	Ans.	Correct / Skipped	Q.	Ans.	Correct / Skipped	Q.	Ans.	Correct / Skipped
81	A	51.97 % / 17.56 %	89	B	57.32 % / 23.91 %	97	A	40.36 % / 24.12 %	105	C	49.45 % / 23.1 %	113	A	75.08 % / 17.05 %
82	C	48.84 % / 21.8 %	90	B	45.61 % / 23.01 %	98	B	12.61 % / 25.94 %	106	D	32.59 % / 23.41 %	114	C	66.2 % / 22.8 %
83	A	25.53 % / 24.12 %	91	D	58.83 % / 23.81 %	99	A	59.03 % / 20.28 %	107	C	22.91 % / 19.98 %	115	D	42.28 % / 21.19 %
84	D	46.52 % / 21.69 %	92	D	40.67 % / 23.61 %	100	B	34.41 % / 20.69 %	108	A	53.08 % / 23.21 %	116	A	26.44 % / 23.11 %
85	D	53.88 % / 23.21 %	93	A	76.59 % / 17.66 %	101	A	41.57 % / 23.11 %	109	D	43.09 % / 18.06 %	117	C	36.83 % / 17.76 %
86	C	39.56 % / 22.9 %	94	B	28.86 % / 23.41 %	102	B	59.74 % / 23.41 %	110	A	26.14 % / 24.72 %	118	C	44.2 % / 23.11 %
87	A	34.11 % / 24.42 %	95	C	47.12 % / 20.59 %	103	C	27.04 % / 24.32 %	111	D	71.85 % / 16.65 %	119	B	34.01 % / 17.15 %
88	C	38.65 % / 23.0 %	96	D	63.98 % / 21.09 %	104	C	37.13 % / 21.4 %	112	C	55.5 % / 22.91 %	120	D	61.96 % / 18.36 %

Performance Analysis

Avg. Score (%)	44.0%
Toppers Score (%)	99.0%
Your Score	

//Hints and Solutions//

1. Section 138 of the Act lays down that a cheque drawn by a person for payment of any amount of money to any other person from out of his account is returned by the bank unpaid, either because the amount of money standing to the credit of the account is insufficient to honor the cheque or it exceeds the amount arranged to be paid from that account by an arrangement made with the bank, such person shall be deemed to have committed an offense under the said section and shall be punished with imprisonment for a term which may extend to one year to with fine which may extend to twice the amount of the cheque, or with both.

Hence, the correct option is (A).

2. All pensioners are required to submit a life certificate in the month of November every year.

Government pensioners are required to submit their life certificate every year in the month of November to ensure that their pension is not stopped. The last date to submit a life certificate to the pension disbursing bank is November 30 every year.

Every Central Government pensioner has to submit a life certificate in the month of November for further continuation of his/her pension. It has been observed that a large number of Central Government pensioners physically visit bank branches for this purpose.

Hence, the correct option is (B).

3. Public Provident Fund accounts for NRI: Non-Resident Indians (NRIs) are not eligible to open an account under The Public Provident Fund Scheme, 1968. However, NRIs, who had invested in the PPF before becoming a non-resident during the maturity period of the account, can continue to subscribe to the Fund till its maturity on a "Non-Repatriation Basis." The PPF rules say: "Non-Resident Indians are not eligible to open an account under the Public Provident Fund Scheme. "Provided that if a resident, who subsequently becomes Non-Resident Indian during the currency of the maturity period prescribed under Public Provident Fund Scheme, may continue to subscribe to the Fund till its maturity on a Non-Repatriation Basis."

Hence, the correct option is (B).

4. A minimum yearly deposit of Rs. 500 is required to open and maintain a PPF account. A PPF account holder can deposit a maximum of Rs. 1.5 lakhs in his/her PPF account (including those accounts where he is the guardian) per financial year.

Hence, the correct option is (C).

5. PPF provides income tax deduction under section 80C for the amount invested (subject to a limit of Rs 1.5 lakh a year). Interest received is exempt from tax and there is no tax on the amount received on maturity of the account.

Hence, the correct option is (D).

6. A Demat account (short for the Dematerialized account) is an account to hold financial securities (equity or debt) in electronic form. In India, Demat accounts are maintained by two depository organizations, National Securities Depository Limited and Central Depository Services Limited. A depository participant, such as a bank, acts as an intermediary between the investor and the depository. India adopted the Demat account for electronic storing, wherein shares and securities are represented and maintained electronically, thus eliminating the troubles associated with paper shares.

A depository is an organization that holds securities (like shares, debentures, bonds, government securities, mutual fund units, etc.) of investors in electronic form at the request of the investors through a registered Depository Participant. It also provides services related to transactions in securities.

Hence, the correct option is (B).

7. The system of marketing information is the structure of people, equipment, and procedures for the generation and processing of information that pertains to marketing. Marketing Information System is a system that analyzes and assesses marketing information, gathered continuously from sources inside and outside an organization. Timely marketing information provides a basis for decisions such as product development or improvement, pricing, packaging, distribution, media selection, and promotion.

Hence, the correct option is (A).

8. Structured Financial Messaging System **(SFMS)** is a secure messaging standard developed to serve as a platform for intra-bank and inter-bank applications. It is an Indian standard similar to SWIFT (Society for Worldwide Interbank Financial Telecommunications) which is the international messaging system used for financial messaging globally.

SFMS can be used for secure communication within the bank and between banks. The SFMS was launched on December 14, 2001, at IDRBT. It allows the definition of message structures, message formats, and authorization of the same for usage by the financial community. SFMS has some features and it is a modularized and web-enabled software, with a flexible architecture facilitating centralized or distributed deployment. The access control is through Smart Card based user access and messages are secured by means of standard encryption and authentication services conforming to ISO standards.

SMS (short message service) is a text messaging service component of most telephone, Internet, and mobile device systems. It uses standardized communication protocols to enable mobile devices to exchange short text messages. An intermediary service can facilitate a text-to-voice conversion to be sent to landlines.

FSMS means the adoption of GMP, GHP, HACCP, and other such practices to be followed by FBOs to ensure food safety. Food Safety Management System (FSMS) cannot be separated from Food Safety because food safety is the reason that there is an FSMS program.

Mutual Fund Service System **(MFSS)** is an online order collection system provided by NSE to its eligible members for placing subscription or redemption orders on the MFSS based on orders received from the investors.

Hence, the correct option is (C).

9. As a **collecting** banker, he collects the proceeds of cheques drawn on other bankers and branches which have been paid in by customers for the credit of their accounts.

Advising Bank is the bank that advises the letter of credit to the beneficiary. Advising banks act upon the request of issuing banks. Generally, advising banks are located in the same country as beneficiaries. That is why issuing banks need their services.

Collecting banker, he collects the proceeds of cheques drawn on other bankers and branches which have been paid in by customers for the credit of their accounts.

The issuing bank is a bank that offers card association branded payment cards directly to consumers, such as credit cards, debit cards, contactless devices such as key fobs as well as prepaid cards. The name is derived from the practice of issuing cards to a consumer.

Hence, the correct option is (A).

10. Financial statements are reports prepared by a company's management to present the financial performance and position at a point in time. A general-purpose set of financial statements usually includes a balance sheet, income statements, statement of owner's equity, and statement of cash flows.

Hence, the correct option is (D).

11. Corporate culture is a set of values, beliefs, goals, norms, and ways of solving problems by the members of the organization that determine how a company's employees and management interact and handle outside business transactions. Often, corporate culture is implied, not expressly defined, and develops organically over time from the cumulative traits of the people the company hires.

Hence, the correct option is (A).

12. In Garnishee Order, Subsequent proceedings of a court are called garnishee absolute. Garnishee proceedings is done in two different stages. The first stage is for the garnishee order nisi, while the second stage is for the garnishee order absolute. It is a special procedure invoked to compel a third party (for instance a bank) who is in possession of the asset of the judgment debtor to forfeit the said asset to the judgment creditor to the tune of the debt in question. It has always been a tug of war between judgment creditors and third-party garnishee.

Hence, the correct option is (B).

13. Risk category is reviewed under KYC has to be undertaken by banks in not less than 6 months.

The KYC directions from the RBI clearly state that the KYC process should follow risk categorization of customers into high, medium, and low risk. The directions also state that the KYC of low-risk customers should be done only once every 10 years if there is no change in the identity or address.

Hence, the correct option is (C).

14. The Paid-up value of shares is defined as the amount which the company has received against its issued shares.

Paid-up capital is created when a company sells its shares on the primary market directly to investors, usually through an initial public offering (IPO).

Hence, the correct option is (A).

15. Volatile Memory is used to store computer programs and data that the CPU needs in real-time and is erased once the computer is switched off. RAM and Cache memory is volatile memory. Whereas Non-volatile memory is static and remains on the computer even if the computer is switched off. ROM and HDD are non-volatile memory.

Read-only memory (ROM) is the permanent memory that is used to store these important control programs and systems software to perform functions such as booting up or starting up programs.

Garbage memory includes data, objects, or other regions of the memory of a computer system (or other system resources), which will not be used in any future computation by the system, or by a program running on it. Because every computer system has a finite amount of memory, and most software produces garbage, it is frequently necessary to deallocate the memory that is occupied by garbage and return it to the heap, or memory pool, for reuse.

Hence, the correct option is (A).

16. Ethics - Moral principles that govern a person's behavior or the conducting of an activity.

Ethical principles: These principles apply to all staff (including those holding honorary appointments), students of UCL, and members of UCL Council. Specific aspects of these principles will apply to UCL contractors and partners where agreements with them require adherence to any of the documents listed in Annex B.

This statement of principles is deliberately short and simple. It is designed to complement Annex A and the documents referred to in Annex B, and to act as an aid to individuals when dealing with decisions at UCL where ethical considerations come into play.

Hence, the correct option is (C).

17. Perform Qualitative Risk Analysis is the process of prioritizing risks for further analysis or action by assessing and combining their probability of occurrence and impact. The key benefit of this process is that it enables project managers to reduce the level of uncertainty and to focus on high-priority risks.

Hence, the correct option is (A).

18.

- Application Software is a program or group of programs designed for end-users. Examples of an application include a word processor, a spreadsheet, an accounting application, a web browser, an email client, a media player, a file viewer, simulators, a console game, or a photo editor.

- An Operating System (OS) is an interface between a computer user and computer hardware. An operating system is a software that performs all the basic tasks like file management, memory management, process management, handling input and output, and controlling peripheral devices such as disk drives and printers.

- System Software is a type of computer program that is designed to run a computer's hardware and application programs. If we think of the computer system as a layered model, the system software is the interface between the hardware and user applications.

- Middleware is computer software that provides services to software applications beyond those available from the operating system. It can be described as "software glue".

Hence, the correct option is (B).

19. Ethical conduct, Environmental practice and Human rights and employee relations are related to the term Corporate Social Responsibility (CSR).

• Corporate Social Responsibility, or CSR is the self declared business model of the various corporate sectors in our economy.

• This CSR mainly includes the maintenance of the sustainability in our society by the corporate world.

• This sustainability includes social ethics, care about environment and also care about the human resource of the corporate sector itself.

• This helps the corporate sectors, to efficiently connect with the human society.

Hence, the correct option is (D).

20. Attach the account, with the garnishee amount, since R is the exclusive owner of the account, during his lifetime.

Non-Resident bank accounts are those, which are maintained by Indian nationals and Persons of Indian origin resident abroad, foreign nationals, and foreign companies in India.

Hence, the correct option is (B).

21. The endorsement is irregular due to which the paying bank is not protected under the provisions of Section 85 of the NI Act. An endorsement may be a signature authorizing the legal transfer of a negotiable instrument between parties. Endorsements can also be amendments to contracts or documents, such as life insurance policies or driver's licenses. Hence, the correct option is (D).

22. The Quality Management Plan documents the necessary information required to effectively manage project quality from project planning to delivery. It defines a project's quality policies, procedures, criteria for and areas of application, and roles, responsibilities, and authorities.

Hence, the correct option is (C).

23. Interestingly, as per the current repo rate, SBI's savings accounts with over Rs 1 lakh deposits will (from May 1, 2019) earn less interest than those with smaller balances in their accounts and also 0.75 percent less than the 4 percent being offered on post office savings account. However, if the repo rate goes above 6.25 percent, then the interest rate for the large SBI savings accounts would be higher than the current 3.5 percent

being earned on smaller accounts, as per the external benchmarking formula.

"Amount of term deposit of Rs.1 lakh minus the balance including interest in the overdraft li limit of Rs. 0.50 lakh against this Term Deposit".

Hence, the correct option is (C).

24. International Factoring is a must need service for the companies engaged in the import and export of goods and services. Companies engaged in international trade, regardless of their size and industry; often face a demand from the importers for an account trade and longer payment terms. This means, getting the payment weeks after the invoice date. Under this system, the transaction involves four parties; exporter, importer, import factor in importer's country, and export factor in exporter's country.

Hence, the correct option is (B).

25. The Offsite Surveillance and Monitoring System (OSMOS) plays a key role in the identification of risks and monitoring banks on a continuous basis. OSMOS consists of a set of 28 structured returns that capture prudential and statistical information of banks at periodical intervals. The RBI requires banks to submit detailed and structured information periodically under OSMOS. On the basis of OSMOS, RBI analyzes the health of the banks.

Following activities can be considered as part of off-site supervision of banks by RBI-

(1) Analysis of statements called by banks

(2) Analysis of the balance sheet of the bank

(3) Meeting with the management periodically

(4) Rating reports of rating agencies

Hence, the correct option is (A).

26. Universal Serial Bus (or USB) Port

- It can connect all kinds of external USB devices such as external hard disk, printer, scanner, mouse, keyboard, etc.

- It was introduced in 1997.

- Most of the computers provide two USB ports as a minimum.

- Data travels at 12 megabits per second.

⇒ USB compliant devices can get power from a USB port.

⇒ The parallel port is a type of interface found on computers for connecting peripherals. The name refers to the way the data is sent; parallel ports send multiple bits of data at once, as opposed to serial communication, in which bits are sent one at a time.

⇒ A smart port is an automated port that uses nascent technologies such as big data, the Internet of Things (IoT), blockchain solutions, and other smart technology-based methods to improve performance and economic competitiveness. With these technologies, smart ports can also improve environmental sustainability.

⇒ A serial port is a serial communication interface through which information transfers in or out sequentially one bit at a time. This is in contrast to a parallel port, which communicates multiple bits simultaneously in parallel.

Hence, the correct option is (A).

27. The Export Credit extended as per the details below would be classified as a priority sector.

Domestic banks	Foreign banks with 20 branches and above	Foreign banks with less than 20 branches
Incremental export credit over the corresponding date of the preceding year. up to 2 percent of ANBC or Credit Equivalent Amount of OH-Balance Sheet Exposure, whichever is higher, effective from April 1, 2015 subject to a sanctioned limit of up to ₹ 25 crores per borrower to units having turnover of up to ₹. 100 crore.	incremental export credit over the corresponding date of the preceding year, up to 2 percent of ANBC or Credit Equivalent Amount of Off-Balance Sheet Exposure, whichever is higher. effective from April 1, 2017 (As per their approved plans, foreign banks with 20 branches and above are allowed to court a certain percentage of export credit Limit as a priority sector till March 2017)	Export credit will be allowed up to 32 Decent of ANEC or Credit Equivalent Amount of Off-Balance Sheet Exposure. Whichever is higher.

Hence, the correct option is (A).

28. The function of a distribution channel does not include product synchronization.

- The synchronize products service method synchronizes all products and related product repositories (that is, artifacts) that need to be synchronized. The related product repositories such as Manufacturers, Product Types, Classifications (categories), and global specifications are referred to as product artifacts.

- In simple terms, the risk is the possibility of something bad happening. Risk involves uncertainty about the effects/implications of activity with respect to something that humans value, often focusing on negative, undesirable consequences. Many different definitions have been proposed.

- Matching of Demand and Supply: The most important function of middlemen is to collect goods and services from many producers so that consumers may select from among a large number of alternatives. Thus, the middlemen play the game of matching demand and supply of goods and services in a market

- Negotiation is a dialogue between two or more people or parties intended to reach a beneficial outcome over one or more issues where a conflict exists with respect to at least one of these issues.

Hence, the correct option is (C).

29. "Phishing" is online fraud to get personal data.

Note- Phishing is a cybercrime in which a target or targets are contacted by email, telephone, or text message by someone posing as a legitimate institution to lure individuals into providing sensitive data such as personally identifiable information, banking, and credit card details and passwords. Hence, the correct option is (C).

30. The locker room should be fully checked before locking the room and this is the responsibility of the custodian of the locker room key.

Note- Every locker has a master key that is held by the bank or private service provider. A duplicate of this key is available only from the vault manufacturer. A second key, for which there is no duplicate, is given to the locker owner.
Hence, the correct option is (A).

31. The main objectives of computerization at the branch level is-

(i) To improve customer service, quality of housekeeping

(ii) Generation of data for better management control

Computerization on branch level should be achieved on any of the following basis-

* Selected branches will have on-line terminals with micro and mini-computers which will be linked with a central main-frame computer to provide counter service and other office-services.

* Personal computers will be installed at counters which will be linked with the Local area network.

* For the third option, the banks will have to depend on Telecom lines.

Hence, the correct option is (D).

32. Banks are required to classify NPAs further into Substandard, Doubtful, and Loss assets.

1. Substandard assets: Assets which has remained NPA for a period less than or equal to 12 months.

2. Doubtful assets: An asset would be classified as doubtful if it has remained in the substandard category for a period of 12 months.

3. Loss assets: As per RBI, "Loss asset is considered uncollectible and of such little value that its continuance as a bankable asset is not warranted, although there may be some salvage or recovery value."
Hence, the correct option is (C).

33. * A positive correlation exists between risk and return: the greater the risk, the higher the potential for profit or loss. Using the risk-reward tradeoff principle, low levels of uncertainty (risk) are associated with low returns and high levels of uncertainty with high returns. An investor needs to understand his individual risk tolerance when constructing a portfolio.

* In statistics, there is a negative relationship or inverse relationship between two variables if higher values of one variable tend to be associated with lower values of the other.

* The relationship between the two variables is generally considered strong when their r value is larger than 0.7. The correlation r measures the strength of the linear relationship

between two quantitative variables. Pearson r: r > 0 indicates a positive association.

* A zero correlation exists when there is no relationship between two variables. For example, there is no relationship between the amount of tea drunk and level of intelligence.

Hence, the correct option is (A).

34. The Banking Codes and Standards Board of India was registered as a society under the Societies Registration Act, 1860 in February 2006. It functions as an independent and autonomous body. Membership of BCSBI is voluntary and open to scheduled banks.

Hence, the correct option is (D).

35. The authorized capital of Regional Rural Banks is Rs. 5 crores which are contributed by Central Government, State Government, and the Sponsor Bank. The Regional Rural Banks is owned by the Central Government, the State Government, and the Sponsor Bank who held shares in the ratios as follows Central Government – 50%, State Government – 15%, and Sponsor Banks – 35%.

Hence, the correct option is (D).

36. 'Kite Flying' refers to Permitting drawls against uncleared cheques. It is an unfair and illegal means of obtaining bank funds by drawing fictitious bills of exchange that have actually no exchange of consideration among the parties and getting the bank to grant a credit against these bills to the parties to the fictitious contract.

Hence, the correct option is (C).

37. National Bank for Agriculture and Rural Development (NABARD) is the apex institution for financing agricultural and rural sectors.

Note- National Bank for Agriculture and Rural Development is an apex development finance institution in India. The bank has been entrusted with "matters concerning policy, planning, and operations in the field of credit for agriculture and other economic activities in rural areas in India".
Hence, the correct option is (C).

38. In the case where the deceased depositor had not made any nomination or for the accounts other than those styled as 'either or survivor' (such as single or jointly operated accounts), banks are advised to adopt a simplified procedure for repayment to the legal heir(s) of the depositor keeping in view the imperative need to avoid inconvenience and undue hardship to the common person. In this context, banks may, keeping in view their risk management systems, fix a minimum threshold limit, for the balance in the account of the deceased depositors, up to which claims in respect of the deceased depositors could be settled without insisting on production of any documentation other than a letter of indemnity.

Hence, the correct option is (D).

39. Code of ethics specifies methods for reporting violations, disciplinary action for violations and the structure of the due process to be followed.

Note- Business ethics is a form of applied ethics or professional ethics, that examines ethical principles and moral or ethical problems that can arise in a business environment. It applies to all aspects of business conduct and is relevant to the conduct of individuals and entire organizations.
Hence, the correct option is (B).

40. Imperfect banknote means any banknote, which is wholly or partially, obliterated, shrunk, washed, altered, or indecipherable but does not include a mutilated banknote.
Hence, the correct option is (C).

41. All the data and files are shared easily in Local Area Network (LAN) because all the data has stored in a server so it is shared easily, fast, and secured. Hence, also save a lot of time and money. Covers Limited Area LAN is only worked in a small working area locality like in offices, schools, banks, etc.

Hence, the correct option is (D).

42. The Banking Ombudsman is appointed by the Reserve Bank in terms of the scheme framed under the Banking Regulation Act. It is a quasi-judicial authority functioning under India's Banking Ombudsman Scheme 2006, and the authority was created pursuant to a decision made by the Government of India to enable resolution of complaints of customers of banks relating to certain services rendered by the banks. The Banking Ombudsman Scheme was first introduced in India in 1995 and was revised in 2002. The current scheme became operative from 1 January 2006 and replaced and superseded the banking Ombudsman Scheme 2002.

Hence, the correct option is (D).

43. A house loan or home loan simply means a sum of money borrowed from a financial institution or bank to purchase a house. Home loans consist of an adjustable or fixed interest rate and payment terms.

A personal loan is a type of unsecured loan and helps you meet your current financial needs. You don't usually need to pledge any security or collateral while availing of a personal loan and your lender provides you with the flexibility to use the funds as per your need.

A car loan (also known as an automobile loan, or auto loan) is a sum of money a consumer borrows in order to purchase a car. Many consumers apply for car loans at their local bank. When applying for a car loan a borrower will usually begin by specifying how much money he or she wants to borrow.

Note- A teaser loan is any loan that offers a lower interest rate for a fixed amount of time as a purchase incentive. Common teaser loans include credit cards with low introductory offers and adjustable-rate mortgages. Borrowers must be aware of the rates that will apply after a teaser rate expires.

A business loan is a loan specifically intended for business purposes. As with all loans, it involves the creation of a debt, which will be repaid with added interest.

Hence, the correct option is (C).

44. This account was introduced as the NRE scheme in 1970. It's a Rupee account and the NRI can remit money to India from the funds abroad. This means that depositor is exposed to the currency rates risk. An NRE-RA account can be opened as saving, current, RD, and FD only because these accounts are opened for the purpose of depositing income earned overseas. The funds held in these accounts can be remitted back overseas freely subject to the terms and conditions of the resident country.

Hence, the correct option is (C).

45. Monetary policy refers to the policy of the Reserve Bank of India with regard to the use of monetary instruments under its control to achieve the goals of GDP growth and lower inflation rate. The RBI is authorized to the made monetary policy under the Reserve Bank of India Act, 1934.

The Monetary Policy Committee (MPC) constituted by the Central Government under Section 45ZB determines the policy interest rate required to achieve the inflation target. The Reserve Bank's Monetary Policy Department (MPD) assists the MPC in formulating the monetary policy.

Hence, the correct option is (B).

46. The liquid has a unique advantage of having low power consumption than the LED or cathode ray tube. The liquid crystal display screen works on the principle of blocking light rather than emitting light. LCDs require a backlight as they do not emit light them.

A liquid-crystal display (LCD) is a flat-panel display or another electronically modulated optical device that uses the light-modulating properties of liquid crystals combined with polarizers. Liquid crystals do not emit light directly, instead of using a backlight or reflector to produce images in color or monochrome. LCDs are available to display arbitrary images (as in a general-purpose computer display) or fixed images with low information content, which can be displayed or hidden, such as preset words, digits, and seven-segment displays, as in a digital clock.

Hence, the correct option is (D).

47. Islamic banking is banking or banking activity that is consistent with the principles of sharia (Islamic law) and it is a practical application through the development of Islamic economics. As such, a more correct term for Islamic banking is sharia-compliant finance. Sharia prohibits acceptance of specific interest or fees for loans of money (known as riba, or usury), whether the payment is fixed or floating.

Hence, the correct option is (C).

48. Establishment Of SEBI

The Securities and Exchange Board of India was established on April 12, 1992, in accordance with the provisions of the Securities and Exchange Board of India Act, 1992.

Preamble

The Preamble of the Securities and Exchange Board of India describes the basic functions of the Securities and Exchange Board of India as "to protect the interests of investors in securities and to promote the development of, and to regulate the securities market and for matters connected therewith or incidental thereto".

Hence, the correct option is (A).

49. Applications Supported by Blocked Amount (ASBA) is a process developed by India's Stock Market Regulator SEBI for applying to IPO. In ASBA, an IPO applicant's account doesn't get debited until shares are allotted to them.
Hence, the correct option is (C).

50. Hindi Day (Hindī Diwas) is national day of India, India celebrate this day every year on14 September. On September 14,1949 Hindi became the official language of India.

Hence, the correct option is (A).

51. The CVV Number ("Card Verification Value") on your credit card or debit card is a 3 digit number on VISA, MasterCard, and Discover branded credit and debit cards.

It is required to complete transactions using cards, but along with that, it also provides added security against scams. All financial institutions that issue credit or debit cards have developed a system in which every card is provided with a unique CVV code. This code is required to complete any monetary transactions that are carried out using the card. CVV number is different from the PIN number which is like a password to complete card transactions. CVV number is present on the backside of your card on the magnetic strip. It verifies that the card is physically available with the individual using it during the transaction.

Hence, the correct option is (B).

52. Letters of credit are indispensable for international transactions since they ensure that payment will be received. Using documentary letters of credit allows the seller to significantly reduce the risk of non-payment for delivered goods, by replacing the risk of the buyer with that of the banks.
Hence, the correct option is (B).

53. Every alliance agreement should include an exit strategy. This does not imply a pessimistic view of the relationship but rather recognizes that all alliances have a natural life. The average lifespan of an alliance is seven years.

Hence, the correct option is (D).

54. Depository receipts allow investors to invest in companies in foreign countries while trading in a local stock exchange in the investor's home country. It is advantageous to investors since shares are not allowed to leave the home country that they trade-in.

Depository receipts were created to minimize the complications of investing in foreign securities.

Previously, if investors wanted to buy shares in a foreign company, they would need to exchange their money into foreign currency and open a foreign brokerage account. Then, they would be able to purchase shares through the brokerage account on a foreign stock exchange.

The creation of depositary receipts eliminates the entire process and makes it simpler and more convenient for investors to invest in international companies.

Hence, the correct option is (A).

55. A minor cannot appoint a nominee in this account. On his behalf nomination will be done by a person legally competent to

act on his behalf. A joint account of a minor is allowed with his guardian.

The nomination is the right conferred upon the holder of a bank account to appoint one or more persons who will be entitled to receive monies upon the death of the account holder. In the event of the death of an account or locker holder, the bank can release the account proceeds or contents to the nominee without insisting upon a succession certificate, letter of administration, or court order. If the nomination is made in favor of a minor, details of the guardian of the minor also need to be mentioned in the nomination form. The guardian should be an adult who will get the amounts in the account on behalf of the minor in case of death of the account holder till the nominee attains majority.

Hence, the correct option is (A).

56. Features of channels for banking services are

(i) Intangibility/inseparability from the seller variability in customer experiences.

(ii) Perishability and non-storability/personal contacts with clients.

Banking Channels:

(i) Automated Teller Machines wherein customers can use the services 24×7 through a Debit Card.

(ii) Through a retail branch wherein customers can go personally and interact with the Bank personnel, and get a solution to their queries.

Hence, the correct option is (D).

57. The prudential limits in respect of both outstanding borrowing and lending transactions in call/notice money mark scheduled commercial banks, co-operative banks, and PDs are as follows:-

Table: Prudential limits for Transactions in Call / Notice Money Market

Sr. No.	Participant	Borrowing	Lending
1	Scheduled Commercial Banks	On a fortnightly average basis, borrowing outstanding should not exceed 100 percent of capital funds (i.e., the sum of Tier 1 and Tier II capital) of the latest audited balance sheet. However, banks are allowed to borrow a maximum of 125 percent of their capital funds on any day, during a fortnight.	On a fortnightly average basis, lending outstanding should not exceed 25 percent of their capital funds. However, banks are allowed to lend a maximum of 50 percent of their capital funds on any day, during a fortnight.
2	Co-operative Banks	Outstanding borrowings of State Cooperative Banks / District Central Cooperative Banks I Urban Co-operative Banks in call / notice money market, on a daily basis, should not exceed 2.0 percent of their aggregate deposits as at end-March of the previous financial year.	No limit.
3	PDs	PDs are allowed to borrow, on average in a reporting fortnight, up to 225 percent of their net owned funds (NOF) as at end-March of the previous financial year.	PDs are allowed to lend in call/notice money market, on average in a reporting fortnight, up to 25 percent of their NOF.

It is the ratio of deposits that banks have to keep with RBI. Under CRR a certain percentage of the total bank deposits has to be kept in the current account with RBI. Banks don't earn anything on that. Banks will not have access to this amount. They cannot use this money for any of their economic or commercial activities. Banks can't lend this portion of the money to corporate or individual borrowers.

Hence, the correct option is (C).

58. Most of the time, debt is classified as non-performing when loan payments have not been made for a period of 90 days (Standard period).

A non-performing asset is a debt obligation where the borrower has not made any previously agreed-upon interest and principal repayments to the designated lender for an extended period of time. A loan can be classified as a non-performing asset at any point during the term of the loan or at its maturity.

Hence, the correct option is (B).

59. Repo Rate refers to the rate at which commercial banks borrow money by selling their securities to the Reserve Bank of India (RBI) to maintain liquidity, in case of shortage of funds or due to some statutory measures.

The current Repo Rate is 4.00%.

The ratio of the liquid assets to the demand and time liabilities is called the Statutory Liquidity Ratio (SLR). The Reserve Bank of India (RBI) has the authority to increase this ratio by up to 40%.

The current Statutory Liquidity Ratio Rate is 18.00%.

Hence, the correct option is (B).

60. ISDN stands for integrated services digital network. It is a design for a completely digital. Telephone/telecommunications network is designed to carry voice, data, images, video, everything you could ever need.

Prior to ISDN, the telephone system consisted of digital links like T1/E1 on the long-distance lines between telephone company offices and analog signals on copper telephone wires to the customers, the "last mile". At the time, the network was viewed as a way to transport voice, with some special services available for data using additional equipment like modems or by providing a

T1 on the customer's location. What became ISDN started as an effort to digitize the last mile, originally under the name "Public Switched Digital Capacity" (PSDC). This would allow call routing to be completed in an all-digital system, while also offering a separate data line. The Basic Rate Interface, or BRI, is the standard last-mile connection in the ISDN system, offering two 64 kbit/s "bearer" lines and a single 16 kbit/s "delta" channel for commands and data.

Hence, the correct option is (D).

61. The second pillar Basel II, i.e. supervisory review rrocess, is a regulatory response to the first pillar, giving regulators better 'tools' over those previously available. It also provides a framework for dealing with systemic risk, pension risk, concentration risk, strategic risk, reputational risk, liquidity risk, and legal risk, which the accord combines under the title of residual risk. Banks can review their risk management system.

Hence, the correct option is (B).

62. In the case of a 'safe custody facility", the bank accepts the responsibility of the safe custody of the sealed boxes and packets. The banker can open such a box only on the duly authorized instructions of that customer.

The legal relationship that arises in the case of safe custody/deposit is that of bailment. The customer, who deposits the things in the box for safe custody with the bank, becomes the 'bailor', and the bank becomes the 'bailee'.

A safe custody facility is offered for an agreed period of time for which the customer is willing to keep and make payment of the necessary changes. The bailee (banker) shall return the contents of the sealed safe custody box to the bailor (customer) as soon as the purpose for which bailment was created is over.

On some occasions, bankers do not charge fees for safe custody facilities for customers who have been associated with them for a long period of time or customers who are maintaining a large amount of balance in their accounts or opening fixed deposits, etc. In such cases, the banker becomes a 'gratuitous bailee". In other cases, where charges are levied, the banker becomes a 'bailee for reward'.

The law of bailment is explained in Section 14,8 of the Contract Act, 1872.

Refer to the judgment given by the Supreme Court in the case of United Commercial Bank vs Hem Chandra Sarkar.

Hence, the correct option is (A).

63. A marketing information system (MKIS) is a management information system (MIS) designed to support marketing decision making. Jobber (2007) defines it as a "system in which marketing data is formally gathered, stored, analyzed, and distributed to managers in accordance with their informational needs on a regular basis."

- An organized collection, storage, and presentation system of data and other knowledge for decision making, progress reporting, and planning and evaluation of programs.

- Information processing is the set of activities, done in a particular sequence by which data produce information. These activities are called processing activities. These processing activities include collecting, collating, analyzing, presenting, and disseminating information. These activities are also known as the sub-processes of an information system. An information system can be either manual or computerized, or a combination of both.

Hence, the correct option is (B).

64. The case can be filed in DRT against the borrower having an outstanding ledger balance of Rs. 20 lacs and above in the NPA/Written-off account.

Procedure for filing of application/ file a case in DRT

The application can be presented by the applicant or by his agent or by an authorized legal practitioner. The application to be presented to the registrar of the tribunal within whose jurisdiction his case falls or can be sent through the registered post addressed to the Registrar.

There are 39 DRTs in the country. The Central government has raised "the pecuniary limit from Rs 10 lacs to Rs 20 lacs for filing an application for recovery of debts in the Debts Recovery Tribunals by such banks and financial institutions," said a Finance Ministry notification.

Hence, the correct option is (C).

65. Financial Intelligence Unit-India (FIU-IND) is the central national agency for receiving, processing, analyzing, and disseminating information relating to suspect financial transactions. FIU-IND is also responsible for coordinating and strengthening efforts of national and international intelligence, investigation, and enforcement agencies in combating money laundering, associated predicate offenses, and terrorist financing. It is an independent body reporting to the Economic Intelligence Council (EIC) headed by the Finance Minister.

The limit of reporting of cash transaction to FIU-
The number of transactions for a single account, which is valued at more than rupees ten lakhs within a month. Non-Profit Organization Transaction Report: Cash transactions of more than rupees ten lakhs involving a non-profit organization as recipient. Hence, the correct option is (B).

66. Encryption is the process in which data is converted from its present form into unrecognizable, encoded information. This way, encrypted messages can only be viewed by those authorized parties that have the way to remove the encryption from the data and see it in its original form.

Encryption is important in today's online marketplace. It helps to protect personal information—banking and credit card information, for example—and keep it viewable only by authorized parties.

Hypertext Transfer Protocol Secure (HTTPS) is the secured variant of HTTP. This URL has the https:// prefix. Secure, in this case, means that all communications between your browser and the website you are visiting are encrypted.

This encryption often uses the Secure Sockets Layer (SSL) Internet protocol, which is a protocol for encrypted communication between a web browser and a website.

Hence, the correct option is (B).

67. A time deposit or term deposit is a deposit in a financial institution with a specific maturity date or a period to maturity, commonly referred to as its "term". Time deposits differ from at-call deposits, such as savings or checking accounts, which can be withdrawn at any time, without any notice or penalty.

A demand deposit is a money deposited into a bank account with funds that can be withdrawn on-demand at any time. The depositor will typically use demand deposit funds to pay for everyday expenses.

Current Deposit refers to a deposit to a bank account or financial institution without a specified maturity date. These types of Current Deposit account generally only earn demand deposit interest.

Deferred deposit means a transaction in which a check casher refrains from depositing a personal check written by a customer until a date after the transaction date, pursuant to a written agreement.

Hence, the correct option is (A).

68. Business Risk Management is a subset of risk management used to evaluate the business risks involved if any changes occur in the business operations, systems, and process. It identifies, prioritizes, and addresses the risk to minimize penalties from unexpected incidents, by keeping them on track. It also enables an integrated response to multiple risks and facilitates a more informed risk-based decision-making capability.

Hence, the correct option is (D).

69. The Reserve Bank has been extending facilities to the public for exchanging cut and mutilated notes at all its Issue Offices and currency chest branches of commercial banks. In order to make the Note Refund Rules easy to understand and to apply, these have been comprehensively revised and simplified. It has also been decided that any officer of the designated branch can adjudicate mutilated notes presented thereat. It is hoped that simplification and liberalization of the Rules would help both, the prescribed officers as well as the tenderers of mutilated notes to easily comprehend the revised Rules and enable the former to apply the Note Refund Rules without leaving any scope for subjectivity.

The facility for exchange of soiled notes is available at all branches of public sector banks and currency chest branches of private sector banks, the facility of exchange of mutilated / cut notes is available only at the currency chest branches of commercial banks.

Hence, the correct option is (D).

70. Code-division multiple access (CDMA) is a channel access method used by various radio communication technologies. CDMA is an example of multiple access, where several transmitters can send information simultaneously over a single communication channel. This allows several users to share a band of frequencies (see bandwidth). To permit this without undue interference between the users, CDMA employs spread-spectrum technology and a special coding scheme (where each transmitter is assigned a code).

CDMA employs analog-to-digital conversion (ADC) in combination with spread spectrum technology. Audio input is first digitized into binary elements. The frequency of the transmitted signal is then made to vary according to a defined pattern (code), so it can be intercepted only by a receiver whose frequency response is programmed with the same code, so it follows exactly along with the transmitter frequency. There are trillions of possible frequency-sequencing codes, which enhances privacy and makes cloning difficult.

Hence, the correct option is (A).

71. The minimum tenure of PPF is 15 years, extendable in blocks of 5 years. Withdrawals not exceeding 50% of 4th-year balance are permitted after a lock-in period of 7 years. PPF also offers loan facilities in specific circumstances. ELSS mutual funds, on the other hand, are the most liquid investments u/s 80C. Hence, the correct option is (D).

72. Core Banking is computerization in which branches are connected to a central host server and its advantages are-

Reliable centralized data repository= A central repository offers trustworthy data in order to produce accurate trend analysis. This increased quality is due to the data being consistently updated as well as standardized across departmental databases.

Provision of Online ATM, telebanking, internet banking= Allows us to easily access the bank and do transactions more smoothly. Hence, the correct option is (D).

73. "LINUX" is an Operating System but it is different from other operating systems in many important ways. First, and perhaps most importantly, Linux is open-source software. The code used to create Linux is free and available to the public to view, edit, and—for users with the appropriate skills—to contribute to.

Linux has been around since the mid-1990s and has since reached a user-base that spans the globe. Linux is actually everywhere: It Is in your phones, your thermostats, in your cars, refrigerators, Roku devices, and televisions. It also runs most of the Internet, all of the world's top 500 supercomputers, and the world's stock exchanges.

Hence, the correct option is (A).

74. 'Windows' applications run on GUI. A graphical user interface is a form of user interface that allows users to interact with electronic devices through graphical icons and audio indicators such as primary notation, instead of text-based user interfaces, typed command labels, or text navigation. Hence, the correct option is (B).

75. Consortium funding is an example of a loan provided by a few banks and the bank with maximum credit extending, act as the main bank.

In the financial world, a consortium refers to several lending institutions that group together to jointly finance a single borrower. These multiple banking arrangements are very similar to loan syndication, although there are structural and operational

differences between the two.
Hence, the correct option is (A).

76. Information explosion, and avoidance of communication gap and to take prompt decisions and to face non-price competition.

Marketing information and research address the need for quicker, yet more accurate, decision making by the marketer. These tools put marketers close to their customers to help them understand who the customers are, what they want, and what competitors are doing.

Hence, the correct option is (C).

77. The Financial Action Task Force (FATF) is an intergovernmental organization that designs and promotes policies and standards to combat financial crime. Recommendations created by the Financial Action Task Force (FATF) target money laundering, terrorist financing, and other threats to the global financial system.

Hence, the correct option is (B).

78. 10,000 to Rs. 50,000 has been provided to marginal farmers (as Flexi KCC) based on the landholding and crops grown including post-harvest warehouse storage-related credit needs and other farm expenses, consumption needs, etc., plus small term loan investments without relating it to the value of the land.
Hence, the correct option is (B).

79. Copy the data from the magnetic strip of cards.

A skimmer is a card reader that can be disguised to look like part of an ATM. The skimmer attachment collects card numbers and PIN codes, which are then replicated into counterfeit cards. Skimming is the type of fraud that occurs when an ATM is compromised by a skimmer.

Hence, the correct option is (B).

80. A Bill is a draft statute that becomes law after it is passed by both the Houses of Parliament and assented to by the President. All legislative proposals are brought before Parliament in the form of Bills.

Non-negotiable refers to the price of a good or security that is firmly established and cannot be adjusted or a part of a contract or deal that is considered a requirement by one or both involved parties.

So on concluding above lines we find that A Government bill is not a negotiable instrument.

Hence, the correct option is (B).

81. A mortgage is taken for a huge amount. Hypothecation is done for a small amount.

A mortgage is done for immovable properties like land, building, warehouse, etc. Hypothecation, on the other hand, is done for movable properties like cars, vehicles, stocks, etc.

Under the mortgage, the interest of the asset would be transferred to the lender first, and then once the amount is paid off, it is re-transferred. But if the borrower isn't able to pay the amount, then the immovable property is sold off. Under hypothecation, the interest of the asset isn't transferred. Rather when the borrower isn't able to pay the amount due, then the movable property is possessed and then sold off to get back the proceeds.

For a mortgage, a mortgage deed is required as a legal document. For hypothecation, the hypothecation deed is required as a legal document.

The tenure of a mortgage is more since the amount of the loan is huge. But in the case of hypothecation, the tenure is lesser since the amount of loan is lower.
Hence, the correct option is (A).

82. Businesses become customer-centric and industry-driven due to Competition.

Client-centric, also known as customer-centric, is an approach to doing business that focuses on creating a positive experience for the customer by maximizing service and/or product offerings and building relationships.
=>customer centric is so important-
Customer centricity is an approach to doing business that focuses on providing a positive customer experience in order to drive profit and gain a competitive advantage. Customer-centricity helps you to build trust and loyalty of your customers, but also a solid reputation.
Hence, the correct option is (C).

83. STP is an initiative used by companies in the financial world to optimize the speed at which transactions are being processed. It is done by electronically connecting participant's internal systems with Central Bank's RTGS System and hence there won't be a need to enter the same pieces of information repeatedly.

STP will increase the efficiency level at the participant's end due to shortened processing cycles. It will also reduce operational errors and moreover curtailed operating expenses because of not reentering transactions in multiple systems. STP is beneficial in decreasing settlement risk. This is because shortening transaction-related processing time will increase the probability that a payment contract /agreement will actually be settled on time. Since the inception of RTGS in many countries, enrollment of direct participants is growing and the volume of transactions is also increasing. It has been foreseen that in the future, the volume of transactions will increase dramatically. This growing volume forcing banks to deploy a gateway application between Core Banking System and Central Bank to improving the performance of financial messages communications channels.

Hence, the correct option is (A).

84. Two duties should not be clubbed with respect to the banking software system.
1) Security administration and security audit:-
A security audit is a systematic evaluation of the security of a company's information system by measuring how well it conforms to a set of established criteria. A Security Administrator is a person who manually administers user access rights to systems. A workflow system may call on a Security Administrator to fulfill an approved request on systems where automated administration agents are not available or have not yet been configured.
2) Security administration and network administration:-
A network administrator is a person designated in an

organization whose responsibility includes maintaining computer infrastructures with emphasis on networking. A Security Administrator is a person who manually administers user access rights to systems. A workflow system may call on a Security Administrator to fulfill an approved request on systems where automated administration agents are not available or have not yet been configured.

3) Systems development and maintenance:-

The modification of a system to correct faults, to improve performance, or to adapt the system to a changing environment or changed requirements.

Hence, the correct option is (D).

85. The basic objective of a Savings Bank Account is to enable the customer to save his/her liquid assets and also earn money on that saving. Savings banks Accounts are preferred by individuals and provide liquidity for private and small businesses sometimes. Saving Accounts have no overdraft facility.

Hence, the correct option is (D).

86. The monetary policy refers to a regulatory policy whereby the central bank maintains its control over the supply of money to achieve general economic goals. The main instruments of the monetary policy are Cash Reserve Ratio, Statutory Liquidity Ratio, Bank Rate, Repo Rate, Reverse Repo Rate, and Open Market Operations. The MPC is required to meet at least four times a year. The quorum for the meeting of the MPC is four members. Each member of the MPC has one vote, and in the event of an equality of votes, the Governor has a second or casting vote.

Hence, the correct option is (C).

87. Account receivable is an example of book debts.

A book debt is a sum of money due to a business in the ordinary course of its business. It has been described as a debt that would normally be entered in the books of the business regardless of whether or not it is in fact entered.

Book debts include sums owed to a business for goods or services supplied or work carried out. Sums due under loans may also be treated as book debts. So we can say that account receivable is an example of book debts.

Hence, the correct option is (A).

88. NPA/Written-off accounts can be settled in Lock Adalat having an outstanding ledger balance up to Rs. 20 Lakhs.

Note- The lock adalat scheme has been formulated in order to make a definite impact on reducing NPAs. The scheme includes all sticky accounts, both suits filed and non-suit filed accounts, which are in the doubtful & loss category, with an outstanding balance of Rs 20 lakhs. No cut-off date has been suggested since the Adalat is an on-going process.

Hence, the correct option is (C).

89. The Special Mention Accounts are usually categorized in terms of duration. For example, in the case of SMA -1, the overdue period is between 31 to 60 days. On the other hand, an overdue between 61 to 90 days will make an asset SMA -2. In the case of SMA -NF, non-financial indications about stress of an asset is considered.

Hence, the correct option is (B).

90. Under the cheque mode of fund payment, there are three parties that are involved in the on-track movement of money through a written paper source.

A) Drawee

It is basically the bank on which the cheque is drawn and is called the "Drawee". Always remember that a cheque is always drawn on a particular banker.

B) Drawer or Maker

He/she is the customer or account holder who issues the cheque.

C) Payee

The individual who is named in the cheque for getting the payment is known as the "Payee". Interestingly, the drawer and the payee can be the same individual in a particular case.

Hence, the correct option is (B).

91. Mobile Banking Features

- 24-hour access to account balances, account history, and transactions.
- Secure mobile check deposit, using the smartphone camera.
- Bill payments.
- Loan payments.
- Money transfers.
- security and fraud alerts.
- Travel services.

Hence, the correct option is (D).

92. The Institute for Development & Research in Banking Technology is an institution exclusively focused on banking technology. Established by the Reserve Bank of India in 1996, the institution works at the intersection of banking and technology. It is located in Hyderabad, India.

The Institute catalyzes utilization of the best technologies in BFSI and has taken a series of big initiatives like creating the nation-wide communication backbone for the Banking Sector - INdian FInancial NETwork (INFINITE); becoming the Certifying Authority for the BFSI; launching of Structured Financial Messaging System (SFMS) for the secure flow of financial messages; instituting Fellowships for Ph. D. in Banking Technology; offering a unique M.Tech. in Banking Technology and Information Security; an intensive Post Graduate Diploma in Banking Technology (PGDBT) and a basket of highly customized Executive Education Programmes.

Hence, the correct option is (D).

93. In India, RBI is referred to as the lender of last resort. Reserve Bank of India is the central bank of India. At the time of liquidity crisis faced by the commercial banks, RBI gives loans to the commercial banks to meet their financial crisis, and thus, it acts as a lender of last resort.

Hence, the correct option is (A).

94. The Information Technology Act, 2000 (also known as ITA-2000, or the IT Act) is an Act of the Indian Parliament (No 21 of 2000) notified on 17 October 2000. It is the primary law in India dealing with cybercrime and electronic commerce.

The Indian Institutes of Information Technology Laws (Amendment) Bill, 2020 was passed in Lok Sabha on 20th March 2020.

Aim- The bill will confer the status of National Importance to five Indian Institutes of Information Technology (IIITs)- Surat, Bhopal, Bhagalpur, Agartala, and Raichur.

The Bill will encourage IIITs to promote the study of information and technology in the country through their innovative and quality methods.

Hence, the correct option is (B).

95. A reverse mortgage is a loan available to homeowners, 62 years or older, that allows them to convert part of the equity in their homes into cash. The loan is called a reverse mortgage because instead of making monthly payments to a lender, as with a traditional mortgage, the lender makes payments to the borrower. Reverse Mortgage Loan provides an additional source of income for senior citizens of India, who have a self-acquired or self-occupied home in India. This product is beneficial for senior citizens who do not have adequate income to support themselves.

Hence, the correct option is (C).

96. The Income-tax Act provides for special status to a Hindu Undivided Family (HUF) and it is assessed to income-tax as a separate unit of assessment. The act has not defined the concept of the Hindu undivided family. For this purpose, we have to depend upon Hindu law.

Generally speaking, the concept of Hindu Undivided Family means a group of persons lineally descended from a common ancestor and- includes their wives and unmarried daughters. It comes into existence due to a certain relationship and it cannot come into existence by an agreement among strangers.

Hindu Undivided Family ('HUF') is treated as a 'person' under section 2(31) of the Income-tax Act, 1961 (Act). HUF is a separate entity for the purpose of assessment under the Act.

Under Hindu Law, a HUF is a family that consists of all persons lineally descended from a common ancestor and includes their wives and unmarried daughters. A HUF cannot be created under a contract, it is created automatically in a Hindu Family.

Jain and Sikh families even though are not governed by the Hindu Law, but are treated as HUF under the Act.

Hence, the correct option is (D).

97. An asset will be straightway classified as Doubtful if the erosion in the value of the security is 50 percent than the value assessed by the bank or accepted by RBI at the time of the last inspection.

Note- A Non-Performing Asset where the erosion in the value of securities is more than 50% of the value as assessed by the bank/ accepted by Reserve Bank of India previously at the time of the last inspection and where the value of securities available is more than 10% of the outstanding liability should be straightaway classified under doubtful category and provisioning should be made as applicable to Doubtful Assets.
Hence, the correct option is (A).

98. The legal act for u/s 141 of the NI Act, offences by companies are-

I) If the person who has committed an offence is a company, then every person responsible for such offence, as well as the company itself, shall be deemed to be guilty of the offence.

II) A person nominated as a director by virtue of his holding any office or employment in the Central or State government, he/she shall not be liable for prosecution.

Note- Section 141 of the said Act, in case of offence by Company, provides for vicarious liability on every person who, at the time the offence was committed, was in charge of, and was responsible to the Company for the conduct of the business of the Company.
Hence, the correct option is (B).

99. One can file an appeal against the award or the decision of the NBFC Ombudsman rejecting the complaint, within 30 days of the date of receipt of communication of Award or rejection of the complaint. The Appellate Authority may, if he/ she is satisfied that the applicant had sufficient cause for not making an application for appeal within time, also allow a further period not exceeding 30 days.

Hence, the correct option is (A).

100. The State Bank of India has signed a memorandum of understanding with the National Investment and Infrastructure Fund to boost the availability of capital for infrastructure projects. The scope of the agreement includes equity investments, project funding, bond financing, renewable energy support, and take-out finance for operating assets.

Hence, the correct option is (B).

101. MCLR (Marginal Cost of Funds based Lending Rate) replaced the earlier base rate system to determine the lending rates for commercial banks. RBI implemented MCLR on 1 April 2016 to determine rates of interest for loans. It is an internal reference rate for banks to determine the interest they can levy on loans. For this, they take into account the additional or incremental cost of arranging an additional rupee for a prospective buyer.

Our Central Bank (RBI) sets a minimum rate for loan borrowers below which banks are not allowed to lend money that is termed as Base rate. This was done to ensure that the customers would receive a lower cost of funds with transparency in the credit market.

Hence, the correct option is (A).

102.

- MSP is a form of market intervention by the GoI to insure agricultural producers against any sharp fall in farm prices.

- The MSP is announced at the beginning of the sowing season for certain crops on the basis of the recommendations of the Commission for Agricultural Costs and Prices (CACP).

- MSP is price fixed to protect the producer – farmers – against excessive fall in price during bumper production years.

- In case the market price for the commodity falls below the announced minimum price due to bumper production and glut in the market, govt. agencies purchase the entire quantity offered by the farmers at the announced minimum price.

- The minimum support prices are a guaranteed price for their produce from the Government.

- The major objectives are to support the farmers from distress sales and to procure food grains for public distribution.

Hence, the correct option is (B).

103. Contingent liabilities including guarantee obligations, while examining audited financials can be studied through Auditor's notes to the account.

Note- Auditors are required to express an opinion on the financial statements as a whole. This includes the notes to the financial statements which are an integral part of the accounts, providing additional information on balances and transactions and other relevant information.

A contingent liability is a liability or a potential loss that may occur in the future depending on the outcome of a specific event. Hence, the correct option is (C).

104. Central Bank generally deals with the public and tries to encourage saving habits among people.

Central Bank of India, a government-owned bank, is one of the oldest and largest commercial banks in India. It is based in Mumbai which is the financial capital of India and the capital city of the state of Maharashtra.

(i) Central Bank regulates currency in accordance with the requirements of business and the general public.

(ii) Central Banks performs general banking and agency service for the state.

Hence, the correct option is (C).

105. Under the National Agriculture Insurance Scheme (NAIS) risk insurance will not cover losses arising out of war & nuclear risks.

Note- The Government of India (GoI) has historically focused on crop insurance as a planned mechanism to mitigate the risks of natural perils on-farm production. The NAIS offers insurance for food crops, oilseeds, and selected commercial crops through a state-owned insurer, Agriculture Insurance Company of India (AICI).
Hence, the correct option is (C).

106. The Reserve Bank of India has a crucial role in the Indian economy as it makes or breaks the economy. Following mentioned are the regions where RBI plays a significant role

1. Development of the banking system

2. Development of financial institutions

3. Development of backward areas

4. Bringing Economic stability

5. Facilitating Economic growth

6. Preparing Proper interest rate structure

Hence, the correct option is (D).

107. Capital budgeting and investment appraisal is the planning process used to determine whether an organization's long term investments such as new machinery, replacement of machinery, new plants, new products, and research development projects are worth the funding of cash through the firm's capitalization structure therefore existing investment in a project is not treated as a sunk cost.

Hence, the correct option is (C).

108. IMEI: International Mobile Equipment Identity; a factory-installed unique serial number that identifies each unit or line of service under GSM (Global System for Mobile Communications) specifications. It is a 15 digit number and is used on non-SIM card capable devices. Motorola phones only have 14 digits so add the number 0 at the end.

The TAC identifies the phone manufacturer and model. TAC is the first 8 digits of IMEI, the next 6 digits are for SNR and the last digit is a kind of checksum.

If your phone is stolen then it can be traced based on IMEI as IMEI is stored in EIR - Equipment Identity Register Database where operators keep records of all the IMEI in 3 categories: Lost/White/Grey.

but first, we need to lodge an FIR and inform the operator so that they mark your IMEI in their database. If you want then they can block your IMEI for being used with any other sim so it's like your phone will not be of any use but in the case to trace it's better not to blacklist it.

In India, every big city police have software through which they can track down phones based on IMEI.

Hence, the correct option is (A).

109. The methods of data transmission for communication can be-

Simplex Operation - In simplex operation, a network cable or communications channel can send information in only one direction; it's a one-way street. For example, a radio station usually sends signals to the audience but never receives signals from them, thus a radio station is a simplex channel.

Half-duplex is a type of communication in which data can flow back and forth between two devices, but not simultaneously. Each device in a half-duplex system can send and receive data, but only one device can transmit at a time. An example of a half-duplex device is a CB (citizens band) radio.
Hence, the correct option is (D).

110. National Scheme for Liberation and Rehabilitation of Scavengers. The Scheme envisages liberating the scavengers engaged in the obnoxious and unclean profession of carrying out night soil on their heads and to rehabilitate them in clean and income-generating professions.

Funding-
1. The scheme provides for funding of projects costing up to Rs. 50,000/- per beneficiary and also for margin money to the extent

of 15% of the project cost at a 4 % rate of interest.

2. For projects costing Rs. 50,000/- the break up would be Rs. 10,000/- subsidy, Rs. 7,500/- margin money from State Scheduled Caste Development Corporations (SCDC)and Rs. 32,500/- loan from the banks.

3. Under the scheme subsidy would be 50 % of the project cost with a minimum ceiling of Rs. 10,000/--.

4. Thus for financial assistance the maximum project cost would be Rs. 50,000/-with 50 % subsidy with a maximum ceiling of Rs. 10,000/- and 15% as margin money.

Hence, the correct option is (A).

111. Following stages of the crop and risks leading to crop loss are covered under the scheme "Pradhan Mantri Fasal Bima Yojana".

a) Prevented Sowing/ Planting Risk: Insured area is prevented from sowing/ planting due to deficit rainfall or adverse seasonal conditions.

b) Standing Crop (Sowing to Harvesting): Comprehensive risk insurance is provided to cover yield losses due to non-preventable risks, viz. Drought, Dry spells, Flood, Inundation, Pests and Diseases, Landslides, Natural Fire and Lightening, Storm, Hailstorm, Cyclone, Typhoon, Tempest, Hurricane and Tornado.

c) Post-Harvest Losses: coverage is available only up to a maximum period of two weeks from harvesting for those crops which are allowed to dry in cut and spread condition in the field after harvesting against specific perils of cyclone and cyclonic rains and unseasonal rains.

d) Localized Calamities: Loss/ damage resulting from occurrence of identified localized risks of hailstorm, landslide, and Inundation affecting isolated farms in the notified area.

Hence, the correct option is (D).

112. A self-help group is a financial intermediary committee usually composed of 10 to 20 local women or men between 18 to 40 years. Most self-help groups are in India, though SHGs can be found in other countries, especially in South Asia and Southeast Asia.

The features of Self-Help Group (SHG) are :

(i) People form their personal groups for the purpose of savings and also lend money among themselves.

(ii) Rate of interest is lower than informal service providers.

(iii) They can also avail of loans from banks if their savings are regular.

(iv) Decisions regarding the savings and loan activities are taken by group members.

Hence, the correct option is (C).

113.

- Hypothecation occurs when an asset is pledged as collateral to secure a loan. The owner of the asset does not give up title, possession, or ownership rights, such as income generated by the asset. However, the lender can seize the asset if the terms of the agreement are

not met. A rental property, for example, may undergo hypothecation as collateral against a mortgage issued by a bank. While the property remains collateral, the bank has no claim on rental income that comes in; however, if the landlord defaults on the loan, the bank may seize the property.

- A mortgage loan or simply mortgage is a loan used either by purchasers of real property to raise funds to buy real estate, or alternatively by existing property owners to raise funds for any purpose while putting a lien on the property being mortgaged.

- A pledge is a bailment that conveys possession title to property owned by a debtor to a creditor to secure repayment for some debt or obligation and to the mutual benefit of both parties. The term is also used to denote the property which constitutes the security. The pledge is a type of security interest.

- A general lien is a possession lien used by the lien-holder to retain any of the debtor's goods in the possession of the lien-holder until any debt due from the debtor has been paid. Insurance brokers, packers, stockbrokers, and bankers have a general lien over the property of their clients or customers.

Hence, the correct option is (A).

114. With more RAM, more of the program instructions can be loaded and there is less need to keep swapping data in and out to the swap file on the hard disk drive. The constant swapping of data slows down the speed at which applications can run, so increasing RAM will increase the speed of operation of the computer.

Read-only memory is a type of non-volatile memory used in computers and other electronic devices. Data stored in ROM cannot be electronically modified after the manufacture of the memory device.

The primary characteristics of an HDD are its capacity and performance. Capacity is specified in unit prefixes corresponding to powers of 1000: a 1-terabyte (TB) drive has a capacity of 1,000 gigabytes (GB; where 1 gigabyte = 1 billion (109) bytes).

Universal Serial Bus is an industry-standard that establishes specifications for cables and connectors and protocols for connection, communication, and power supply between computers, peripherals, and other computers.

Hence, the correct option is (C).

115. VSAT (Very Small Aperture Terminal) is a satellite communications system that serves home and business users. A VSAT end-user needs a box that interfaces between the user's computer and an outside antenna with a transceiver. The transceiver receives or sends a signal to a satellite transponder in the sky.

The following applications which are possible on VSAT Network for banks are-

(i) Anywhere/Anytime banking/Electronic Fund Transfer.

(ii) Plastic cards implementation/Treasury Management.
Hence, the correct option is (D).

116. Business ethics refers to implementing appropriate business policies and practices with regard to arguably controversial subjects. Some issues that come up in a discussion of ethics include corporate governance, insider trading, bribery, discrimination, social responsibility, and fiduciary responsibilities.

A **code of conduct** is a set of rules outlining the norms, rules, and responsibilities or proper practices of an individual party or an organization.
Hence, the correct option is (A).

117. The correct answer is option C which is "Bank has no right to appropriate the funds except to meet the cheque amount as stated by Mr. Hilton".

Note- SMA-0 are loans where principal and interest are overdue for less than 31 days or showing initial signs of stress.
->Section 59 in The Indian Contract Act, 1872
Application of payment where debt to be discharged is indicated.—Where a debtor, owing to several distinct debts to one person, makes a payment to him, either with express intimation or under circumstances implying, that the payment is to be applied to the discharge of some particular debt, the payment, if accepted, must be applied accordingly. —Where a debtor, owing to several distinct debts to one person, makes a payment to him, either with express intimation or under circumstances implying, that the payment is to be applied to the discharge of some particular debt, the payment, if accepted, must be applied accordingly."
Hence, the correct option is (C).

118. Cloud computing is offered in three different service models which each satisfy a unique set of business requirements. These three models are known as Software as a Service (SaaS), Platform as a Service (PaaS), and Infrastructure as a Service (IaaS).

Hence, the correct option is (C).

119. A code of conduct is a set of rules outlining the norms, rules, and responsibilities or proper practices of an individual party or an organization.

Business ethics refers to implementing appropriate business policies and practices with regard to arguably controversial subjects. Some issues that come up in a discussion of ethics include corporate governance, insider trading, bribery, discrimination, social responsibility, and fiduciary responsibilities.

Hence, the correct option is (B).

120. A garnishee order is a common form of enforcing a judgment debt against a creditor to recover money. Put simply, the court directs a third party that owes money to the judgment debtor to instead pay the judgment creditor. The third-party is called a 'garnishee'.

Attachable under Garnishee Orders are-

(i) The specified amount in the garnishee order.

(ii) If the amount is unspecified, then the account is frozen and no payment is allowed.
Hence, the correct option is (D).

Q.1 Where a minor is admitted for benefit in a partnership firm and he attains majority and decides to join the firm as a partner, his liability begins from

A. date of his majority.

B. date of his decision to join the firm.

C. date of information to him that he was admitted for benefits.

D. when he was admitted for benefits.

Q.2 Which of the following amount can be sent abroad by an NRI from his NRO account?

(a) Interest credited by the bank.

(b) Amount of dividend received.

(c) Principal in the account.

A. (a) and (b)　　　　**B.** (b) and (c)

C. (a) and (c)　　　　**D.** Any of the above

Q.3 In the _________ the subscription and repurchase is available on a continuous basis.

A. growth fund　　　　**B.** open-ended fund

C. close-ended fund　　　　**D.** debt-oriented fund

Q.4 The Integrated Grievance Management System (IGMS) is an online consumer complaints registration system which is created by:

A. RBI　　　**B.** IRDAI　　　**C.** SEBI　　　**D.** LIC

Q.5 The process of maintenance of account books, discounting of bills and collection of bills on the due date is called by a person other than by the seller?

A. Securitization　　　　**B.** Factoring

C. Forfaiting　　　　**D.** Take out finance

Q.6 RBI is managed by a Board which consists of

(i) governor

(ii) 4 deputy governors

(iii) all nominated by the Central Govt. and RBI

Which of these is correct?

A. Only (i) and (ii)　　　　**B.** Only (i) and (iii)

C. Only (ii) and (iii)　　　　**D.** (i), (ii) and (iii)

Q.7 A withdrawal slip is a

A. cheque.　　　　**B.** bill of Exchange.

C. promissory Note.　　　　**D.** None of these

Q.8 Which of the following is the internal factor influencing pricing?

A. Price elasticity of the demand of the product

B. Competitors' policy

C. Bargaining power of suppliers

D. Social considerations

Q.9 The marketing concept is rested on four main pillars. Which of the following is not amongst four pillars?

A. Target Market

B. Customer needs

C. Segregated Marketing

D. Profitability

Q.10 Bailor – bailee relationship is applicable in

A. cash deposited with a cashier by customer.

B. safe deposits locker.

C. demand draft issued by the bank.

D. keeping articles in safe custody with a bank.

Q.11 Digital Banking is characterised by

A. visiting the branch office for doing transactions and using digital devices available at branches.

B. use of computers and core banking solutions by the banks for effective customer services.

C. alternative electronic channels which can be used by customers at their convenience to carry out banking operations.

D. use of Electronic ledgers and digital tools for book maintenance and transactions by the banks.

Q.12 The difference between the ATM card and the debit card is

A. both are same and no difference.

B. ATM card can be used in both online transactions, POS and ATM withdrawals whereas debit cards can be used only for ATM with drawls.

C. a debit card can be used in online transactions, POS transactions and ATM withdrawals whereas ATM cards can be used only for ATM withdrawals.

D. ATM, the card is used in POS terminals only whereas debit cards can be used in all type of transactions.

Q.13 Which of the following is India's first Credit Information Company?

A. CRISIL　　　**B.** CIBIL　　　**C.** SMERA　　　**D.** CERSAI

Q.14 Which of the following is an Example for Prepaid card?

(i) Travelcard

(ii) Creditcard

(iii) Giftcard

A. Only (i) and (ii)　　　　**B.** Only (i) and (iii)

C. Only (ii) and (iii)　　　　**D.** (i), (ii) and (iii)

Q.15 When were the draft guidelines for building grievance redressal mechanism within NBFCs (Non-Banking Financial Companies) published?

A. April 5, 2006　　　　**B.** May 26, 2006

C. June 29, 2007　　　　**D.** September 30, 2005

Q.16 Regional rural banks re-licensed for banking business under

A. a Special Statute.

B. Companies Act.

C. Co-operative Societies Act.

D. Banking Regulation Act.

Q.17 Pradhan Mantri Jeevan Jyoti Bima Yojana (PMJJBY) is a renewable insurance scheme. The upper age limit for this scheme is ______.

A. 55 years   **B.** 50 years   **C.** 60 years   **D.** 65 years

Q.18 When a bank lends money to the corporate person the relationship between the bank and the corporate person is

A. borrower and lender.

B. creditor-debtor.

C. debtor-creditor.

D. customer and client.

Q.19 An electronic database of certificates, the equivalent of digital Yellow Pages is called

A. certificates chest.

B. certificates depositor.

C. repository.

D. certificate warehouse.

Q.20 When did the Government of India set up the Export-Import Bank of India?

A. January 1982   **B.** January, 1993

C. March, 1971   **D.** June 1969

Q.21 What is meant by A/B testing in marketing?

A. Testing of 2 different products.

B. Testing 2 versions of an advertisement to see which elicits the best response.

C. Clinical testing of medical products before legally allowing them for sale.

D. Testing via 2 mediums, such as radio and television.

Q.22 When was IDBI transformed into a commercial bank from a Developmental Financial Institution?

A. 2004   **B.** 2005   **C.** 1964   **D.** 1980

Q.23 What place does Pricing have in marketing?

A. Higher prices guarantee a higher revenue stream

B. The company should actively market how much their products cost

C. Different pricing levels can be tested to see what elicits the best consumer response

D. Marketing based on the pricing level relative to the competition is important

Q.24 Which among the following made the initial contribution for setting up the Financial Inclusion Fund (FIF) and Financial Inclusion Technology Fund (FITF)?

A. Government of India, NABARD, and RBI

B. NABARD, UTI, and RBI

C. SIDBI, Government of India and IDBI Bank

D. SIDBI, NABARD, and UTI

Q.25 Social networks have an enormous information-sharing capacity. As such, they are a great distribution channel for

A. customer feedback.

B. viral content.

C. exclusive coupons.

D. marketing messages.

Q.26 A debit card can be used for

(i) cash withdrawal from ATMs.

(ii) for making payment in POS terminals.

(iii) making payment in e-commerce portals by providing card number, expiry date, and CVV number.

A. Only (i) and (ii)   **B.** Only (i) and (iii)

C. Only (ii) and (iii)   **D.** (i), (ii) and (iii)

Q.27 The ________ of the computer that makes use of primary memory.

A. storage unit

B. central processing unit

C. output devices

D. All of the above

Q.28 Which of the following products in retail banking do not fall under retail deposit products?

A. No frill accounts

B. Deposit accounts of senior citizens

C. Depository services

D. All of the above

Q.29 According to marketing four Ps, credit term be classified as

A. place.   **B.** price.

C. product.   **D.** promotion.

Q.30 From the buyer's point of view, the product is considered as

A. customers cost.

B. customer solution.

C. convenient availability.

D. communication.

Q.31 Bancassurance is not

(i) an insurance scheme to insure bank deposits.
(ii) a composite financial service offering both bank and insurance products.
(iii) an insurance scheme to insure bank advances.

A. Only (i) and (ii)   **B.** Only (i) and (iii)

C. Only (ii) and (iii)   **D.** (i), (ii) and (iii)

Q.32 As per which guidelines did the Government pick up the entire SBI shares held by the RBI?

A. National Stock Exchange of India

B. Securities Commission

C. Financial Regulations

D. Securities and Exchange Board of India (SEBI)

Q.33 Which of the following is NOT a credit rating agency in India?

A. CARE   **B.** RBI   **C.** ICRA   **D.** CRISIL

Q.34 The minimum percentage of Priority Sector advances to be maintained by Domestic commercial banks

A. 40%   **B.** 18%   **C.** 32%   **D.** 60%

Q.35 Loans to corporates directly engaged in Agriculture and Allied Activities to an aggregate limit of more than 2 crores is covered under Priority Sector as _____ advances.
A. direct agriculture
B. indirect agriculture
C. self-employment scheme
D. allied to indirect Agriculture

Q.36 Bank loans to Primary Agricultural Credit Societies (PACS) are covered under Priority Sector as _____ advances.
A. direct agriculture
B. indirect agriculture
C. self-employment scheme
D. allied to indirect agriculture

Q.37 The rural co-operative credit system in India is primarily mandated to ensure the flow of credit to
A. women sector.
B. industries sector.
C. corporate sector.
D. agriculture sector.

Q.38 What is Reverse Repo?
(i) It is a method of borrowing against certain securities for a short period.
(ii) It is a process where the lender levels against the securities with a commitment to take back the securities from the borrower against payment at a specified price.
(iii) It is helpful in contracting liquidity in the system.
A. Only (i) and (ii)
B. Only (i) and (iii)
C. Only (ii) and (iii)
D. (i), (ii) and (iii)

Q.39 Marketing channel doesn't refer to
(i) a set of independent organizations involved in the process of making a product or service available for use or consumption.
(ii) a physical channel for the movement of goods from the seller to the buyer.
(iii) a set of firms who handle the physical movement of goods from one point to another.
A. Only (i) and (ii)
B. Only (i) and (iii)
C. Only (ii) and (iii)
D. (i), (ii) and (iii)

Q.40 Business market strategies stimulate a customer to take action towards the buying decision is known as
A. promotional market.
B. related market.
C. digital market.
D. virtual market.

Q.41 When Marginal utility diminishes, total utility
A. diminishes.
B. increases.
C. remains constant.
D. increases at a diminishing rate.

Q.42 When was the Insurance Regulatory and Development Authority constituted?
A. 1938
B. 1971
C. 1993
D. 1999

Q.43 Reserve Bank of India will make available the National Electronic Funds Transfer system on a 24 ×7 basis from
_________.
A. January 2020
B. December 2019

C. November 2019
D. October 2019

Q.44 Mr. X maintains an SB account with your bank. He has given a POA to his son, to operate his SB account. The relationship between the bank and Mr. X is
A. debtor and creditor.
B. principal and agent.
C. donor and donee.
D. None of the above

Q.45 Match the following:

i) Classification of Assets	a. Narasimham
ii) Allonge	b. Endorsement
iii) Funds Transfer	c. EFT
iv) Crossed cheques	d. Collecting banker

A. i-A,ii-B,iii-C,iv-D
B. i-D,ii-C,iii-A,iv-B
C. i-A,ii-D,iii-B,iv-C
D. i-B,ii-A,iii-C,iv-D

Q.46 Which of the following is not true in respect of Joint Hindu Family?
A. It is governed by two schools of Hindu law–Dayabhaga & Mitakshara
B. Under Mitakshara, every son/daughter of a coparcener acquire a right in JHF by birth
C. Under Dayabhaga School he/she acquires the right in JHF only after her father's death
D. All members of the family are called coparceners including mother and daughter-in-law

Q.47 Deposits mobilized by the banks are utilized for
(i) loans and advances.
(ii) investment in government and other approved securities in fulfillment of liquidity stipulation.
(iii) investment in commercial paper, shares, debentures up to stipulated ceilings.
A. Only (i)
B. Both (ii) and (iii)
C. All the above
D. None of the above

Q.48 The ombudsman signifies
A. an institution established to content and prevent abuses of power by public official.
B. redress individual grievances.
C. acts as an external agency to probe into administration faults.
D. All of the above

Q.49 Maximum No of Partners in a banking partnership firm is _____ in terms of _____.
A. 10, Indian Partnership Act 1932
B. 20, Indian Partnership Act 1932
C. 10, Companies Act 1956
D. 20, Companies Act 1956

Q.50 Find the odd one out from the following?
A. National Bank for Agriculture and Rural development
B. Industrial Finance Corporation of India
C. Industrial Investment Bank of India
D. IDBI bank

Q.51 Which amongst the following is not term deposit issued by commercial banks?
A. Current account

B. Fixed deposit

C. Recurring deposit

D. Reinvestment deposit

Q.52 Find the odd one out from the following?

A. Non-resident external account

B. Non-resident ordinary account

C. FCNR account

D. Savings bank

Q.53 The minimum period for opening an FCNR deposit account is

A. six months.

B. three months.

C. one year.

D. two years.

Q.54 Asian Development Bank(ADB) has signed an agreement to invest _________ million in non-convertible debentures(NCD) being issued by GRIL.

A. $32   **B.** $12   **C.** $18   **D.** $23

Q.55 Which of the following can be taken as part of Off-balance sheet items?

A. Take out finance in the books of the taking over the institution

B. Outstanding foreign exchange contracts

C. Open position in gold

D. All of the above

Q.56 Initial Public Offering (IPO) means that an unlisted company makes to the public for the first time
(i) a fresh issue of securities.
(ii) offers its existing securities for sale.

A. Only (i)

B. Only (ii)

C. Either (i) or (ii)

D. Both (i) and (ii)

Q.57 The legal status of a mutual fund is in the form of a

A. partnership firm.

B. proprietorship.

C. joint-stock company.

D. trust.

Q.58 Sales of an MSME unit for the previous year were Rs. 200 lakhs. These are projected at Rs. 300 lakhs for next year. As per the Nayak Committee, the level of minimum bank working capital limits to be sanctioned would be

A. Rs. 40 lakhs.

B. Rs. 60 lakhs.

C. Rs. 20 lakhs.

D. Rs. 100 lakhs.

Q.59 A forward exchange contract is a firm contract for the purchase/sale of a specified quantity of a stated foreign currency at a predetermined exchange rate between the bank and its
(i) exporters.
(ii) importers.

A. Only (i)

B. Only (ii)

C. Either (i) or (ii)

D. Both (i) and (ii)

Q.60 Forfaiting enables the exporter to avoid the following risks
(i) interest-rate risk.
(ii) currency risk.
(iii) credit risk and political risk.

A. Only (i) and (ii)

B. Only (i) and (iii)

C. Only (ii) and (iii)

D. (i), (ii) and (iii)

Q.61 A computer network is used for which of the following?

A. To share date

B. To share software

C. To share hardware

D. All of the above

Q.62 Those terminals that are attached to a server in a computer network system, are called

A. CPU, nodes, and clients.

B. Only the CPU and clients.

C. Only clients and nodes.

D. Only the CPU and nodes.

Q.63 Which of the following statement is false?

A. In a stored value card monetary value is stored in the card itself

B. In stored value card credit limits are generally provided by the card issuer

C. A stored-value card is a prepaid card and the card issuer is not a bank but a service provider

D. In prepaid card, the value of the card lying in the deposit account linked at the back end

Q.64 Under National Electronic Funds Transfer (NEFT), the bank to afford credit to beneficiary accounts immediately upon completion of a batch or else return the transactions within_________of completion of batch settlement, if credits are unable to be afforded.

A. immediately

B. half an-hour

C. one hour

D. 2 hours

Q.65 KCC scheme has been implemented on recommendations of which of the following committee?

A. Narsgiman committee

B. Gadgil committee

C. Anantgitte committee

D. R. V. Gupta committee

Q.66 State Bank of India has reduced its benchmark lending rate by _________ bps for all loan tenures.

A. 6.2   **B.** 6   **C.** 4.5   **D.** 5

Q.67 A Fund of Funds is a scheme that invests primarily

A. in money market instruments.

B. in other schemes of the same mutual fund or other mutual funds.

C. in the bullion market.

D. only in the primary market.

Q.68 The headquarters of Investment Information & Credit Rating Agency (ICRA) Limited is located in?

A. Mumbai

B. Gurugram

C. Noida

D. New Delhi

Q.69 What does the letter 'R' denote in the abbreviation 'BR Act' which controls banking activities in the country?

A. Reclamation

B. Reformation

C. Regulation

D. Rule

Q.70 To address customer grievances in respect of insurance contracts on personal lives, there is an institution called

A. insurance ombudsman.

B. insurance regulator.

C. insurance intermediary.

D. insurance regulatory and development authority.

Q.71 The minimum capital to start a new Insurance company in India is

A. Rs. 100 crores.　　B. Rs. 75 crores.

C. Rs. 50 crores.　　D. Rs. 10 crores.

Q.72 Which is a full-service credit rating agency exclusively set up for micro, small and medium enterprises?

A. SMERA　　B. ICRA

C. ONICRA　　D. CRISIL

Q.73 If there is a default of repayment by the buyer in case of factoring and the factor is able to recover the amount from the seller, it is called

A. non-recourse factoring.

B. without recourse factoring.

C. recourse factoring.

D. bills discounting.

Q.74 A bank can exercise its right of general lien u/s 171 if
(a) the goods are received in the normal course of business.
(b) in the capacity of a banker.
(c) whether as security for a loan or for safe custody.
(d) the loan is due for recovery.

A. (a) to (d) all correct

B. (a), (b), and (c) correct

C. (a),(b) and (d) correct

D. (b), (c) and (d) correct

Q.75 The rule in the Clayton case becomes applicable in banking transactions in the following cases
(a) when the death of a customer takes place.
(b) when the partner retires.
(c) when the guarantor withdraws his guarantee.
(d) when the director of a company dies who has been operating the account.

A. (a), (b) and (c) only　　B. (b), (c) and (d) only

C. (a), (c) and (d) only　　D. (a) to (d) all

Q.76 X received a bearer cheque from Y for valuable consideration and in good faith. Actually, Y had stolen this cheque from Z. X would get the title of

A. a holder only.

B. a holder for value.

C. a holder in due course.

D. an endorsee.

Q.77 SMERA is a joint initiative between _____.

A. SIDBI & Leading Public Sector Banks

B. Dun & Bradstreet Information Services India Private Limited (D&B) & Leading Private Banks

C. RBI & SEBI

D. Both (A) and (B)

Q.78 In the balance sheet of a bank, the off-balance sheet items are shown as

A. assets.

B. liability.

C. asset or liability as per its nature.

D. notes to the balance sheet.

Q.79 Out of the following, which does not match?

A. A cheque is received by a trust as a donation from Mr. X - Trust is a holder only

B. A cheque is given by Mr. X to Mrs. Y as a gift on her marriage – Y is a holder in due course

C. X delivers to Y a bearer cheque after getting the value from Y - Y is a holder in due courses

D. A finds a cheque drawn in favor of B - A is not the holder

Q.80 Which of the following is not true in respect of the common seal?

A. The common Seal of the company can only be of metal and not a rubber stamp

B. Fact that it is a common seal & the name of the company should be engraved in it in legible characters in English only

C. The common seal can be affixed only with the authority of the Board of directors as provided in AOA

D. Subsequent board resolution will not validate documents where the common seal is affixed without a board of directors' authority

Q.81 Pledge of movable assets by a company can be searched at

A. register of charges maintained by a company at the registered office.

B. registrar of companies of the state where the registered office of the company is situated.

C. Both (A) and (B)

D. Neither (A) nor (B)

Q.82 Search for corporate guarantee is given in relation to any other corporate body can be made at

A. register of guarantees maintained by a company at the registered office.

B. registrar of companies of the state where the registered office of the company is situated.

C. Both (A) and (B)

D. Neither (A) nor (B)

Q.83 Which of the following charge over assets of the company is not required to be registered with the registrar of companies?

A. Equitable mortgage

B. Hypothecation

C. Pledge

D. Charge on book debts

Q.84 A charge created on the assets of the company is required to be registered with Roc within how many days?

A. 30 days from the date of sanction

B. 60 days from the date of sanction

C. 30 days from the date of creation of charge

D. 60 days from the date of creation of charge

Q.85 The role of banking ombudsman is

A. resolution of complaints against banks regarding deficiency in services.

B. it is an external agency that includes mediation persuasion and adjudication.

C. it is an external agency having an independent identity.

D. All of the above

Q.86 Who can participate in Call/Notice money market?

A. Scheduled commercial banks

B. Co-operative banks

C. Primary Dealers

D. All of these

Q.87 FERA was replaced by FEMA with effect from _______.

A. 01.01.1999   B. 01.06.1999

C. 01.01.2000   D. 01.06.2000

Q.88 The tenor of issue of CDs can be upto_______months.

A. 3   B. 6   C. 9   D. 12

Q.89 There are_______types of possible errors during screening of ideas.

A. 1   B. 2   C. 3   D. 4

Q.90 One of the objectives of feature improvement is

A. reliability.   B. safety.

C. aesthetic appeal.   D. speed.

Q.91 An audiocassette manufacturer enters into fax machines or diet products businesses is an example of

A. concentric diversification.

B. horizontal diversification.

C. conglomerate diversification.

D. None of the above

Q.92 Minimum and maximum number of shareholders in a public limited company?

A. 2, 50   B. 10, 50

C. 7, no limit   D. 7, 50

Q.93 The data processing NEFT clearing center National Clearing Cell (NCC), of the RBI, is located at

A. New Delhi.   B. Mumbai.

C. Calcutta.   D. Chennai.

Q.94 CHIPS started its operation in

A. 1960   B. 1970   C. 1980   D. 1990

Q.95 In credit cards, the period of interest-free credit ranges from_______days.

A. 15 to 50   B. 16 to 51   C. 15 to 51   D. 16 to 50

Q.96 Narasimhan committee was related to which of the following reforms?

A. High education reforms

B. Tax structure reforms

C. Banking structure reforms

D. Planning implementation reforms

Q.97 What are we going to do? And, how are we going to do? In which of the following categories these two questions fall?

A. Researching   B. Planning

C. Controlling   D. Managing

Q.98 Which of the following is true when death/ insolvency/ retirement or expulsion of any partner takes place in a partnership firm?

A. The firm is compulsorily dissolved

B. The firm is reconstituted

C. Continuation of the firm depends upon the provisions made in the partnership deed

D. Both (B) or (C)

Q.99 Which of the following is the instrument of payment called Plastic Money?

(i) Debit card.

(ii) Credit card.

(iii) Banker's cheque.

A. Only (i) and (ii)   B. Only (i) and (iii)

C. Only (ii) and (iii)   D. (i), (ii) and (iii)

Q.100 The T-bill is quoted in the secondary market with a minimum tradable amount of Rs._______.

A. 100   B. 10000   C. 25000   D. 50000

Q.101 When was the Decimal currency system introduced in India?

A. January 1955   B. April 1955

C. April 1951   D. April 1957

Q.102 The Indian rupee is a legal tender in two other countries. One is Nepal. The other is

A. Pakistan.   B. Sri Lanka.

C. Bhutan.   D. Afghanistan.

Q.103 Which category of banks are under the dual control of Govt. and RBI:

A. Private banks   B. Public sector banks

C. RRBs   D. Cooperative banks

Q.104 Which of the following taxes is the largest source of revenue for the Government of India?

A. Excise   B. Customs

C. Income tax   D. Corporation tax

Q.105 The National Stock Exchange (NSE) is located at

A. Mumbai.   B. New Delhi.

C. Madras.   D. Calcutta.

Q.106 What happens to marginal cost when average cost increases?

A. The marginal cost is below the average cost

B. Marginal cost is above average cost

C. Marginal cost is equal to average variable cost

D. Marginal cost is equal to the average cost

Q.107 Does development mean economic growth with

A. price stability.   B. social change.

C. inflation.   D. deflation.

Q.108 Which one of the following is more effective in controlling prices in the long run?

A. The decrease in production
B. Increase in production
C. The decrease in the rate of interest
D. Increase in the rate of employment

Q.109 Through open market operations, the RBI purchase and sell

A. foreign exchange.
B. gold.
C. government securities.
D. All of these

Q.110 A firm is said to be of optimum size when

A. average total cost is at a minimum.
B. marginal cost is at a minimum.
C. marginal cost is equal to marginal revenue.
D. the firm is maximizing its profit.

Q.111 All revenues received, loans raised, and money received in repayment of loans by the union government go into

A. the public account of India.
B. a contingency fund of India.
C. consolidated fund of India.
D. None of the above

Q.112 The law of demand states that

A. demand increases with an increase in income.
B. when income and prices rise, the demand also rises.
C. when the price falls, demand increases.
D. when price increases, demand increases.

Q.113 The balance of payment comprises

A. a current account of goods and services only.
B. a capital account of financial assets only.
C. official settlement accounts only.
D. All of these

Q.114 What is Net National Product?

A. The money value of final goods and services produced annually in the economy
B. The money value of annual service generation in the economy
C. The money value of tangible goods produced annually in the economy
D. The money value of tangible goods available in the economy

Q.115 Which bank is otherwise called an Investment bank?

A. Exchange Bank
B. Reserve Bank of India
C. Agricultural Bank
D. Industrial Bank

Q.116 Deflation is________.

A. deficit budget.
B. reduction in taxation.
C. the contraction in the volume of money or credit that results in a decline in the price level.

D. increase in public expenditure.

Q.117 Does bank rate mean

A. the interest rate charged by moneylenders.
B. the interest rate charged by scheduled banks.
C. rate of profit of the banking institution.
D. the official rate of interest charged by the central bank of the country.

Q.118 Which agency estimates the national income of India?

A. Reserve Bank of India
B. Planning Commission
C. Ministry of Finance
D. Central Statistical Organization

Q.119 What is the gross national product?

A. The total output of goods and services produced by the country's economy
B. The total domestic and foreign output claimed by residents of the country
C. The sum of gross domestic product and investment
D. National income minus national expenditure

Q.120 The Government of India acquired the ownership and control of major banks in 1969 whose deposits were not less than

A. Rs. 40 crores.
B. Rs. 50 crores.
C. Rs. 60 crores.
D. Rs. 80 crores.

// Smart Answer Sheet //

Correct — Indicates percentage of students who answered questions correctly.

Skipped — Indicates percentage of students who skipped questions.

Q.	Ans.	Correct / Skipped	Q.	Ans.	Correct / Skipped	Q.	Ans.	Correct / Skipped	Q.	Ans.	Correct / Skipped	Q.	Ans.	Correct / Skipped
1	D	20.69 % / 12.38 %	17	B	30.09 % / 25.4 %	33	B	52.35 % / 14.89 %	49	C	21.0 % / 26.02 %	65	D	27.9 % / 24.61 %
2	A	24.61 % / 23.98 %	18	B	52.98 % / 24.92 %	34	A	55.96 % / 25.07 %	50	D	32.45 % / 23.82 %	66	D	25.08 % / 24.14 %
3	B	57.84 % / 21.16 %	19	C	38.71 % / 8.78 %	35	B	23.67 % / 21.94 %	51	A	58.62 % / 21.0 %	67	B	43.1 % / 25.4 %
4	B	16.46 % / 25.7 %	20	A	39.97 % / 19.9 %	36	B	22.73 % / 21.78 %	52	D	63.95 % / 19.75 %	68	B	22.57 % / 25.39 %
5	B	47.02 % / 24.77 %	21	B	48.75 % / 18.8 %	37	D	57.84 % / 25.86 %	53	C	32.6 % / 25.71 %	69	C	62.85 % / 25.71 %
6	D	57.68 % / 23.35 %	22	A	31.82 % / 25.08 %	38	B	17.4 % / 24.45 %	54	D	15.99 % / 23.98 %	70	A	26.18 % / 25.07 %
7	D	26.02 % / 24.92 %	23	C	31.66 % / 13.64 %	39	C	22.26 % / 25.7 %	55	D	55.8 % / 22.41 %	71	A	65.67 % / 15.21 %
8	A	40.28 % / 25.39 %	24	A	45.3 % / 25.7 %	40	A	49.53 % / 25.23 %	56	D	23.51 % / 25.55 %	72	A	46.39 % / 20.54 %
9	C	38.71 % / 26.34 %	25	D	32.29 % / 25.7 %	41	D	25.39 % / 18.97 %	57	D	41.54 % / 25.07 %	73	C	44.36 % / 26.33 %
10	D	50.47 % / 23.82 %	26	D	65.67 % / 25.4 %	42	D	26.96 % / 25.23 %	58	B	30.56 % / 24.77 %	74	C	16.46 % / 24.61 %
11	C	46.39 % / 22.11 %	27	B	48.59 % / 17.71 %	43	B	28.37 % / 21.16 %	59	D	39.81 % / 22.26 %	75	A	12.38 % / 25.55 %
12	C	36.52 % / 24.92 %	28	C	30.72 % / 25.86 %	44	A	25.08 % / 25.7 %	60	D	40.6 % / 20.22 %	76	C	40.6 % / 23.04 %
13	B	42.63 % / 18.97 %	29	B	53.45 % / 18.96 %	45	A	51.25 % / 20.22 %	61	D	42.16 % / 25.55 %	77	D	28.21 % / 25.71 %
14	B	46.71 % / 25.23 %	30	A	29.47 % / 23.35 %	46	D	38.09 % / 26.02 %	62	C	32.92 % / 23.98 %	78	D	39.81 % / 23.83 %
15	B	27.74 % / 21.63 %	31	B	44.83 % / 22.25 %	47	C	51.41 % / 22.57 %	63	B	13.95 % / 23.04 %	79	B	24.61 % / 15.99 %
16	D	47.18 % / 21.16 %	32	D	41.54 % / 21.47 %	48	D	55.33 % / 25.55 %	64	D	33.39 % / 25.07 %	80	B	26.33 % / 21.79 %

Q.	Ans.	Correct	Skipped		Q.	Ans.	Correct	Skipped		Q.	Ans.	Correct	Skipped		Q.	Ans.	Correct	Skipped		Q.	Ans.	Correct	Skipped
81	A	15.2 %	18.34 %		89	B	29.15 %	26.02 %		97	B	52.51 %	26.02 %		105	A	56.74 %	25.39 %		113	D	58.46 %	18.03 %
82	A	10.5 %	24.14 %		90	B	14.11 %	25.39 %		98	D	42.63 %	25.08 %		106	B	21.32 %	25.7 %		114	A	43.42 %	25.86 %
83	C	19.59 %	25.39 %		91	C	39.81 %	25.55 %		99	A	67.08 %	22.89 %		107	B	24.45 %	21.16 %		115	D	25.86 %	23.2 %
84	C	40.13 %	23.66 %		92	C	56.27 %	25.55 %		100	C	28.37 %	21.94 %		108	B	35.74 %	25.7 %		116	A	10.5 %	25.24 %
85	D	47.65 %	25.86 %		93	B	63.48 %	19.28 %		101	D	17.08 %	26.65 %		109	D	46.87 %	18.96 %		117	D	57.68 %	16.77 %
86	D	31.19 %	24.92 %		94	B	20.38 %	26.64 %		102	C	53.13 %	25.08 %		110	A	10.03 %	25.08 %		118	D	41.69 %	24.92 %
87	D	20.85 %	25.86 %		95	C	23.2 %	23.04 %		103	D	29.94 %	26.02 %		111	C	38.71 %	16.31 %		119	B	19.75 %	16.93 %
88	D	50.31 %	25.08 %		96	C	39.97 %	23.98 %		104	D	21.16 %	23.35 %		112	C	37.62 %	25.39 %		120	B	51.88 %	20.53 %

Performance Analysis

Avg. Score (%)	36.0%
Toppers Score (%)	99.0%
Your Score	

//Hints and Solutions//

1. Section 30 of the Indian Partnership Act, provides that though a minor cannot be a partner in a firm, with the consent of all the partners, for the time being, he may be admitted to the benefits of the partnership by an agreement executed through his guardian with the other partners.

Liabilities of a Minor Partner

i. A minor cannot be held personally liable for the losses of the firm. And if the firm declares insolvency the minor's share is kept with the Official Receiver.

ii. After turning 18 the minor partner can choose to become a partner of the firm. But he may choose to not become a partner. In this case, the minor partner has to give public notice about this decision. And the notice has to be given within 6 months of gaining a majority. If such a notice is not given even after 6 months then the minor partner will become liable for all acts done by the other partners till the date of such notice.

iii. Should the minor partner choose to become a partner he will be liable to all the third parties for the acts done by any and all partners since he was admitted to the benefits of the partnership.

iv. If he becomes a full-time partner he will be treated as a normal partner and have all the liabilities of one. His share in the profits and property of the firm will remain the same as it was when he was a minor partner.

Hence, the correct option is (D).

2. (a) Interest credited by the bank - At present, the interest is credited in savings bank accounts on a half-yearly basis. "Interest on savings deposit shall be credited at quarterly or shorter intervals (on domestic savings deposits)," the RBI said in a master circular issued on March 3.

(b) Amount of dividend received - Essentially, the investors receiving the dividend from the fund are reducing their holding value, which gets reflected in the reduced NAV on the ex-dividend date.

Hence, the correct option is (A).

3. Open-ended Fund - An open-ended fund or scheme is one that is available for subscription and repurchase on a continuous basis. These schemes do not have a fixed maturity period. Investors can conveniently buy and sell units at Net Asset Value (NAV) related prices which are declared on a daily basis. The key feature of open-end schemes is liquidity.

A mutual fund scheme can be classified into an open-ended scheme or close-ended scheme depending on its maturity period.

Close-ended Fund - A close-ended fund or scheme has a stipulated maturity period e.g. 5-7 years. The fund is open for subscription only during a specified period at the time of launch of the scheme. Investors can invest in the scheme at the time of the initial public issue and thereafter they can buy or sell the units of the scheme on the stock exchanges where the units are listed. In order to provide an exit route to the investors, some close-ended funds give an option of selling back the units to the mutual fund through periodic repurchase at NAV related prices.

Growth Fund -The aim of growth funds is to provide capital appreciation over the medium to long- term. Such schemes normally invest a major part of their corpus inequities. Such funds have comparatively high risks. These schemes provide different options to the investors like dividend option, capital appreciation, etc.

Debt Oriented Fund - The aim of income funds is to provide a regular and steady income to investors. Such schemes generally invest in fixed income securities such as bonds, corporate debentures, Government securities and money market instruments. Such funds are less risky compared to equity schemes.

Hence, the correct option is (B).

4. The Integrated Grievance Management System (IGMS) facilitates online registration of policyholders' complaints and helps track their status. It is created by the Insurance Regulatory and Development Authority (IRDAI).

Policyholders can register their complaints online with their insurance company and track the progress of complaint resolution. IRDAI monitors the complaints and their progress in real-time through IGMS.

Hence, the correct option is (B).

5. Factoring, receivables factoring or debtor financing, is when a company buys a debt or invoice from another company. Factoring is also seen as a form of invoice discounting in many markets and is very similar but just within a different context. In this purchase, accounts receivable are discounted in order to allow the buyer to make a profit upon the settlement of the debt. Essentially factoring transfers the ownership of accounts to another party that then chases up the debt.

Hence, the correct option is (B).

6. The RBI Central Board at present comprises 18 members, including five official directors: Governor Urjit Patel and four deputy governors, N S Vishwanathan, Viral Acharya, BP Kanungo and Mahesh Kumar Jain. The Governor and deputy governors generally get a five-year term, but it can also be less as in the case of Raghuram Rajan who just served for three years. He didn't get any extension. In this current board, Subhash Chandra Garg, Economic Affairs Secretary, and Rajiv Kumar, Financial Services Secretary are the nominees of the government.

In the CBD, there are official and non-official members. Five members are official members and are from the RBI – the Governor and the four Deputy Governors. The government can nominate the remaining 14 who are non-official members from different fields. Of these, four are from Local Boards of the RBI.

Official Directors: The Governor and four deputy governors are automatically members of the CBD and they are known as the official directors.

Non-official Directors: RBI Act empowers the government to nominate non-official directors comprised of:

Ten Directors from various fields and Two Government Officials.

Four Directors – one each from four local boards.

Among the ten nominated members, two will be Government officials representing the Government, who are usually the Finance Secretary/Economic Affairs Secretary to the Government and remain on the Board 'during the pleasure of the Central Government'.

Hence, the correct option is (D).

7. A withdrawal slip, as the name suggests, is a form that is required to withdraw money from your account. If you are at a branch to withdraw funds from your account, you have to fill up a withdrawal form. A withdrawal slip is a written instruction to the bank to pay the said amount to the account holder. The funds are debited from the account number mentioned.

Withdrawal slip is used to take money out of your account by visiting a branch of the bank. As cheque books are normally not issued for Savings Account, withdrawal from such accounts necessitate the use of a withdrawal slip (Alternately, you can withdraw from an ATM).

Hence, the correct option is (D).

8. A firm can determine the expected price in a few test-markets by trying different prices in different markets and comparing the results with a controlled market in which price is not altered. If the demand for the product is inelastic, high prices may be fixed. On the other hand, if demand is elastic, the firm should not fix high prices, rather it should fix lower prices than that of the competitors.

Hence, the correct option is (A).

9. Segregated Marketing

Segregation became a rule in the securities industry in the late 1960s and was solidified with the advent of the Security and Exchange Commission's consumer protection rule, the Securities Exchange Act (SEA) Rule 15c3-3. Other rules require firms to file monthly reports regarding the proper segregation of investor funds.

Market Segmentation can be defined as a methodology that companies use to segregate targeted consumer markets into smaller units or segments, similar in preferences and attributes, to streamline the promotional, marketing and sales strategies to attain required results. In this article, we will see in-depth the different types of market segmentation.

Marketing Concept holds that the key to achieving organizational goals consists of the company being more effective than its competitors in creating, delivering, and communicating customers value to its chosen target markets.

Four pillars are-

- Target Market
- Customer Needs
- Segregated or Integrated Marketing
- Profitability

Target Market

Companies do best when they choose their target market's carefully and prepare a tailored marketing program.

Customer Needs

A company can carefully define its target market yet fail to correctly understand the customer's needs. Clearly, understanding customers need and want is not always simple. Some customers have needs of which they are not fully conscious:; some articulates these needs or use words that require some interpretations.

Profitability

The ultimate purpose of the marketing concept is to help organizations achieve their objectives. In the case of private firms, the major objective is profits; in the case of nonprofit and public organizations, it is surviving and attracting enough funds to perform useful work. Private firms should aim to achieve profits as a consequence of creating superior customer value, by satisfying customer needs better than competitors.

Hence, the correct option is (C).

10. The legal relationship that arises in case of safe custody/deposit is that of bailment. The customer, who deposits the things in the box for safe custody with the bank, becomes the 'bailor', and the bank becomes the 'bailee'. In such cases, the banker becomes a 'gratuitous bailee'.

Hence, the correct option is (D).

11. Digital banking involves high levels of process automation and web-based services and may include APIs enabling cross-institutional service composition to deliver banking products and provide transactions. It provides the ability for users to access financial data through desktop, mobile and ATM services.

Core banking refers to a centralized system established by a bank which allows its customers to conduct their business irrespective of the bank's branch. Thus, it removes the impediments of geo-specific transactions. In fact, CORE is an acronym for "Centralized Online Real-time Exchange", thus the bank's branches can access applications from the centralized data centre.

Hence, the correct option is (C).

12. These terms cannot be used interchangeably. The key difference between ATM card and debit card is the kind of transactions allowed by these cards. An ATM card only allows withdrawal of cash. With a debit card, in addition to cash withdrawal, you can pay for goods or services, utility bills etc.

ATM Cards

Automated Teller Machine (ATM) cards are the simplest cards. They are offered by banks and some credit unions and are primarily used to withdraw cash and make basic banking transactions at ATMs located in many places. Most issuers will charge a user fee if the card is used to withdraw funds from a different bank. These cards typically cannot be used to make purchases at stores, as they do not have the major credit card network logos on them.

Ideal for: Access to cash, limiting everyday spending.

Debit Cards

Debit cards, also known as check cards, do everything ATM cards do but can also be used for purchases anywhere credit cards are

accepted, including retail stores and online sites. The funds from these transactions are taken directly from your checking account. The issuer of these cards will often charge a monthly fee for the convenience of using the debit card instead of paper checks.

Hence, the correct option is (C).

13. Credit Information Bureau Limited (CIBIL) is the first Credit Information Company in India.

TransUnion CIBIL Limited (Formerly: Credit Information Bureau (India) Limited) is India's first Credit Information Company (CIC) founded in August 2000.

It collects and maintains records of individuals' and non-individuals' (commercial entities) payments pertaining to loans and credit cards.

These records are submitted to the credit bureau by banks and other lenders on a monthly basis; using this information a Credit Information Report (CIR) and Credit Score is developed, enabling lenders to evaluate and approve loan applications.

CIBIL was promoted by the State Bank of India (SBI), Housing Development Finance Corporation (HDFC), Dun & Bradstreet Information Services India Private Limited (D&B), and TransUnion International Inc. (TransUnion).

CIBIL

Founded: August 2000; 16 years ago

Headquarter: Mumbai, India

Current Head: M.V. Nair (Chairman), Satish Pillai (Managing Director)

Hence, the correct option is (B).

14. A prepaid card is a card you can use to pay for things. You buy a card with money loaded on it. Then you can use the card to spend up to that amount. A prepaid card is also called a prepaid debit card, or a stored-value card.

A travel card is a type of credit card that is specifically designed keeping in mind the needs of a traveller. A normal credit card gives you rewards in form of cashback or points which can be redeemed for gift cards, merchandise and discounts. A travel credit card offers travel-specific benefits.

Gift cards are a form of prepaid debit cards loaded with funds for future use. In some situations, they can be used to pay for a portion of the purchase with cash, debit, or credit used to balance the expense.

A credit card is a thin rectangular piece of plastic or metal issued by a bank or financial services company, that allows cardholders to borrow funds with which to pay for goods and services with merchants that accept cards for payment.

Hence, the correct option is (B).

15. The Reserve Bank of India (RBI) published the draft guidelines for building grievance redressal mechanism within NBFCs (Non-Banking Financial Companies) on May 26, 2006. The grievance redressal mechanism would be used to resolve disputes arising out of the decisions of the lending institutions' functionaries.

Guidelines have also been outlined by the RBI for putting in place the Fair Practices Codes by all NBFCs.

Hence, the correct option is (B).

16. The Banking Regulation act, 1949 is a legislation in India that regulates all banking firms in India. Passed as the Banking Companies Act 1949, it came into force from 16 March 1949 and changed to Banking Regulation Act 1949 from 1 March 1966. It is applicable in Jammu and Kashmir since 1956.

The Banking Companies Act, 1949 is a very well-crafted law, the eminent economist said adding it reflects the sophistication of the founders of modern India. Basu, however, noted that times have changed and there are reasons to amend some parts of it.

Hence, the correct option is (D).

17. PMJJBY is available to people in the age group of 18 to 50 years (life cover up to age 55) having a savings bank account who give their consent to join and enable auto-debit. Under the PMJJBY scheme, a life cover of Rs.2 lakhs is available at a premium of Rs.330 per annum per member and is renewable every year.

Hence, the correct option is (B).

18. A creditor is a term used in accounting to describe an entity (can either be a person, organization, or a government body) that is owed money, as they have provided goods or services to another entity. Sometimes, this entity will charge interest on money borrowed as a way to make money. This could be interesting on bank loan repayments or credit card payments.

Examples of creditors:

Trade creditors – money you owe to suppliers.

A loan from a bank or entity.

A debtor is a term used in accounting to describe the opposite of a creditor an individual that owes money, or who is in debt to an organization or person. For example, a debtor is somebody who has taken out a loan at a bank for a new car.

Examples of debtors:

Trade debtors – money owed from customers.

Staff loans.

Assume that a company borrows money from its bank. The company is the debtor and the bank is the creditor. If a manufacturer sells merchandise to a retailer with terms of net 30 days, the manufacturer is the creditor and the retailer is the debtor.

Hence, the correct option is (B).

19. A repository is "an electronic database of certificates accessible to all parties desiring to correspond with the subscriber. The equivalent of [an online] digital Yellow Pages" accessible to the general public. However, unlike the Yellow Pages, a user may be charged for access to the information.

Electronic Yellow Pages are online versions of traditional printed business directories produced by telephone companies around the world. Typical functionalities of online yellow pages include the alphabetical listings of businesses and search functionality of the business database by name, business, or location. Since Electronic Yellow Pages are not limited by space considerations, they often contain far more comprehensive business information such as vicinity maps, company profiles, product information, and more.

Hence, the correct option is (C).

20. In January 1982 recognising the importance of exports in India's development programmes, the Government of India set up the Export-Import Bank of India as a statutory corporation owned completely by the Union Government.

Hence, the correct option is (A).

21. AB testing is essentially an experiment where two or more variants of a page are shown to users at random, and statistical analysis is used to determine which variation performs better for a given conversion goal.

Hence, the correct option is (B).

22. Industrial Development Bank of India (IDBI) was constituted under the Industrial Development Bank of India Act, 1964 as a Development Financial Institution and came into being as of July 01, 1964.

It continued to serve as a DFI for 40 years till the year 2004 when it was transformed into a Bank.

Subsequently, in September 2004, the Reserve Bank of India incorporated IDBI as a 'scheduled bank' under the RBI Act, 1934.

Consequently, IDBI formally entered the portals of banking business as IDBI Ltd. from 1st October 2004.

The commercial banking arm, IDBI BANK, was merged into IDBI in 2005.

In 2006, IDBI Bank acquired United Western Bank (headquartered at Satara).

IDBI - Industrial Development Bank of India

Founded: July 1, 1964

Headquarters: Mumbai, India

Current head: Mr Kishor Kharat (MD & CEO)

Hence, the correct option is (A).

23. Pricing and the Marketing Mix: Pricing might not be as glamorous as promotion, but it is the most important decision a marketer can make. Price is important to marketers because it represents marketers' assessment of the value customers see in the product or service and are willing to pay for a product or service.

Hence, the correct option is (C).

24. FIF(Financial Inclusion Fund)

The objectives of the FIF shall be to support developmental and promotional activities with a view to securing greater financial inclusion, particularly among weaker sections, low-income groups, and in backward regions/hitherto unbanked areas.

FITF(Financial Inclusion Technology Fund)

The objectives of FITF shall be to enhance investment in Information Communication Technology (ICT) aimed at promoting financial inclusion, stimulate the transfer of research and technology in financial inclusion, increase the technological absorption capacity of financial service providers/users and encourage an environment of innovation and cooperation among stakeholders.

Hence, the correct option is (A).

25. A marketing message is any media or communication that is designed to influence customers. They are often used to generate demand, build brand awareness, and sell. The following are the basic types of marketing messages.

Hence, the correct option is (D).

26. A debit card can be used for

(i) Cash withdrawal from ATMs - These include free transactions from 5 SBI ATMs and 3 ATMs of any other bank. Non-metro cities get 10 free ATM transactions, in which 5-5 transactions can be made from SBI and other banks. It then levies Rs.20 + GST for cash transactions and Rs.8 + GST for non-cash transactions.

(ii) Most merchants will have a separate point of sale (POS) machine that you will need to use to swipe your debit card. If your debit card has a chip on one side, you will need to insert your chip into the bottom gap in the POS machine for the transaction to process.

(iii) It depends if he knows your card PIN too and/or he has somehow the access of your mobile number which is linked to a bank account. For online transactions through the card, only card number and CVV are not sufficient, they can be used to initiate a transaction.

Hence, the correct option is (D).

27. Primary Memory: Primary memory is computer memory that is accessed directly by the CPU. This includes several types of memory, such as the processor cache and system ROM. However, in most cases, primary memory refers to system RAM.

Hence, the correct option is (B).

28. Depository services are services in which the securities of investors are kept in an electronic form just as the bank keeps all your cash in its account and provides all services related to the transaction of cash, similarly, we help you out in performing the service through a Demat account.

Retail banking, also known as consumer banking or personal banking, is banking that provides financial services to consumers as individuals, not businesses. Retail banking is a way for individual consumers to manage their money, have access to credit, and deposit their money in a secure manner. Services offered by retail banks include checking and savings accounts, mortgages, personal loans, credit cards, and certificates of deposit (CDs).

Hence, the correct option is (C).

29. The four Ps are the four essential factors involved in marketing a good or service to the public. These are the four Ps :

the product (the good or service), the price (what the consumer pays), the place (the location where a product is marketed), and promotion (the advertising).

Hence, the correct option is (B).

30. Customer cost refers not only to the price of a product, but it also encompasses the purchase costs, uses Customer cost refers not only to the price of a product, but it also encompasses the purchase costs, uses costs, and the post-use costs. Purchase costs consist of the cost of searching for a product, gathering information about the product, and the cost of obtaining that information costs and the post-use costs. Purchase costs consist of the cost of searching for a product, gathering information about the product, and the cost of obtaining that information.

Hence, the correct option is (A).

31. In 1999, most of the Glass-Steagall Act was repealed, allowing bancassurance, also known as Allianz. However, it still has not been fully accepted as a practice for most forms of insurance. Bankassurance is controversial, with opponents believing that it gives banks too much control over the financial industry.

Bancassurance is not :

(i) An insurance scheme to insure bank deposits - Currently, as per the RBI guidelines, deposits with all commercial banks and cooperative banks are insured under the Deposit Insurance and Credit Guarantee Corporation (DICGC). Only Primary Cooperative Societies are not covered under DICGC.

(ii) An insurance scheme to insure bank advances - The DICGC is a wholly-owned subsidiary of the Reserve Bank of India and in case of a bank failure, the DICGC provides protection to bank deposits that are payable in India. Banks are required to compulsorily enrol for the deposit insurance scheme and no bank can withdraw from it.

Hence, the correct option is (B).

32. As per the guidelines of the Securities and Exchange Board of India (SEBI), the Government picked up the entire SBI shares held by the RBI at a price of Rs. 1,130.35 a share.

SEBI is the regulatory authority for the securities market in India.

Powers for the discharge of its functions efficiently, SEBI has been vested with the following powers:

- to approve by-laws of stock exchanges.
- to require the stock exchange to amend their by-laws.
- inspect the books of accounts and call for periodical returns from recognized stock exchanges.
- inspect the books of accounts of financial intermediaries.
- compel certain companies to list their shares in one or more stock exchanges.
- registration of brokers.

Hence, the correct option is (D).

33. RBI is not a credit rating agency in India.

- Reserve Bank of India (RBI) is India's central bank, which is responsible for issuing and distributing the Indian rupee and controlling the Indian banking system.
- It also operates the key payment networks of the nation and works to facilitate its economic growth.
- RBI began its operations on 1 April 1935 in compliance with the Reserve Bank of India Act, 1934.
- The RBI was nationalized on 1 January 1949 following India's independence on 15 August 1947.

Hence, the correct option is (B).

34. Every Domestic Commercial Bank and Every Foreign Bank operating in India with more than 20 branches needs to provide 40% of their total loans to the priority sector.

Hence, the correct option is (A).

35. Loans to corporates directly engaged in Agriculture and Allied Activities to an aggregate limit of more than 2 crores is covered under Priority Sector as Indirect Agriculture advances.

Hence, the correct option is (B).

36. Bank loans to Primary Agricultural Credit Societies (PACS) are covered under Priority Sector as Indirect Agriculture advances.

Hence, the correct option is (B).

37. The rural co-operative credit system in India is primarily mandated to ensure the flow of credit to the agriculture sector. It comprises short-term and long-term co-operative credit structures.

Hence, the correct option is (D).

38. Reverse repo rate is the rate at which the central bank of a country (Reserve Bank of India in the case of India) borrows money from commercial banks within the country. It is a monetary policy instrument that can be used to control the money supply in the country.

(i) It is a method of borrowing against certain securities for a short period.

(ii) It is helpful in contracting liquidity in the system.

Hence, the correct option is (B).

39. Marketing channel doesn't refer to

(i) a physical channel for the movement of goods from the seller to the buyer.

(ii) a set of firms who handle the physical movement of goods from one point to another.

Hence, the correct option is (C).

40. Promotion marketing is any message that includes an incentive to persuade the target audience to take immediate action, thereby driving some form of brand interaction that leads to a current or future purchase. Promotional marketing is an often-misused tool when placed into inexperienced hands.

Business market strategies stimulate a customer to take action towards the buying decision is known as the Promotional market. Hence, the correct option is (A).

41. Marginal utility is the derivative of total utility with respect to quantity demanded. This means that if marginal utility decreases, total utility will still increase because the marginal utility is greater than 0, so the consumer still derives satisfaction from consuming that extra product.

Hence, the correct option is (D).

42. Insurance Regulatory and Development Authority of India (IRDAI), is a statutory body formed under an Act of Parliament, i.e., Insurance Regulatory and Development Authority Act, 1999 (IRDAI Act 1999) for overall supervision and development of the Insurance sector in India.

Hence, the correct option is (D).

43. The Reserve Bank of India will make available the National Electronic Funds Transfer system on a 24 ×7 basis from December 2019 as per the Payment System Vision 2021 document. Presently, the transfer of funds via NEFT can only be done during banks' working hours. The facility of electronic transfer of funds is available from 8 am to 7 pm on all working days, except the second and the fourth Saturday of the month. The move will revolutionize the retail payments system of the country. It will also reduce the number of cheques while making payments and will also increase efficiency in businesses.

Hence, the correct option is (B).

44. CMR. X maintains an SB account with your bank. He has given a POA to his son, to operate his SB account. The relationship between the bank and Mr. X is debtor and creditor.

- debtor and creditor are correct because - A debtor is a term used in accounting to describe the opposite of a creditor an individual that owes money, or who is in debt to an organization or person. For example, a debtor is somebody who has taken out a loan at a bank for a new car.

- principal and agent are incorrect because-The principal-agent relationship is an arrangement in which one entity legally appoints another to act on its behalf. In a principal-agent relationship, the agent acts on behalf of the principal and should not have a conflict of interest in carrying out the act.

- donor and donee are incorrect because-A a donor, in general, is a person, organization, or government that donates something voluntarily. In business law, a donor is someone who is giving the gift (law), and a donee the person receiving the gift.

Hence, the correct option is (A).

45.

i) Classification of Assets	a. Narasimham
ii) Allonge	b. Endorsement
iii) Funds Transfer	c. EFT
iv) Crossed cheques	d. Collecting banker

i) In line with the recommendations of the **Narasimham Committee**, the Reserve Bank of India advised the banks in 1991-92 to **classify their assets** into four categories, (i) standard assets, (ii) substandard assets, (iii) doubtful debts and (iv) loss assets.

ii) Additional paper firmly attached to Commercial Paper, such as a promissory note, to provide room to write endorsements. An **allonge** is necessary when there is insufficient space on the document itself for the **endorsements**.

iii) **Electronic funds transfer (EFT)** is the electronic transfer of money from one bank account to another, either within a single financial institution or across multiple institutions, via computer-based systems, without the direct intervention of bank staff.

iv) According to Section 127, where a **cheque is crossed** specially to more than one banker, except when that bank to whom it has been specially crossed makes another special crossing in the name of another bank for the **purpose of collection, the banker** on whom it is drawn shall refuse payment thereof.

Hence, the correct option is (A).

46. Option A) This is true because -The Dayabhaga and The Mitakshara are the two schools of law that govern the law of succession of the Hindu Undivided Family under Indian Law. They collectively have co-ownership/Coparcenary in the Joint Family. Thus a son by birth acquires an interest in the ancestral property of the joint family.

Option B) Is true because - Daughter of a coparcener in a Hindu joint family governed by Mitakshara Law now is coparcener by birth in her own right in the same manner as a son; she has right of claim by survivorship and has same liabilities and disabilities as a son; now coparcenary property to be divided and allotted in equal share.

Option C) Is true because - Dayabhaga School is based on the code of yagnavalkya commented by Jimutuvahana,Inheritance is based on the principle of spiritual benefit. It arises by pinda offering i.e. rice balloffering to deceased ancestors. This school is followed in Bengal state only. Sapinda relation is bypanda offerings. The right to Hindu joint family property is not by birth but only on the death of thefather. The system of devolution of property is by inheritance. The legal heirs (sons) have definiteshares after the death of the father. Each brother has ownership over a definite fraction of the jointfamily property and so can transfer his share.

Option D) Is false because- A coparcener is a person who acquires interest in the joint family property by birth. The essential difference between a 'coparcener' and a 'member' of a HUF is that a coparcener can enforce the partition of the HUF, while a member cannot prior to the year 2005, a HUF was understood as a family with a common ancestor and all lineal male descendants together with their wives and unmarried daughters. The 2005 Amendment to the Hindu Succession Act, 1956 however brought about a vital change to the concept of a HUF. Prior to the Amendment of 2005, only lineal male descendants were regarded as coparceners whereas daughters merely attained the status of members on birth and not coparceners. The Amendment of 2005 however has conferred equal rights upon daughters. Daughters, just as sons, become coparceners of their father's HUFs on birth, with the result that they have equal rights as sons in the properties of the HUF.

Hence, the correct option is (D).

47. Deposits mobilized by the banks are utilized for loans and advances, investment in government and other approved securities in fulfillment of liquidity stipulation, and investment in commercial papers, shares, debentures up to stipulated ceilings. After the nationalization of major commercial banks in the country, there has been a marked expansion in their business, both with regard to the bank deposits as well as the bank credit. The accretion of deposits was primarily on account of time deposits which increased substantially despite the downward movement of the interest rates and reflected the "safe haven" sentiment.

Hence, the correct option is (C).

48. An ombudsman is an official, usually appointed by the government, who investigates complaints (usually lodged by private citizens) against businesses, financial institutions, or government departments, or other public entities, and attempts to resolve the conflicts or concerns raised, either by mediation or by making recommendations. Ombudsmen may be called by different names in some countries, including titles such as a public advocate or national defender.

Hence, the correct option is (D).

49. 10, Companies Act 1956 is correct because the new Companies Act 2013 has prescribed the maximum number of members in case of a partnership firm should not be more than 100 in case of partnerships. As per the previous Companies Act 1956, the maximum limit in the case of partnerships was 10 and 20 for banking business and other businesses respectively.

Hence, the correct option is (C).

50. National Bank for Agriculture and Rural Development, Industrial Finance Corporation of India, and Industrial Investment Bank of India are Financial Institutions while IDBI is a bank.

Industrial Development Bank of India (IDBI Bank Limited or IDBI Bank or IDBI) was established in 1964 to provide credit and other financial facilities for the development of the fledgeling Indian industry. Many national institutes find their roots in IDBI like SIDBI, India Exim Bank, National Stock Exchange of India and National Securities Depository Limited.

Hence, the correct option is (D).

51. Commercial banks accept various types of deposits from the public especially from its clients, including saving account deposits, recurring account deposits, reinvestment deposits, and fixed deposits. These deposits are returned whenever the customer demands it or after a certain time period. Hence, the correct option is (A).

52. There are various types of NRI accounts that are available to an NRI Investor. Some of the major ones are-

- Non-Resident Ordinary (NRO) Savings Account/ Fixed Deposit Account.

- Non-Resident External (NRE) Savings Account/ Fixed Deposit Account.

- Foreign Currency Non -Resident (FCNR) Fixed Deposit Account.

Given below is a list of comprehensive features of each type of account-

NRE Savings Account /Fixed Deposit Account

NRE Accounts are maintained in INR. this means that when you deposit the money in the NRE Account, the foreign currency is converted to Indian rupees at the prevailing foreign exchange rates.

- It is mainly used to house your savings from the income that you have earned abroad.

- The principal amount, as well as the interest, are fully repatriable, i.e., transferable.

- The interest income earned on the amount in an NRE account is non-taxable in India.

You can have other NRIs or Resident Indian (who is a close relative as per Companies Act 2013) as joint account holders in NRE Accounts. In case Resident Indian is added as Joint holder the mode of operation will be 'Former or Survivor'.

NRO Savings Account/Fixed Deposit Account

NRO Accounts are maintained in INR this means that when you deposit the money in the NRO Account, the foreign currency is converted to Indian rupees at the prevailing foreign exchange rates.

- It is used to house funds from the income that you have earned from India or abroad.

- Income like rent, dividend, pension, etc. can be sent abroad through the NRO Account.

- Interest income earned on the amount in an NRO Account is liable for TDS or Tax Deductible at Source.

You can have other NRIs or Resident Indian as joint account holders in NRO Accounts. In case Resident Indian is added as Joint holder the mode of operation will be 'Former or Survivor' FCNR Account.

Foreign Currency **Non-Resident Accounts** have to be opened and maintained in foreign currency.

Your principal amount and the interest in an FCNR Account are fully repatriable, i.e., transferable

Interest income earned on your money in an FCNR account is non-taxable in India.

You can also opt for other products like NRE/NRO Current account, NRE Recurring Deposit RFC Savings/ RFC Deposits, etc.

A savings bank is a financial institution whose primary purpose is accepting savings deposits and paying interest on those deposits.

Hence, the correct option is (D).

53. The minimum maturity period of the deposit under the FCNR(B) scheme, which was initially six months, was raised to one year, effective October 1999. From July 26, 2005, banks were allowed to accept FCNR (B) deposits up to a maximum maturity period of five years, against the earlier maximum limit of three years.

Hence, the correct option is (C).

54. In order to support road sector investment plans of the Indian government, Asian Development Bank(ADB) has signed an agreement to invest $23 million in non-convertible debentures(NCD) being issued by GRIL(GR Infraprojects Limited). This investment will promote the GRIL ability for the construction of roads and highways in India through the purchase of new building equipment & help execute its existing order book of $ 2.78 billion and enable it to bid for larger and more complex infrastructure projects. The agreement was signed by Michael Barrow, Director General of ADB's Private Sector Operations Department and Vinod Kumar Agarwal, GRIL Chairman and Managing Director.

Hence, the correct option is (D).

55. Off-balance sheet (OBS) items is a term for assets or liabilities that do not appear on a company's balance sheet. Although not recorded on the balance sheet, they are still assets and liabilities of the company. Off-balance sheet items are typically those not owned by or are a direct obligation of the company.

Hence, the correct option is (D).

56.

- An initial public offering (IPO) refers to the process of offering shares of a private corporation to the public in a new stock issuance.

- Companies must meet requirements by exchanges and the Securities and Exchange Commission (SEC) to hold an initial public offering (IPO).

- IPOs provide companies with an opportunity to obtain capital by offering shares through the primary market.

- Companies hire investment banks to market, gauge demand, set the IPO price and date, and more.

- An IPO can be seen as an exit strategy for the company's founders and early investors, realizing the full profit from their private investment.

Hence, the correct option is (D).

57. Trust is correct- Mutual funds are not just a type of investment but are actually legal entities, often formed as a business trust or corporation.

A partnership firm is an organization that is formed with two or more persons to run a business with a view to earning a profit. Each member of such a group is known as a partner and collectively known as a partnership firm. These firms are governed by the Indian Partnership Act, 1932.

The sole proprietorship is the simplest business form under which one can operate a business. The sole proprietorship is not a legal entity. It simply refers to a person who owns the business and is personally responsible for its debts.

A joint-stock company is a business owned collectively by its shareholders. Historically, a joint-stock company was not incorporated and thus its shareholders could bear unlimited liability for debts owed by the company.

Hence, the correct option is (D).

58. Banks in India have evolved their own method of lending as they have been given free hand by the Central Bank (that is RBI) to decide the lending methods. The method of assessment of working capital limits up to Rs. 2 crores (Rs.7.50 Crore for SME) assessed under turn over method is called as limits assessed under Nayak Committee Norms. Under the turnover method, the aggregate fund-based working capital limits are computed on the basis of Minimum of 20% of their projected annual turnover.

Thus, As per the Nayak Committee, the level of minimum bank working capital limits to be sanctioned would be Rs.60 lakhs.

Hence, the correct option is (B).

59. A forward exchange contract is a firm contract for the purchase/sale of a specified quantity of a stated foreign currency at a predetermined exchange rate between the bank and its exporters and importers.

A forward exchange contract is an agreement between two parties to exchange two designated currencies at a specific time in the future.

Forward contracts are not traded on exchanges, and standard amounts of currency are not traded in these agreements.

Forward exchange contracts are a mutual hedge against risk as it protects both parties from unexpected or adverse movements in the currencies' future spot rates.

Hence, the correct option is (D).

60. (i) interest-rate risk - Interest rate risk is the risk that arises for bond owners from fluctuating interest rates. How much interest rate risk a bond has depends on how sensitive its price is to interest rate changes in the market. The sensitivity depends on two things, the bond's time to maturity, and the coupon rate of the bond.

(ii) currency risk - Currency Risk, sometimes referred to as exchange rate risk, is the possibility that currency depreciation will negatively affect the value of one's assets, investments, and related interest and dividend payment streams, especially those securities denominated in foreign currency.

(iii) credit risk and political risk - Credit insurance is the provision of insurance against the non-payment of the customer against an insured occurrence (i.e. contractual disagreements and insolvency). Political risk insurance plays the role of an insurance policy for businesses that are purchasing from potentially unstable countries.

Hence, the correct option is (D).

61. Computer networks share common devices, functions, and features including servers, clients, transmission media, shared data, shared printers and other hardware and software resources, network interface card(NIC), local operating system(LOS), and the network operating system (NOS).

Hence, the correct option is (D).

62. The other workstations are referred to as client computers, and this is a server/client network. You may also find terminals

connected as nodes on a network (terminals have only a screen and a keyboard, and no processing power; they connect over the network to a computer that does the actual processing).

Hence, the correct option is (C).

63. A stored-value card (SVC) is a payment card with a monetary value stored on the card itself, not in an external account maintained by a financial institution. This means no network access is required by the payment collection terminals as funds can be withdrawn and deposited straight from the card.

Hence, the correct option is (B).

64. Under National Electronic Funds Transfer (NEFT), the bank to afford credit to beneficiary accounts immediately upon completion of a batch or you may expect a timeline of two hours from the batch settlement within which beneficiary's account should be credited.

Hence, the correct option is (D).

65. The Kisan Credit Card (KCC) scheme is a credit scheme introduced in August 1998 by Indian banks. This model scheme was prepared by the National Bank for Agriculture and Rural Development (NABARD) on the recommendations of the R.V. GUPTA committee to provide term loans for agricultural needs.

Hence, the correct option is (D).

66. State Bank of India has reduced its benchmark lending rate by 5 bps across all loan tenures. The lender's one-year marginal cost of funds based lending rate (MCLR) will be 8.4% compared with 8.45%.

Hence, the correct option is (D).

67. A scheme that invests primarily in other schemes of the same mutual fund or other mutual funds is known as an FoF scheme. An FoF scheme enables investors to achieve greater diversification through one scheme. It spreads risks across a greater universe.
Hence, the correct option is (B).

68. ICRA Limited (ICRA) is an Indian independent and professional investment information and credit rating agency.

It was established in 1991 and was originally named Investment Information and Credit Rating Agency of India Limited (IICRA India).

It was a joint-venture between Moody's and various Indian commercial banks and financial services companies.

The company changed its name to ICRA Limited, and went public on 13 April 2007, with a listing on the Bombay Stock Exchange and the National Stock Exchange.

ICRA is the second-largest Indian rating company in terms of the customer base.

ICRA

Founded: 1991

Headquarters: Gurugram, Haryana

Current Head: Naresh Takkar (CEO)

Hence, the correct option is (B).

69. Winding up of a banking company is done under the provisions of the Banking Regulation Act, 1949. The reasons for this are inability to pay its debts, moratorium placed on the bank or failure to comply with minimum capital adequacy, failure to comply with requirements of the Banking Regulation Act.

Hence, the correct option is (C).

70. Option A) Insurance Ombudsman is correct because - The **Insurance Ombudsman** scheme was created by the Government of India for individual policyholders to have their complaints settled out of the courts' system in a cost-effective, efficient, and impartial way. There are at present 17 Insurance Ombudsman in different locations and any person who has a grievance against an insurer, may himself or through his legal heirs, nominee or assignee, make a complaint in writing to the Insurance Ombudsman within whose territorial jurisdiction the branch or office of the insurer complained against or the residential address or place of residence of the complainant is located.

Option B) Insurance regulator - An **insurance regulator** is any authority that initiates and develops legislation and/or non-legislative regulation (i.e. rulemaking) to address these rationales in the insurance sector context, in consultation with the supervisor and other stakeholders.

Option C) Insurance Intermediary - An **Insurance Intermediary** means individual agents, corporate agents including banks and brokers, insurance marketing firm. Insurance Intermediary also includes Surveyors and Third Party Administrators but these intermediaries are not involved in the procurement of business.

Option D) Insurance Regulatory and Development Authority (IRDA) Act, 1999 spells out the Mission of IRDAI as:

"to protect the interests of the policyholders, to regulate, promote and ensure orderly growth of the insurance industry and for matters connected therewith or incidental thereto"

Functions and Duties of IRDAI

Section 14 of the IRDA Act, 1999 lays down the duties, powers, and functions of IRDA.

- Registering and regulating insurance companies
- Protecting policyholders' interests
- Licensing and establishing norms for insurance intermediaries
- Promoting professional organizations in insurance
- Regulating and overseeing premium rates and terms of non-life insurance covers
- Specifying financial reporting norms of insurance companies
- Regulating investment of policyholders' funds by insurance companies
- Ensuring the maintenance of solvency margin by insurance companies
- Ensuring insurance coverage in rural areas and of vulnerable sections of society

Hence, the correct option is (A).

71. Guidelines for starting a new Insurance company in India is-

At least, one-third of the directors on the board should be independent directors. The minimum capital requirement for insurance companies is Rs. 100 crores. There are two kinds of capital involved minimum capital requirement and solvency capital requirement. Solvency capital requirement depends on capital burn based on growth and the kind of business. It varies from business to product and distribution network.
Hence, the correct option is (A).

72. SMERA Ratings Limited (formerly SME Rating Agency of India Ltd.) is a full-service credit rating agency exclusively set up for micro, small and medium enterprises.

It provides ratings that enable MSME, SMEs, and Corporate to raise bank loans at competitive rates of interest.

SMERA

Founded: 2005

Headquarter: Mumbai, India

Current Head: Sankar Chakraborty (CEO)

Hence, the correct option is (A).

73. Recourse factoring is correct because -Recourse factoring is an agreement between the client and the factor in which the client is required to buy back the unpaid bills receivable from the factor. Thus, the credit risk stays with the client in case of non-payment by the debtor. If there is a default of repayment by the buyer in case of factoring and the factor is able to recover the amount from the seller.

Under non-recourse factoring, the client and the factor enter into an agreement where the factor shall bear the obligation of absorbing those bills receivable which remain unpaid. Thus, the business remains unaffected by the unpaid invoices.

Without recourse factoring- Without recourse can mean that the buyer of a promissory note or other negotiable instrument assumes the risk of default. A sale that is with recourse means that the seller bears responsibility for the sold asset if it turns out to be defective, and the buyer can seek recourse from the seller.

Bills discounting- Bill Discounting is a method of trading the bill of exchange to the financial institution before it gets matured, at a price that is in a smaller amount than its par value. The discount on the bill of exchange will be based on the remaining time for its maturity and also the risk concerned in it.Hence, the correct option is (C).

74. Section 171 of the Indian Contract Act, 1872, confers the right of general lien on the bankers as follows: "Bankers may, in the absence of a contract to the contrary, retain as a security for a general balance of the account, any goods bailed to them."

A bank can exercise its right of general lien u/s 171 if the goods are received in the normal course of business in the capacity of a banker the loan is due for recovery.

Hence, the correct option is (C).

75. From Clayton's case, the following rules are:

- A debtor making a payment has a right to appropriate it to the discharge of any debt due to the creditor,

- if at the time of payment there is no express or implied appropriation thereof by the debtor, then the creditor has a right to make the appropriation,

- in the absence of any appropriation by either debtor or creditor, an appropriation is made by the presumption of law, according to the items of account, the first item on the debit side being the item discharged or reduced by the first item on the credit side.

The rule in the Clayton case becomes applicable in banking transactions in the following cases when the death of a customer takes place when the partner retires when the guarantor withdraws his guarantee.

Hence, the correct option is (A).

76. A holder in due course- X received a bearer cheque from Y for valuable consideration and in good faith. Actually, Y had stolen this cheque from Z. X would get the title of A holder in due course.

In commercial law, a holder in due course is someone who accepts a negotiable instrument in a value-for-value exchange without reason to doubt its legitimacy. A holder in due course acquires the right to make a claim for the instrument's value against its originator and intermediate holders.
Hence, the correct option is (C).

77. SMERA Ratings Limited (formerly SME Rating Agency of India Ltd.) is a joint initiative of Small Industries Development Bank of India (SIDBI), Dun & Bradstreet Information Services India Private Limited (D&B), and leading public and private sector banks in India.
Hence, the correct option is (D).

78. The notes (or footnotes) to the balance sheet and to the other financial statements are considered to be part of the financial statements. The notes inform the readers about such things as significant accounting policies, commitments made by the company, and potential liabilities and potential losses. Off-balance sheet (OBS) items is a term for assets or liabilities that do not appear on a company's balance sheet. Although not recorded on the balance sheet, they are still assets and liabilities of the company. Off-balance sheet items are typically those not owned by or are a direct obligation of the company.
Hence, the correct option is (D).

79.

- A cheque is received by a trust as a donation from Mr. X - Trust is a holder only.

- X delivers to Y a bearer cheque after getting the value from Y - Y is a holder in due courses.

- A finds a cheque drawn in favor of B - A is not a holder.

- A cheque is given by Mr. X to Mrs. Y as a gift on her marriage – Y is a holder in due course does not match.

Hence, the correct option is (B).

80. A company seal (sometimes referred to as the corporate seal or common seal) is an official seal used by a company. Company

seals were predominantly used by companies in common law jurisdictions, although in modern times, most countries have done away with the use of seals.

- Common Seal of the Company can only be of metal and not a rubber stamp.
- Common Seal can be affixed only with the authority of the Board of Directors as provided in AoA.
- Subsequent Board resolution will not validate documents where Common Seal is affixed without Board of Directors Authority.

Hence, the correct option is (B).

81. Earlier there was a list of the transaction on which charge was required to create. With the enactment of the Companies Act, 2013, tire list of charges requiring registration done away with. Thus, in the absence of a specific list of charges to be registered, and the wide definition of the word "charge", 'pledges' and 'liens' was also required to be registered.

Hence, the correct option is (A).

82. A search for corporate guarantee is given in relation to any other corporate body can be made at the register of guarantees maintained by a company at the registered office.

A corporate guarantee is an official letter where a guarantor becomes responsible for handling debt payments or takes overall responsibility for debt repayment in case the debtor defaults on the loan.

Hence, the correct option is (A).

83. As per section 125(4) of the Companies Act 1956, the following charges are required to be filed with the Registrar of Companies (ROC).

- a charge for the purpose of securing any issue of debentures;
- a charge on the uncalled share capital of the company;
- a charge on any immovable property, wherever situate, or any interest therein;
- a charge on any book debts of the company;
- a charge, not being a pledge, on any movable property of the company
- a floating charge on the undertaking or any property of the company including stock in trade
- a charge on calls made but not paid;
- a charge on a ship or any share in a ship;
- a charge on goodwill, on a patent or a license under a patent, on a trademark, or on a copyright or a license under copyright.

Hence, the correct option is (C).

84. A charge created by a company is required to be registered with the Registrar within 30 days of its creation in such form and on payment of such fees as may be prescribed.

Hence, the correct option is (C).

85. The Banking Ombudsman is a senior officer appointed by the Reserve Bank of India to resolve the grievance of banking customers. Any person aggrieved by the decision of the bank can file a complaint, either himself or through his representative other than through an advocate.

Resolution of complaints against banks regarding deficiency in services.

It is an external agency that includes mediation persuasion and adjudication.

It is an external agency having an independent identity.

Hence, the correct option is (D).

86. Scheduled commercial banks, Co-operative banks (other than Land Development Banks), and Primary Dealers (PDs), are permitted to participate in the Call/Notice money market both as borrowers and lenders. Participants in the call money market are banks and related entities specified by the RBI.

Hence, the correct option is (D).

87. FERA was replaced by FEMA with effect from 01.06.2000

Foreign Exchange Regulation Act (FERA) was replaced by the Foreign Exchange Management Act (FEMA), 1999 which came into effect from 1st June 2000 in India.

Hence, the correct option is (D).

88. The tenor of issue can range from 7 days to 1 year. However, most CDs are issued by banks for 3, 6, and 12 months. CDs can be issued to individuals, corporations, companies, trusts, funds, associations, etc. Non-Resident Indians may also subscribe to CDs.

Hence, the correct option is (D).

89. When the company collect ideas from different resources the stage comes to screen the entire ideas. In screening company must avoid two types of errors:

1. Drop Error It means that when a company drop a good idea if a company dismiss many drops errors its standards are too conservative.
2. Go Error It occurs when a company allow a poor idea to move in development and commercialization.

Hence, the correct option is (B).

90. One of the objectives of Feature improvement is Safety.

The objective of a Safety Management System is to provide a structured management approach to control safety risks in operations. Effective safety management must take into account the organisation's specific structures and processes related to the safety of operations.

Hence, the correct option is (B).

91. An audiocassette manufacturer enters into fax machines or diet products businesses is an example of Conglomerate diversification.

Conglomerate diversification is a growth strategy that involves adding new products or services that are significantly different from the organization's present products or services. Conglomerate diversification occurs when the firm diversifies into an area(s) totally unrelated to the organization's current business.

Hence, the correct option is (C).

92. There are various rules and regulations prescribed under the companies act, 2013 for the formation of a public limited company. Here is what you should keep in mind when registering a public limited company:

-Minimum number of shareholders is 7 and there is no limit on the maximum number of shareholders.

-Minimum of 3 directors is required to form a public limited company.

-The minimum share capital of Rs. 5 lakhs is required.

Hence, the correct option is (C).

93. The National Clearing Cell, Reserve Bank of India, Nariman Point, Mumbai has been designated as the NEFT Clearing Centre (NCC) for purposes of the NEFT System.

Hence, the correct option is (B).

94. CHIPS started its operation in 1970.

However, the CHIPS focus has shifted to domestic business since CHIPS introduced intraday settlement in January 2001. Until January 2001, CHIPS conducted all of its settlings at the end of the business day. Now, however, CHIPS provides intraday payment finality through a real-time system.

Hence, the correct option is (B).

95. In credit cards, the period of interest-free credit ranges from 15 to 51 days.

The payment due date on your credit card can be between 18 and 25 days after the statement date, the day when the statement is made. So, the interest-free credit period can range from 18-48 days to 25-55 days depending on your credit card's payment due date.

Hence, the correct option is (C).

96. Narasimhan Committee is related to Banking structure reforms. The Narasimham Committee was established under former RBI Governor M. Narasimham in August 1991 to look into all aspects of the financial system in India

Hence, the correct option is (C).

97. Planning involves some basic questions:

- What are the needs of the community?
- What is the purpose of the library related to community needs?
- Where are we now?
- Where do we want to go?
- How will we get there?
- How will we know what we accomplished?

Hence, the correct option is (B).

98. When death/insolvency/retirement or expulsion of any partner takes place in a partnership firm.

The firm is a reconstituted-Any change in the existing agreement is known as reconstitution of the partnership firm. Reconstitution of a partnership firm takes place whenever there is a change in the profit-sharing ratio among the partners, admission of a new partner, retirement of a partner, and death or insolvency of a partner.

Continuation of the firm depends upon the provisions made in the partnership deed. Partnerships are one of the easiest business structures when it comes to formation and management. Minimum compliance requirement and straightforward dissolution rules make it one of the preferred choices for the small-scale business.

Hence, the correct option is (D).

99. (i) Debit card - A debit card is a payment card that deducts money directly from a consumer's checking account to pay for a purchase. Debit cards eliminate the need to carry cash or physical checks to make purchases directly from your savings.

(ii) Credit card- Issued by financial institutions, credit cards give customers a pre-set credit limit which he can use to pay for their purchases without having to pay in cash or issuing a cheque. The credit limit of the card is decided by the financial institution depending on the customer's credit score and monthly income. Hence, the correct option is (A).

100. The T-bill is quoted in the secondary market with a minimum tradable amount of Rs. 25000.

T-bills are one of the safest investments, but their returns are low compared to most other investments. When deciding if T-bills are a good fit for a retirement portfolio, opportunity cost and risk need to be considered. In general, T-bills may be appropriate for investors who are nearing or in retirement.

Hence, the correct option is (C).

101. India changed from the rupee, anna, pie system to decimal currency on 1st April 1957. Yemen Arab Republic introduced coinage system of 1 North Yemeni rial=100 fils in 1974, to replace former system of 1 rial = 40 buqsha = 80 halala = 160 zakat. The country was one of the last to convert its coinage.

Hence, the correct option is (D).

102. While China is actively pursuing a policy of Renminbi internationalisation, India appears to be on the path of de-internationalisation of the Indian rupee (INR). Of the two countries which had adopted the INR as legal tender, Nepal and Bhutan, one had to ban the use of notes above Rs.100 as legal tender. Considering the demand from people engaged in the trade and tourism links between the two countries, Nepal has now requested the Reserve Bank of India (RBI) to allow the use of higher denomination rupee notes in Nepal. The RBI should agree.

Hence, the correct option is (C).

103. Union Cabinet clears changes in Banking Regulation Act to give RBI wider powers. Cooperative banks are under the dual control of the Registrar of Cooperative Societies and RBI. The Union Cabinet on approved changes to the Banking Regulation

Act to give the Reserve Bank of India wider powers to regulate cooperative lenders and prevent frauds such as the one seen at Punjab and Maharashtra Co-operative Bank Ltd. Once the amendment is cleared by Parliament, cooperative banks will be audited according to RBI's norms and the central bank can supersede the board, in consultation with the state government, if any cooperative bank is under stress.

Hence, the correct option is (D).

104. According to the Budget for 2019-20 presented in Parliament by Finance Minister Nirmala Sitharaman, Goods and Services Tax collections will contribute 19 paise in every rupee revenue. Corporation tax is the single largest source of income, contributing 21 paise to each rupee earned.

Hence, the correct option is (D).

105. The National Stock Exchange of India Limited (NSE) is the leading stock exchange of India, located in Mumbai. The NSE was established in 1992 as the first dematerialized electronic exchange in the country.

Hence, the correct option is (A).

106. The curves show how each cost changes with an increase in the product price and quantity produced. When the average cost declines, the marginal cost is less than the average cost. When the average cost increases, the marginal cost is greater than the average cost.

Hence, the correct option is (B).

107. The Pursuit of Development provides a concise account of what development means and how it can be achieved. It draws on scholarly and policy debates to show how nations escape poverty and achieve economic and social progress.
Hence, the correct option is (B).

108. Production is a process of combining various material inputs and immaterial inputs in order to make something for consumption. It is the act of creating output, a good or service that has value and contributes to the utility of individuals. An increase in production is more effective in controlling prices in the long run.

Hence, the correct option is (B).

109. The foreign exchange market is a global decentralized or over-the-counter market for the trading of currencies. This market determines foreign exchange rates for every currency. It includes all aspects of buying, selling, and exchanging currencies at current or determined prices.

Government securities are debt instruments that a sovereign government. They sell these products to finance day-to-day governmental operations and provide funding for special infrastructure and military projects. These investments work in much the same way as a corporate debt issue.

Hence, the correct option is (D).

110. The LAC curve is the locus of all the points denoting the least cost for producing that level of output. It is a planning curve because on the basis of this the producer decides what the size

of the plant should be in order to produce optimally. This optimal point is the minimum point of the long-run average cost curve.

Hence, the correct option is (A).

111. All revenues received, loans raised and all money received by repayment of loans are credited to the consolidated fund of India. All other money received by or on behalf of the government is credited to the Public Account.

Hence, the correct option is (C).

112. The law of demand states that other factors being constant (Cetris Peribus), price and quantity demand of any good and service are inversely related to each other. When the price of a product increases, the demand for the same product will fall.

Hence, the correct option is (C).

113. The balance of payments includes both the current account and capital account. The current account includes a nation's net trade in goods and services, its net earnings on cross-border investments, and its net transfer payments. The capital account consists of a nation's imports and exports of capital and foreign aid.

Hence, the correct option is (D).

114. Net national product (NNP) is the monetary value of finished goods and services produced by a country's citizens, overseas and domestically, in a given period. It is the equivalent of the gross national product (GNP), the total value of a nation's annual output, minus the amount of GNP required to purchase new goods to maintain existing stock, otherwise known as depreciation.
Hence, the correct option is (A).

115. Industrial Bank is otherwise called as Investment banks.

Industrial banks sell certificates that are labeled as investment shares. This helps the public to invest in such bonds and certificates through industrial banks. So, Industrial banks are also known as investment banks.

An investment bank is a financial services company that acts as an intermediary in large and complex financial transactions.

Hence, the correct option is (D).

116. A budget deficit occurs when expenses exceed revenue and indicate the financial health of a country. The government generally uses the term budget deficit when referring to spending rather than businesses or individuals. Budget deficits may occur in response to certain unanticipated events and policies.

Hence, the correct option is (A).

117. The official rate of interest charged by the central bank of the country.

Definition of 'Bank Rate' Definition: Bank rate is the rate charged by the central bank for lending funds to commercial banks. Description: Bank rates influence the lending rates of commercial banks. Base rate is the minimum rate set by the Reserve Bank of India below which banks are not allowed to lend to their customers.

Hence, the correct option is (D).

118. The main functions of C.S.O (Central Statistical Organization) are to provide advisory services to other statistical agencies, keeping liaison (public relation) with international statistical bodies, preparing and publishing national accounts statistics, industrial statistics, conducting an economic census and training statistical personal in official statistics etc.

Hence, the correct option is (D).

119. Gross National Product (GNP) is the total value of all finished goods and services produced by a country's citizens in a given financial year, irrespective of their location. GNP also measures the output generated by a country's businesses located domestically or abroad.

Hence, the correct option is (B).

120. The Government of India acquired ownership and control of major banks in 1969 with deposits of not less than Rs. 50 crores.

Thereafter, the Government of India issued the Banking Companies (Acquisition and Transfer of Undertakings) Ordinance, 1969, and nationalized the 14 largest commercial banks with effect from midnight of 19 July 1969. These banks contained 85% of bank deposits in the country.

Hence, the correct option is (B).

Q.1 Why bank take signature on the backside of a bearer cheque?

A. Identify the person

B. Acknowledgement of receipt

C. KYC guidelines

D. As a matter of practice

Q.2 How many accounts a person can open under the PPF scheme?

A. 1   **B.** 2   **C.** 3   **D.** No limit

Q.3 Under SCSS no tax deduction at source need to be made if the interest payment does not exceed Rs. __________.

A. 5,000   **B.** 10,000   **C.** 20,000   **D.** 7,500

Q.4 Conversion of Demat shares to physical sharers is called ______.

A. Dematerialization   **B.** Demat

C. Rematerialization   **D.** Both (A) and (B)

Q.5 Which public sector bank has been authorized to issue the 11th tranche of Electoral Bonds sale in India?

A. State Bank of India

B. Indian Bank

C. Canara Bank

D. Indian Overseas Bank

Q.6 Under the Nepal remittance Scheme remittance up to Rs. 50,000 can be made a maximum of______ times a year.

A. 12   **B.** 15   **C.** 20   **D.** 24

Q.7 In the cheque truncation system clearing the physical cheque is kept with the ______.

A. Presenting banker   **B.** Drawee banker

C. Beneficiary   **D.** Repository

Q.8 On which rate base, overnight money is needed by the bank from RBI?

A. MSF   **B.** Repo rate

C. Reverse repo   **D.** Bank rate

Q.9 Global Bank allows one of its clients to withdraw against the clearing of a cheque. The banker is called ______.

A. Collecting and paying banker

B. Holder in due course

C. Holder for value

D. Reimbursement banker

Q.10 What would be the sum assured under the scheme "PRADHAN MANTRI SURAKSHA BIMA YOJANA" in case of Total and irrecoverable loss of both eyes or loss of use of both hands or feet or loss of sight of one eye and loss of use of hand or foot?

A. Rs. 1 Lakh   **B.** Rs. 2 Lakhs

C. Rs. 3 Lakhs   **D.** Rs. 5 Lakhs

Q.11 The bank to first set up a merchant banking division in 1967 in India was ________.

A. Grindlays Bank

B. American Express Bank

C. SBI

D. Canara Bank

Q.12 When the foreign exchange is bought in spot & sold in forward simultaneously is called ______.

A. Swap   **B.** Future   **C.** Option   **D.** Forward

Q.13 To control the inflationary situation in the economy, RBI can increase which one or more of these monetary tools?

A. CRR   **B.** SLR

C. Bank Rate   **D.** All the above

Q.14 Which of the following customers does not fall under the low-risk category under the KYC guideline?

A. Salaried person

B. Persons from lower srata of society

C. Govt departments

D. Trusts

Q.15 Data Mining is a technique to reveal the strategic information hidden in Data Warehouses. It helps in exposing the patterns that are critical to business and provides an advantage through insight and knowledge of:

A. Predictions of customer behaviour, highly targeted market focus, maximized operational effectiveness

B. Unsound predictions of customer behaviour, optimal return on investment, and minimum operational effectiveness

C. Allows banks to capitalize on the investments made in constructing and managing data warehouses and maximizing return on investments

D. None

Q.16 In India, the normal transit period is prescribed by ___ from time to time.

A. RBI   **B.** DGFT   **C.** FEDAI   **D.** Bank

Q.17 What is the priority sector loan target for foreign banks with 20 or more branches in India?

A. 32% of ANBC or credit equivalent of off-balance sheet exposure, whichever is lower

B. 32% of ANBC or credit equivalent of off-balance sheet exposure, whichever is higher

C. 40% of adjusted net bank credit or credit equivalent of off-balance sheet exposure, whichever is lower

D. 40% of adjusted net bank credit or credit equivalent of off-balance sheet exposure, whichever is higher

Q.18 The amount of loan under retail lending normally range between ________.

A. Rs. 20,000 to Rs. 1 lakhs

B. Rs. 20,000 to Rs. 100 lakhs

C. Rs. 40,000 to Rs. 100 lakhs
D. Rs. 30,000 to Rs. 100 lakhs

Q.19 In the concept of balance of payment, which of the following is not part of visible trade?

A. Financial service
B. Air service
C. Shipping service
D. All of the above

Q.20 ABC Bank Ltd has made aggressive publicity for locker facilities to new bank customers due to the occurrence of many thefts in the locality. A number of new customers availed of the facility. Bank was closed half day on Saturday, Sunday, and also on Monday (due to Ganpati Day) and there was percolation of rainwater nallah, inside the basement area, where lockers were kept, due to the overflow of rainwater, which was flowing near the bank premises. Resultantly, all paper material inside the lockers got spoiled. All the customers complained about the loss suffered by them due to the bank's negligence. Bank expressed regret for the loss suffered by them but stated (choose the correct one).

A. The bank is not responsible since it was an act of God.

B. By bank is not responsible as a bailee since bank had taken enough care of the articles bailed in the lockers as a man of ordinary prudence, under similar circumstances, would take of his own goods. Overflow of nallah water was not a regular feature and bank had taken enough care in protecting them from any mishaps or insecurity as covered under section 151 of Contract Act, 1872

C. Bank was not responsible since the bank had given on hire the place in the locker, which is not destroyed or spoiled at all, due to overflow of water inside the locker-cabinets. Bank does not know the contents of the locker and hence is not responsible for any loss suffered by customers under section 177 of Contract Act, 1872 as pawnor

D. It is not the duty of the bank to return the goods bailed/or stored in the safe deposit lockers, and the customer would be responsible for the loss, destruction, or deterioration

Q.21 The Retail loans given by commercial banks are generally for a duration of five to seven years with housing loans granted for a longer duration of _________ years.

A. 10 - 20
B. 15 - 20
C. 15 - 30
D. 16 - 40

Q.22 The experience of banks in India in recent years under retail lending has shown that the following loans had the least level of impairment (defaults).

A. Home loans portfolio
B. Consumer loans portfolio
C. Vehicle loans portfolio
D. None of these

Q.23 When the delivery under a forex deal is completed by the 2nd banking day following the date of the contract, the rate is called?

A. TT rate
B. Buy rate
C. Forward rate
D. Spot rate

Q.24 Since advances to Tea Industry are considered/governed by the norms as applicable for agricultural advances, such advances will be considered as NPA if interest/principal remains overdue for_________crop season.

A. One
B. Two
C. Three
D. None

Q.25 ___________ is useful in situations which cannot be predicted. The system allows the creation of simulations under various conditions and helps the management in analysing situations under different conditions. e.g. incretion of simulations under various conditions and helps the manage analysing situations under different conditions. e.g. in CRR/SLR require pricing of services and products, etc.

A. Computer based decision systems
B. Data mining
C. Decision support system
D. Management support system

Q.26 What type of ethical issue does a green company resolve?

A. Environmental
B. Financial
C. Labor
D. Social

Q.27 Wholesale banking refers to doing banking business with _________.

A. Individuals
B. Industrial and business entities - including government and public sector companies
C. Both (A) and (B)
D. None of these

Q.28 A foreign exchange transaction is a ___ to exchange funds in one ___ for funds in another currency at an agreed rate and on an arranged basis.

A. Currency, Currency
B. Arrangement, Currency
C. Currency, Agreement
D. Contract, Currency

Q.29 While opening a trust account we must collect______.

A. Copy of trust deed certified by trustees
B. Copy of trust deed certified by Br. Manager
C. Copy of trust deed certified by sub-registrar
D. Copy of trust deed certified by gazetted officer

Q.30 Mohammed Aslam Shah who does not like to earn any interest on his money, entered the ABC Bank Ltd., and desired to open an account without payment of interest for deposits for withdrawal sometimes but not as a trader, but for saving and liquidity. The Branch Manager offered to open Savings Bank A/c but expressed inability to exempt payment of interest thereon. What can the branch manager do in this case?

A. To open Saving account in the name of Mohammed Aslam Shah and go on depositing the money for liquidity and savings

B. To open Current Account in the name of the depositor and take an undertaking from Mohammed Aslam Shah that no interest be paid in the account and interest credit be blocked in the computers

C. To refuse to open such an account, without interest. However, an arrangement could be made by him for awarding scholarships to needy students out of the interest earned on deposits; if agreed to by Mohammed Aslam Shah.

D. R.B.I. be approached for making regulations for such depositors, who are unwilling to earn any interest thereon

Q.31 Ranking Operations in recent years are becoming increasingly customer-focused and, in a way, getting attuned to the ever-growing______.
- **A.** Regulatory prescriptions
- **B.** IT challenges
- **C.** Customers' incomes
- **D.** Customers' preferences

Q.32 Participatory notes are issued by ______ registered with SEBI.
- **A.** Brokers
- **B.** Foreign institutional investores
- **C.** Both (A) and (B)
- **D.** None of these

Q.33 A clean bill is one which ______.
- **A.** Does not contain any superimposed clauses regarding the manner of its payment
- **B.** Does not indicate the defective condition of the goods or packing
- **C.** Is not accompanied by any document of title to goods
- **D.** Allows for interest for an overdue period at the rate applicable to clean advances

Q.34 BCSBI formed in the year 2006 on the recommendation of the "Committee on Procedure & Performance Audit of Public Services" constituted under the chairmanship of ______.
- **A.** Sri T.M. Bhasin
- **B.** Sri M. Damodaran
- **C.** Sri S. S. Tarapore
- **D.** Sri R. K. Talwar

Q.35 Banks are using through________new avenues to market their products and services, dissemination of information, financial advice, non-banking activities, the node for commerce, etc.; name this platform.
- **A.** Web-sites
- **B.** MIS
- **C.** DSS
- **D.** EDI

Q.36 Information Technology (IT) has broadly been used under two different avenues in banking. One is communication and connectivity, and the other is ______.
- **A.** Digital Rights Management (DRM)
- **B.** Business Process Re-engineering (BPR)
- **C.** Intellectual Property Rights (IPR)
- **D.** Data Leak Prevention (DLP)

Q.37 Marketing is ______.
- **A.** The process is the sale of goods or services to the customers
- **B.** The process of serving as a link between a society's needs and its pattern of industrial response
- **C.** The process of planning and executing, the conception, pricing, promotion, and distribution of goods, services, and ideas that satisfy customers
- **D.** The process of Converting customer needs into profitable dis-opportunities

Q.38 The main function of SEBI is ______.
- **A.** To protect the interests of investors in securities
- **B.** To regulate the securities market
- **C.** To promote the development of the securities market

- **D.** All the above

Q.39 What is the rate of commission for collection of the premium amount under Pradhan Mantri Fasal Bima Yojana?
- **A.** 5% & 4% of the premium collected from loanee farmers & non-loanee farmers respectively
- **B.** 3% & 2% of the premium collected from loanee farmers & non-loanee farmers respectively
- **C.** 4% of the premium collected either from loanee or non-loanee farmers
- **D.** None of the above

Q.40 Banks and other institutions have issued debit and credit cards; the purpose of both are:
- **A.** The same, to make paperless payments
- **B.** Different, since in credit card, the account is credited with the amount in debit card the account is debited
- **C.** The same, there is risk weightage of 125% in both the cards
- **D.** Different, since in debit cards interest for a delayed period is charged while in credit cards no such interest is charged by banks

Q.41 RBI's Committees on Mechanisation in the Banking Industry (1984) and on Computerisation in Banks (1988) were headed by:
- **A.** Shri YH Malegam
- **B.** Dr C. Rangarajan
- **C.** Shri WS Saraf
- **D.** Shri M. Narasimham

Q.42 EMV stands for ____.
- **A.** Europay, Master card & Value
- **B.** Europay, Master card & Visa
- **C.** Europay, Mestro card & Visa
- **D.** Euro, Master card & Visa

Q.43 SEBI in respect of certain matters has the same powers ____.
- **A.** As are vested in a criminal court under the Criminal Procedure Code while trying a suit
- **B.** As are vested in a civil court under the Code of Civil Procedure, 1908 (5 of 1908), while trying a suit
- **C.** Both (A) and (B)
- **D.** None of these

Q.44 What is the priority sector loan target for domestic banks?
- **A.** 40% of adjusted net bank credit
- **B.** 40% of credit equivalent of off- balance sheet exposure
- **C.** 40% of adjusted net bank credit or credit equivalent of off-balance sheet exposure, whichever is lower
- **D.** 40% of adjusted net bank credit or credit equivalent of off-balance sheet exposure, whichever is higher

Q.45 Name the concept/system of paperless office extensively used for interoffice and interoffice correspondence:
- **A.** E-Banking
- **B.** E-B to B
- **C.** E-Mail
- **D.** E-Commerce

Q.46 Intellectual Property Right (IPR) allows its creator/innovator to use the IP for his or her own benefit and______.

A. Only allows the government also to use such work
B. Prohibits any third party use of such work
C. Allows anyone else for non-prohibited use
D. Dilutes the credibility and confidence in the business space

Q.47 Which of the following functions are carried by IRDA in India?

(i) Regulator of insurance companies.
(ii) Regulator of insurance products.
(iii) Supervision of the general insurance market.

A. Only (i) and (ii)
B. Only (i) and (iii)
C. Only (ii) and (iii)
D. (i) (ii) and (iii)

Q.48 Which is not part of social media?

A. Pinterest
B. Instagram
C. Facebook
D. Wikipedia

Q.49 The gestation period of long-term crop is________ .

A. More than 6 months
B. More than 12 months
C. More than 18 months
D. More than 24 months

Q.50 Can the cheque-returning memo be treated as evidence in offences under the Negotiable Instruments Act?

A. It is secondary evidence, banker could be called in court
B. It is prima facie evidence, banker need not be called in court
C. It is affidavit evidence, banker to tender affidavit
D. None

Q.51 What is the CRR ratio of the scheduled bank?

A. 3%   B. 5%   C. 15%   D. 18%

Q.52 Suspicious Transaction Report (STR) to be submitted within______.

A. 7 days   B. 15 days   C. 30 days   D. 60 days

Q.53 One of the following categories of investors need not obtain a certificate of registration from SEBI in order to buy, sell, or deal in securities ________.

A. Investment adviser
B. Retail investor
C. Both (A) and (B)
D. None of these

Q.54 While opening the account of Limited company we must take ________.

A. Certified copy of articles of association
B. Certified copy of the memorandum of association
C. Copy of the certificate of incorporation in the case of public companies
D. All of the above

Q.55 The data stored have got characteristics of customer-oriented/integrated and absence of inconsistencies/non-volatile and time-variant for longer storage of say 5 to 10 years in banks. This database system is called:

A. Data Mining

B. Wata Warehouse
C. Gateway for Electronic Data Interchange services
D. Data Message

Q.56 What is the meaning of liquidity with the banker in the banking system?

A. Cash in hand
B. Cash and bank balances
C. Short term current assets which can be converted into cash within 12 months
D. All of the above

Q.57 If there are declining sales leading to declining profits and no possibility of increasing and improving them, which of the following strategy will be adopted by an organization?

A. Product modification
B. More of product modification and some production elimination
C. Some production modification and more of production elimination
D. Product elimination

Q.58 A customer of the bank lost their FDR, which of the following document he needs to be executed?

A. Government bond
B. Agreement
C. Promissory note
D. Indemnity bond

Q.59 The ownership, management, and trading functions of a stock exchange are clearly segregated in respect of ________.

A. Demutualized exchange
B. Corporatized exchange
C. Stock exchange
D. None of these

Q.60 As per the provisions of section 138 of Negotiable Instruments Act, 1881, payee of a cheque may initiate criminal action, if the cheque is returned for the reason is:

A. Refer to the drawer
B. Payment stopped by the drawer
C. Post-dated
D. Insufficient funds

Q.61 Priority sector targets are linked to (A) adjusted net bank credit (B) credit equivalent of off-balance sheet exposure (whichever is lower (C) whichever is higher.

A. Only (A)
B. (A) and (B) both
C. (A) and (C) both
D. (A) (B) and (C) together

Q.62 What does an Ethical Foundation for an organization embody?

(i) The structure, operation, and conduct of the activities of the organization.
(ii) The basic principles which govern the external and internal relations of the organization.

A. Only (i)
B. Only (ii)
C. Either (i) or (ii)
D. Both (i) and (ii)

Q.63 A bank received the payment of an outstation bill on behalf of its customer, but before the money could be credited to the customer's account the bank failed. What is the relationship between the bank and the customer?

A. Creditor & Debtor

B. Principal & Agent

C. Bailer & Bailee

D. Trustee & Beneficiary

Q.64 The issue of new securities to existing shareholders at a ratio to those already held is known as _______.

A. Rights issue

B. Rights shares

C. Both the above

D. None of these

Q.65 As per the Information Technology Act, 2000, the importance of electronic transmission of messages has gone up heavily in e-commerce. The digital images are required for authenticity, integrity, and non-repudiation. The concept is known as:

A. RTGS

B. Electronic Fund Transfer

C. Packet Assembler/Dissembler

D. Digital Signature

Q.66 What is CVV?

A. Card Verification Value

B. Card Validation Value

C. Card Valid Verification

D. Card Value Verification

Q.67 Compared to a manual system, the consequences of an error in a computerized system are more serious due to:

(A) Errors being generated at high speed will involve a higher cost to correct them.

(B) Computer system processes more data.

(C) Users of computer systems perceive the computer output to be always correct.

A. A to C all

B. Only B and C

C. Only A and B

D. Only A

Q.68 Which ethical principle specifies to do what is good?

A. Beneficence

B. Least harm

C. Respect for autonomy

D. None of the above

Q.69 For the opening of the Partnership account documents to be obtained?

A. Letter of Partner

B. (A) and (D) both

C. Only Registered Deed

D. Partnership Deed (registered/Not registered)

Q.70 Bancassurance means _____.

A. Bank assures the customer of the best services

B. Bank has to be assured or guaranteed repayment of advances

C. A package of financial services that can fulfil both the banking and insurance needs of the customer at the same time

D. A kind of insurance policy

Q.71 Where non marriage certificate is required?

A. Only in case of family pension as family pension will be stopped after the marriage of the family pension holder who can be widow, widower or unmarried daughter.

B. Only in case of family pension as family pension will be stopped after the marriage of the family pension holder who can be the unmarried daughter.

C. Only in case of family pension as family pension will be stopped after the marriage of the family pension holder who can be a widow.

D. None of above

Q.72 What was the State Bank of India called before it was created through SBI Act?

A. Bank of Hindustan

B. Bank of Madras

C. Imperial Bank of India

D. Imperial Bank of Calcutta

Q.73 There is no need to give notice to the customer, of the bank's intention exercise?

A. Right of set-off

B. Right to sell the pledged goods

C. Bankers lien

D. Contingent contracts

Q.74 As per revised guidelines, loans to individual women beneficiaries up to Rs. ___ per borrower are covered under the weaker section.

A. 25,000   **B.** 50,000   **C.** 1,00,000   **D.** 2,00,000

Q.75 As per RBI guidelines bank have to earmark the following day as the customer day _________.

A. 15th of every month

B. last day of every month

C. 1st day of every month

D. Last Friday of month

Q.76 Which one is the correct name of depositories presently functioning in India?

A. NSDL

B. CDSL

C. Both (A) and (B)

D. None of above

Q.77 Preference share is called so because _______.

A. It is received from the preferred few people

B. Shares are allotted on preference

C. It is never paid back preferred only for business for ever

D. Preference of payment of interest and at winding up

Q.78 A red-flagged account is a _____________ account.

A. Potential non-performing assets

B. Willful defaulter

C. Fraud prone

D. Loss account

Q.79 Credit proposals of these borrowers whose names are appearing in the non-willful defaulter's list published by RBI/CIBIL?

A. Should not be entertained

B. Should be considered with due diligence, care and caution

C. Should be considered only after ensuring 100% collateral

D. Should be considered only in retail credit proposals

Q.80 Recently, Reserve Bank relaxed the leverage ratio (LR) for Domestic Systemically Important Banks (DSIBs). It is____.

A. 2.4%   **B.** 3.8%   **C.** 5%   **D.** 4%

Q.81 What is the loan limit for education under the priority sector?

A. 10 lakhs   **B.** 15 lakhs   **C.** 20 lakhs   **D.** 25 lakhs

Q.82 What is the applicable limit and purpose for social infrastructure loans under the priority sector?

A. 40 million   **B.** 60 million

C. 50 million   **D.** 70 million

Q.83 Under PM Fasal Bima Yojna, what is the premium rate for Kharif crops?

A. 2% of sum insured or actuarial rate, whichever is less

B. 1.5% of sum insured or actuarial rate, whichever is less

C. 5% of sum insured or actuarial rate, whichever is less

D. None of the above

Q.84 The models which have been permitted to be adopted by banks for outsourcing are the following _________.

A. Business facilitators

B. Business correspondents

C. Service providers in non-core activities

D. Both (A) and (B)

Q.85 A product means something that can be offered to satisfy a want or need which can be physical goods, services, persons, places, ideas, etc. Which of the following does not match?

A. Idea- adult education

B. Places- Goa, Kashmir

C. Persons- Bismilla Khan

D. Services- toothpaste

Q.86 Which of the following does not belong to the major general insurance private sector companies in India?

A. Bajaj Allianz General Insurance

B. Reliance General Insurance

C. Royal Sundaram Alliance Insurance

D. The Oriental Insurance Company

Q.87 Internal Rate of Return i.e. IRR is:

A. The rate at which the present value of future inflows from the project will be equal to the outflow for the project.

B. The rate at which the net present value of project inflows and outflows will be zero.

C. Rate of return which matches the cost of funds of the project.

D. Both (A) and (B)

Q.88 What is the full form of TIBOR?

A. Tokyo Interbank Offered Rate

B. Tokyo-India Bureau Of Regulations

C. The Interbank Offered Rate

D. The Interbank Offered Rights

Q.89 In the case of a long term crop loan, the account will become NPA if the instalment of principal or interest remains overdue for_________.

A. One crop season   **B.** Two crop season

C. Three crop season   **D.** None

Q.90 Onsite inspection of banks and financial institutions is based on:

A. CAMELS – Capital adequacy / asset quality / management /earning appraisal / liquidity and system controls

B. ACB – Audit Committee of the Board

C. K.Y.C. – know your customer

D. OSMOS – On sit monitoring system

Q.91 Nomination in current account can be done _________.

A. Only by an individual

B. Only by the sole proprietor

C. Both (A) and (B)

D. Partnership firm

Q.92 What does the letter 'M' mean in the term SME as used in the financial world?

A. Maximum   **B.** Medium

C. Market   **D.** Mutual

Q.93 Under which act, Yoga was included in the ambit of charitable purposes as announced in the Union Budget 2015-16?

A. Income Tax Act

B. Fundamental Rights Act

C. Co-operative Societies Act

D. Emergency Provisions Act

Q.94 Which among the following is a component of promotion mix:

(A) Advertising

(B) Personal selling

(C) Public relations

(D) Sales promotion

A. A to D all   **B.** A, B and C only

C. A, B and D only   **D.** A, C and D only

Q.95 Swarnjayanti Gram Swarozgar Yojana (SGSY), has been renamed as _________.

A. National Gram Swarozgar Yojana (NGSY)

B. Swarnjayanti Rural Livelihood Mission (SRLM)

C. National Rural Livelihood Mission (NRLM)

D. National Rural Mission Yojana (NRMY)

Q.96 What type of tax has been abolished with a CESS in this budget 2015-16?

A. Entertainment Tax   **B.** Income Tax

C. Transaction Tax   **D.** Wealth Tax

Q.97 When more than one banks allow credit facilities to one party in coordination with each other, the process is called as _________.

A. Amortization   **B.** Consortium

C. Moratorium   **D.** Subvention

Q.98 From which year, the Goods and Service Tax will be rolled out in India?

A. 2014   **B.** 2015   **C.** 2016   **D.** 2017

Q.99 Key elements of KYC Policy in lending are _____.

A. Customer acceptance policy
B. Customer Identification procedure
C. Monitoring of transaction
D. All of the above

Q.100 Large scale computer network spread over the sizable geographic area is called _____.

A. Local Area Network   **B.** Wide Area Network
C. Topology   **D.** RDBMS

Q.101 Lending to which of the following activities is part of priority sector (1) agriculture (2) micro and small enterprises (3) renewable energy (4) social infrastructure (5) export credit?

A. 1 to 5 all   **B.** 1 to 4 all
C. 1,2 and 4 only   **D.** 1,2,3 and 5 only

Q.102 Reserve Bank of India through its notification dated June 2, 2016, advised all commercial banks in India to have in place a cyber-security policy with the approval of their Boards. RBI gave a timeframe to the commercial banks to set up such cybersecurity policy of approximately:

A. 2 months   **B.** 4 months
C. 8 months   **D.** 12 months

Q.103 Who acts as the regulator for the insurance companies in India?

A. RBI   **B.** SEBI   **C.** IRDAI   **D.** GOI

Q.104 Which one of the following is a valid document available to the bank for customer identification?

A. Voter's ID Card   **B.** Ration Card
C. Bank's Pass Book   **D.** All the above

Q.105 Name the card which is having features of accumulation of transactions over a period of time and the total amount charged to the account, once a month:

A. Debit card   **B.** Charge card
C. Credit card   **D.** Smart card

Q.106 In the case of a short term crop loan, the account will become NPA if the installment of principal or interest remains overdue for________.

A. One crop season   **B.** Two crop season
C. Three crop season   **D.** None

Q.107 VSAT stands for:

A. Value Small Aperture Terminal
B. Very Small Aperture Terminal
C. Very Systematic Aperture Terminal
D. Very Small Aperture Transmission

Q.108 SWIFT for:

A. Trading of securities
B. Electronic funds transfers

C. Foreign exchange rate calculation
D. Link to CBS with foreign banks

Q.109 An asset will be classified Doubtful-1 if it has remainded in substandard category for more than________months.

A. 24   **B.** 18   **C.** 12   **D.** 6

Q.110 Which is that card that looks like any other plastic card or an ATM card with an integrated circuit (IC-Chip)?

A. Member card   **B.** Charge card
C. Credit card   **D.** Smart card

Q.111 A Usance Bill is presented for acceptance to the drawee. Does he have to accept it:

A. Within 24 hours   **B.** Within 48 hours
C. Within 72 hours   **D.** No time limit

Q.112 The custodian key of the locker is to be kept overnight in:

A. Strong room under joint custody
B. With the manager
C. The nearest branch
D. None of the above

Q.113 Safe deposit facility cannot be granted to:

A. Blind person.   **B.** Trusts
C. Minors   **D.** Both (A) and (B)

Q.114 The system of marketing information is _____ that pertains to marketing.

A. The structure of people, equipment and procedures for generation and processing of Information
B. The software used for the collection of information
C. The computer hardware which is used for handling database
D. The set of inputs to collate the information

Q.115 ________is the largest wide area network, provides access to the satellite, and operates from 650 VSAT terminals, access is through leased lines as well as dial-up connectivity.

A. INET   **B.** NICNET
C. INDONET   **D.** INFINET

Q.116 Mr. Ram is maintaining a saving bank account which is showing a credit balance of Rs. 15000 on 30.01.2019 you receive a cheque of Rs. 15000 issued by Mr. ram in clearing what would be the course of action?

A. Bank has to pay the cheque if it is in order
B. Bank will not make payment advising the drawer maintain minimum balance as per rules
C. The bank has to make the payment as there is sufficient balance in the account to meet the cheque under section 31 of NI act
D. Bank makes a noting in recognizing slip to "refer to drawer"

Q.117 To prevent or minimize cyber threats, it is recommended that individuals must NOT set their passwords which are?

A. Simple   **B.** Unique   **C.** Secret   **D.** Complex

Q.118 Priority sector lending certificates (PSLC) can be issued with a standard lot size of ________and multiples there of.

A. Rs. 10 lakhs   **B.** Rs. 25 lakhs
C. Rs. 50 lakhs   **D.** Rs. 100 lakhs

Q.119 Name a system/organization which operates with an objective of creating a unified international transaction processing and transmission to meet the ever-growing telecommunications requirements of the banking industry?

A. SWIFT   **B.** Internet   **C.** CHIPS   **D.** CHATS

Q.120 In case of death of the safe deposit locker holder, the nominee of a Safe Deposit locker has to produce the following document to enable the bank to settle the claim _______.

A. Will
B. Succession certificate
C. Probate
D. Death certificate

// Smart Answer Sheet //

Correct — Indicates percentage of students who answered questions correctly.

Skipped — Indicates percentage of students who skipped questions.

Q.	Ans.	Correct / Skipped
1	B	55.28 % / 5.72 %
2	A	65.65 % / 17.89 %
3	A	16.1 % / 18.43 %
4	A	36.14 % / 19.14 %
5	A	55.99 % / 19.32 %
6	A	60.82 % / 19.68 %
7	A	54.38 % / 20.22 %
8	A	40.25 % / 20.93 %
9	C	14.31 % / 20.93 %
10	D	45.44 % / 21.29 %
11	A	27.55 % / 21.11 %
12	A	34.88 % / 20.76 %
13	D	63.33 % / 20.75 %
14	D	52.59 % / 21.47 %
15	A	32.92 % / 21.82 %
16	C	15.03 % / 21.46 %

Q.	Ans.	Correct / Skipped
17	D	31.13 % / 22.18 %
18	B	55.1 % / 21.82 %
19	D	38.28 % / 18.25 %
20	B	38.46 % / 20.57 %
21	B	27.73 % / 21.82 %
22	A	51.52 % / 22.72 %
23	D	29.16 % / 20.39 %
24	B	44.01 % / 22.36 %
25	C	21.47 % / 23.43 %
26	A	61.0 % / 22.9 %
27	B	34.35 % / 22.36 %
28	D	35.78 % / 23.08 %
29	C	34.7 % / 22.55 %
30	A	26.65 % / 23.26 %
31	D	48.48 % / 23.26 %
32	C	41.14 % / 23.62 %

Q.	Ans.	Correct / Skipped
33	C	23.08 % / 22.72 %
34	C	50.63 % / 23.25 %
35	A	42.93 % / 23.62 %
36	B	28.09 % / 23.97 %
37	C	64.04 % / 24.51 %
38	D	66.19 % / 24.33 %
39	C	18.78 % / 24.33 %
40	A	42.58 % / 24.5 %
41	B	43.29 % / 23.79 %
42	B	48.66 % / 24.69 %
43	B	22.9 % / 24.51 %
44	D	35.42 % / 25.4 %
45	C	39.0 % / 24.51 %
46	B	42.04 % / 25.4 %
47	D	62.43 % / 24.69 %
48	D	55.28 % / 25.04 %

Q.	Ans.	Correct / Skipped
49	B	35.96 % / 25.76 %
50	B	43.83 % / 24.86 %
51	A	36.14 % / 24.33 %
52	A	46.87 % / 24.87 %
53	B	25.94 % / 25.94 %
54	D	63.86 % / 25.59 %
55	B	40.43 % / 25.76 %
56	D	55.46 % / 25.94 %
57	D	22.54 % / 26.48 %
58	D	63.51 % / 25.94 %
59	A	33.99 % / 25.76 %
60	D	50.45 % / 24.86 %
61	D	29.16 % / 25.94 %
62	B	12.16 % / 26.12 %
63	B	26.65 % / 25.59 %
64	C	28.8 % / 25.76 %

Q.	Ans.	Correct / Skipped
65	D	47.23 % / 25.4 %
66	A	57.42 % / 25.76 %
67	A	43.29 % / 26.66 %
68	A	22.36 % / 27.37 %
69	B	40.79 % / 27.01 %
70	C	62.25 % / 27.02 %
71	A	32.02 % / 25.76 %
72	C	43.29 % / 25.4 %
73	A	38.46 % / 27.19 %
74	C	23.97 % / 26.84 %
75	A	45.26 % / 26.3 %
76	C	59.39 % / 26.12 %
77	D	34.35 % / 26.65 %
78	C	49.37 % / 26.84 %
79	B	38.46 % / 25.4 %
80	D	26.12 % / 25.94 %

Q.	Ans.	Correct / Skipped	Q.	Ans.	Correct / Skipped	Q.	Ans.	Correct / Skipped	Q.	Ans.	Correct / Skipped	Q.	Ans.	Correct / Skipped
81	C	37.21 % / 25.76 %	89	A	28.62 % / 26.48 %	97	B	48.12 % / 26.66 %	105	B	20.21 % / 26.3 %	113	C	41.86 % / 25.4 %
82	C	34.53 % / 26.29 %	90	A	46.69 % / 26.48 %	98	C	26.12 % / 27.01 %	106	B	45.62 % / 26.29 %	114	A	57.78 % / 26.84 %
83	A	42.75 % / 27.02 %	91	C	54.38 % / 25.94 %	99	D	59.93 % / 26.3 %	107	B	47.41 % / 25.4 %	115	B	15.03 % / 25.94 %
84	D	52.77 % / 26.12 %	92	B	49.02 % / 27.01 %	100	B	58.32 % / 25.94 %	108	B	41.32 % / 25.94 %	116	C	44.72 % / 25.94 %
85	D	48.12 % / 27.19 %	93	A	36.85 % / 26.12 %	101	A	33.45 % / 26.3 %	109	C	56.35 % / 25.58 %	117	A	55.28 % / 24.86 %
86	D	29.52 % / 26.65 %	94	A	45.44 % / 26.65 %	102	B	23.97 % / 26.66 %	110	D	35.78 % / 26.12 %	118	B	21.82 % / 25.76 %
87	D	42.75 % / 26.48 %	95	C	52.59 % / 26.3 %	103	C	67.8 % / 25.76 %	111	B	28.62 % / 25.05 %	119	A	55.81 % / 24.69 %
88	A	45.62 % / 26.83 %	96	D	36.49 % / 26.3 %	104	A	37.21 % / 25.76 %	112	A	52.59 % / 26.12 %	120	D	58.32 % / 23.97 %

Performance Analysis

Performance Analysis	
Avg. Score (%)	39.0%
Toppers Score (%)	98.0%
Your Score	

//Hints and Solutions//

1. Case 1: When you draw a cheque and submit over the counter to withdraw cash. You are asked to sign on the back of the cheque. That is actually your acknowledgement of getting the cash.

Case 2: When you draw a cheque favouring someone without crossing as account payee and the payee submits the cheque over the counter then there is no any way we can verify whether that holder/bearer is "holder in due course" or "not" so in this case, you (drawer of cheque) need to attest the signature of payee and write a line "Signature Attested" along with your sign. So in this case drawer sign twice one in front while drawing and second in the back while attesting. Similarly, the payee also signs twice once for the purpose of attestation and second as an acknowledgement of getting the cash over the counter.

Hence, the correct option is (B).

2. PPF rules are very clear that one can't open more than one account if someone still opens a second account, he or she will not be eligible for any interest on invested amount, said Rajan Pathak, Mumbai-based independent financial advisor. The second account will have to be closed down. The person can approach the respective bank branch or post office and ask them to close the account, said a senior official from National Small Savings Institute.

Hence, the correct option is (A).

3. TDS has to be applied if the interest paid or payable exceeds Rs 5,000 during the financial year. It said that under the SCSS an individual of 65 years of age or above needs to furnish a declaration in Form No. 15H to the bank or post office if the tax on his estimated income for the financial year is nil.

Hence, the correct option is (A).

4. Dematerialization (Commonly known as 'Demat') signifies the conversion of a share certificate from its present physical form to electronic form for the same number of holding.
Dematerialization of shares is optional and an investor can still hold shares in physical form.

Hence, the correct option is (A).

5. The Finance Ministry of India has launched the 11th tranche of Electoral Bonds sale from July 1-10. In this regard, India's largest Public Sector Bank (PSB), State Bank of India (SBI) has been authorized to issue and encash electoral bonds in the XI phase of sale through its 29 branches. This is the first issuance of electoral bonds after the formation of the new government.

Hence, the correct option is (A).

6. The remittance is limited to 12 transactions a year per sender with a maximum amount of Rs. 50,000 per transaction with a normal transaction fee of Rs. 50 for an amount less than Rs. 5,000 and Rs. 75 for the amount above Rs. 5,000.

There is also no limit on the minimum or maximum amount of funds that could be transferred using NEFT. However, the maximum amount per transaction is limited to Rs 50,000 for cash-based remittances within India and also for remittances to Nepal under the Indo-Nepal Remittance Facility Scheme.

Hence, the correct option is (A).

7. Under cheque truncation system (CTS) the physical cheques are retained at the presenting bank and do not move to the paying banks. In case a customer desires, banks can provide images of cheques duly certified authenticated. In case, however, a customer desires to see/get the physical cheque, it would need to be sourced from the presenting bank, for which a request has to be made to his/her bank.

Hence, the correct option is (A).

8. Marginal Standing Facility (MSF) rate refers to the rate at which the banks can borrow funds overnight from RBI against government securities. MSF is a very short term borrowing scheme for scheduled commercial banks. Banks may borrow funds through MSF during severe cash shortages or acute shortages of liquidity.

Hence, the correct option is (A).

9. A holder for value is a holder of e.g., a bill of exchange, for which value has been given at some time. However, he can only claim from persons who were parties to the bill, up to the time value was last given, and cannot claim a better title than that of the person from whom he took the bill.

Hence, the correct option is (C).

10. In case of total and irreparable loss of both eyes or loss of use of both hands or feet or loss of sight of one eye or loss of use of hands or feet, the sum assured under the scheme "PRADHAN MANTRI SURAKSHA BIMA YOJANA" is Rs. 2 Lakhs. Upon the happening of any event which may give rise to a claim under this policy, written notice with full particulars must be given to the company immediately. In case of death,written notice unless reasonable cause is shown, be so given within seven days after the death, and inthe event of loss of sight or amputation of limbs, written notice thereof must also be given within onecalendar month after such loss of sight or amputation.

Hence, the correct option is (B).

11. Merchant Banking in India was started by the Grindlays Bank in 1967. Since then, many private and public banks such as the State Bank of India, Citibank, ICICI Bank, etc., and other national and international firms have set up their own Merchant Banking services.

Hence, the correct option is (A).

12. In finance, a foreign exchange swap, forex swap, or FX swap is a simultaneous purchase and sale of identical amounts of one currency for another with two different value dates (normally spot to forward) and may use foreign exchange derivatives. An FX swap allows sums of a certain currency to be used to fund charges designated in another currency without acquiring foreign exchange risk. It permits companies that have funds in different currencies to manage them efficiently.

Hence, the correct option is (A).

13. "Our best tool to control inflation is the interest rate," he said, adding that the government too has tools like increasing agricultural production and improving supply. "Both need to work together and will work together. We were expecting some increase in the CPI number because of the seasonal effects from vegetable prices, but it came more than anticipated by the consensus forecast. We will study them in greater detail.

Hence, the correct option is (D).

14. The objective of the KYC guidelines is to prevent banks from being used, intentionally or unintentionally, by criminal elements for money laundering activities. One of the elements of the KYC guidelines is the Customer Acceptance Policy (CAP), Which indicates the criteria for acceptance of customers to be followed by the bank.

Hence, the correct option is (D).

15. Data mining is looking for hidden, valid, and potentially useful patterns in huge data sets. Data Mining is all about discovering unsuspected/ previously unknown relationships amongst the data. It is a multi-disciplinary skill that uses machine learning, statistics, AI, and database technology. The insights extracted via Data mining can be used for marketing, fraud detection, and scientific discovery, etc.

Predictions of customer behaviour, highly targeted market focus, maximized operational effectiveness.

Hence, the correct option is (A).

16. In India, the NTP for foreign currency and Rupee bills as prescribed by the Foreign Exchange Dealers Association of India (FEDAI). The details are as under-NTP for Foreign currency bills, For all foreign Currency bills in 25 days.

In India, the normal transit period is prescribed by FEDAI from time to time.

Hence, the correct option is (C).

17. The Reserve Bank of India (RBI) on Thursday brought foreign banks with at least 20 branches in India under the ambit of compulsory targeted lending to small farmers and micro-enterprises.

The PSL norms mandate foreign banks to eventually lend 40% of their total loan book to the priority sector, such as agriculture, rural infra, and medium, small and micro enterprises (MSMEs) among others from April 2020.

Therefore, the correct option is "40% of adjusted net bank credit or credit equivalent of off-balance sheet exposure, whichever is higher".

Hence, the correct option is (D).

18. The loans are marketed under attractive brand names to differentiate the products offered by different banks. As the Report on Trend and Progress of India, 2003-04 has shown that the loan values of these retail lending typically range between Rs. 20,000 to Rs. 100 lakhs.

Hence, the correct option is (B).

19. Financial services are the economic services provided by the finance industry, which encompasses a broad range of businesses that manage money, including credit unions, banks, credit-card companies, insurance companies, accountancy companies, consumer-finance companies, stock brokerages, investment funds, individual managers, and some government-sponsored enterprises. Financial services companies are present in all economically developed geographic locations and tend to cluster in local, national, regional, and international financial centres such as London, New York City, and Tokyo.

Hence, the correct option is (D).

20. By Bank is not responsible as a bailee since the bank had taken enough care of the articles bailed in the lockers as a man of ordinary prudence, under similar circumstances, would take of his own goods. Overflow of nallah water was not a regular feature and the bank had taken enough care in protecting them from any mishaps or insecurity as covered under section 151 of Contract Act, 1872.

In all cases of bailment, the bailee is bound to take as much care of the goods bailed to him as a man of ordinary prudence would, under similar circumstances, take of his own goods of the same bulk, quantity, and value as the goods bailed.
Hence, the correct option is (B).

21. The loans are generally for a duration of five to seven years with housing loans granted for a longer duration of 15 years.

Hence, the correct option is (B).

22. Retail loan is estimated to have accounted for nearly one-fifth of all banks. For the last few years, it has become synonymous with mainstream banking India, 2003-04 has shown that the loan values of these retail lending typically. In the retail segment, the housing loans had the least gross asset impairment.

Hence, the correct option is (A).

23. In finance, a spot contract, spot transaction, or simply spot, is a contract of buying or selling a commodity, security, or currency for immediate settlement (payment and delivery) on the spot date, which is normally two business days after the trade date. The settlement price (or rate) is called spot price (or spot rate). A spot contract is in contrast with a forward contract or futures contract where contract terms are agreed now but delivery and payment will occur at a future date.

Hence, the correct option is (D).

24. Since advances to Tea Industry are considered/governed by the norms as applicable for agricultural advances, such advances will be considered as NPA if interest/principal remains overdue for two crop seasons.

The agricultural crop year in India is from June to July. The Indian cropping season is classified into two main seasons-(i) Kharif and (ii) Rabi based on the monsoon. The Kharif cropping season is from July–October during the south-west monsoon and the Rabi cropping season is from October-March (winter).

Hence, the correct option is (B).

25. The decision support system is useful in situations that cannot be predicted. The system allows the creation of simulations under various conditions and helps the management in analyzing situations under different conditions. e.g. incretion of simulations under various conditions and helps the manage analyzing situations under different conditions. e.g. in CRR/SLR require pricing of services and products, etc.

A decision support system (DSS) is a computerized program used to support determinations, judgments, and courses of action in an organization or a business. A DSS shifts through and analyzes massive amounts of data, compiling comprehensive information that can be used to solve problems and in decision-making.

Hence, the correct option is (C).

26. The natural environment encompasses all living and non-living things occurring naturally, meaning in this case not artificial. The term is most often applied to the Earth or some parts of Earth.

Hence, the correct option is (A).

27. Wholesale banking refers to banking services sold to large clients, such as other banks, other financial institutions, government agencies, large corporations, and real estate developers. It is the opposite of retail banking, which focuses on individual clients and small businesses.

Therefore, the correct option is "Industrial and business entities - including government and public sector companies".

Hence, the correct option is (B).

28. A foreign exchange transaction is a contract to exchange funds in one currency for funds in another currency at an agreed rate and on an arranged basis. A foreign currency swap, also known as an FX swap, is an agreement to exchange currency between two foreign parties. The agreement consists of swapping principal and interest payments on a loan made in one currency for principal and interest payments of a loan of equal value in another currency.

Hence, the correct option is (D).

29. Copy of Trust Deed Certified by sub-registrar. The first step to register a trust starts with the drafting of a trust deed. The trust deed is to be executed on appropriate non-judicial stamp paper, the rate of stamp duty differs from state to state. The next step is to seek an appointment with the sub-registrar office having jurisdiction based on the registered office of the trust, and the government registration fee is to be paid after that.

Hence, the correct option is (C).

30. Liquidity means how quickly you can get your hands on your cash. In simpler terms, liquidity is to get your money whenever you need it. Cash, savings account, checkable account are liquid assets because they can be easily converted into cash as and when required.

To open a Saving Account in the name of Mohammed Aslam Shah and go on depositing the money for liquidity and savings.

Hence, the correct option is (A).

31. Customer preferences are expectations, likes, dislikes, motivations, and inclinations that drive customer purchasing decisions. They complement customer needs in explaining customer behaviour. For example, a customer needs shoes and they'd prefer a particular style, brand, and colour.

Hence, the correct option is (D).

32. Participatory notes are offshore derivative instruments with Indian shares as underlying assets. Brokers and foreign institutional investors registered with the Securities and Exchange Board of India (SEBI) issue the participatory notes and invest on behalf of the foreign investors. Brokers must report their participatory note issuance status to the regulatory board each quarter. The notes allow foreign investors with high net worth, hedge funds, and other investors, to participate in the Indian markets without registering with the SEBI. Investors save time, money, and scrutiny associated with direct registration. Hence, the correct option is (C).

33. A clean bill of lading is one type of bill of lading signed by the carrier and the shipper. It guarantees the goods received and placed on the vessel are in good condition with no apparent damage or defect. Any and all damages, defects, and/or changes in quantity are outlined in the claused or foul bill.

Hence, the correct option is (C).

34. As this is my first address to you from my desk, it is only appropriate that I begin at the very beginning and underline the single most important concern that permeates my thoughts as Chairman, Banking Codes and Standards Board of India (BCSBI). And that is, how do we enhance awareness of BCSBI and the Codes that it has developed for banks to follow when they deal with customers. It is a matter of concern that more than half a decade after BCSBI was established in response to the recommendations of the Committee on Procedures and Performance Audit on Public Services (CPPAPS) under the Chairmanship of Shri S. S. Tarapore, a vast majority of the bank functionaries and the customer population has little awareness of what BCSBI is about, what its mandate is, and even more crucially, how BCSBI can impact the life of the ordinary person who has a banking account.

Hence, the correct option is (C).

35. A website (also written as a web site) is a collection of web pages and related content that is identified by a common domain name and published on at least one web server. Notable examples are wikipedia.org, google.com, and amazon.com.

Banks are using through Web-sites new avenues to market their products and services, dissemination of information, financial advice, non-banking activities, the node for commerce, etc.; name this platform.

Hence, the correct option is (A).

36. Information Technology has basically been used under two different avenues in Banking. One is Communication and Connectivity and the other is Business Process Re-engineering. The research shows a positive correlation between the levels of implemented IT and both profitability and cost savings.

Hence, the correct option is (B).

37. Marketing research is the function that links the consumer, customer, and public to the marketer through information–information used to identify and define marketing opportunities and problems; generate, refine, and evaluate marketing actions; monitor marketing performance; and improve understanding of marketing as a process. Marketing research specifies the information required to address these issues, designs the method for collecting information, manages and implements the data collection process, analyzes the results, and communicates the findings and their implications.

Therefore, marketing is the "The process of planning and executing, the conception, pricing, promotion, and distribution of goods, services, and ideas that satisfy customers".

Hence, the correct option is (C).

38. Securities and Exchange Board of India (SEBI) is a statutory regulatory body entrusted with the responsibility to regulate the Indian capital markets. It monitors and regulates the securities market and protects the interests of the investors by enforcing certain rules and regulations.

Hence, the correct option is (D).

39. 4% of the premium collected either from loanee or non-loanee farmers. All farmers including sharecroppers and tenant farmers growing the notified crops in the notified areas are eligible for coverage. However, farmers should have an insurable interest in the insured crops. The non-loanee farmers are required to submit necessary documentary evidence of land records prevailing in the State (Records of Right (RoR), Land possession Certificate (LPC), etc.) and/or applicable contract/agreement details (in case of sharecroppers/tenant farmers).

Hence, the correct option is (C).

40. It is safe to say that in today's world of payment processing, it is all about digital. Between personal and professional needs, society is rapidly moving into a fully digital landscape across the map. The convenience and efficiency of some of these programs are hard to match with any physical or paper equivalent, particularly when it comes to business and paperless payment processing.

Hence, the correct option is (A).

41. In 1984, a committee set up by the RBI and chaired by Dr C.Rangarajan (who was then deputy governor of RBI and later became governor of RBI) was set up to present a roadmap for computerization of the banking industry for the five year period 1984 to 1989.
Hence, the correct option is (B).

42. EMV is short for Europay, MasterCard, and Visa, the 1994 founders. The EMV standard is a secure technology that is used worldwide for all payments done with credit, debit, and prepaid EMV smart cards.

Hence, the correct option is (B).

43. As are vested in a civil court under the Code of Civil Procedure, 1908 (5 of 1908), while trying a suit. Provided that the State Government concerned may, by notification in the Official Gazette, extend the provisions of this Code or any of them to the whole or part of the State of Nagaland or such tribal areas, as the case may be, with such supplemental, incidental or consequential modifications as may be specified in the notification.

Hence, the correct option is (B).

44. 40 per cent of adjusted net bank credit or credit equivalent amount of off-balance sheet exposure, whichever is higher. Within the 18 per cent target for agriculture, a target of 8 per cent of ANBC or credit equivalent amount of off-balance sheet exposure, whichever is higher is prescribed for small and marginal farmers.

40% of adjusted net bank credit or credit equivalent of off-balance sheet exposure, whichever is higher.

Hence, the correct option is (D).

45. Electronic mail (email or e-mail) is a method of exchanging messages ("mail") between people using electronic devices. The email entered limited use in the 1960 s, but users could only send to users of the same computer, and some early email systems required the author and the recipient to both be online simultaneously, similar to instant messaging. Ray Tomlinson is credited as the inventor of email in 1971, he developed the first system able to send mail between users on different hosts across the ARPANET, using the @ sign to link the user name with a destination server. By the mid-1970s, this was the form recognized as email.

Hence, the correct option is (C).

46. Intellectual property rights are like any other property right. They allow creators, or owners, of patents, trademarks, or copyrighted works to benefit from their own work or investment in a creation.

Hence, the correct option is (B).

47. IRDA issues the registration certificates to insurance companies and regulates them. It protects the interest of policyholders. It provides a license to insurance intermediaries such as agents and brokers after specifying the required qualifications and set norms/codes of conduct for them.

Hence, the correct option is (D).

48. Wikipedia is a free, open content online encyclopedia created through the collaborative effort of a community of users known as Wikipedians. Anyone registered on the site can create an article for publication; registration is not required to edit articles. Wikipedia was the only non-commercial site of the top ten.
Hence, the correct option is (D).

49. The gestation period of the long-term crop is more than 12 months. For the purpose of these guidelines, 'long duration' crops would be crops with crop season longer than one year and crops, which are not 'long duration' crops, would be treated as 'short duration' crops.

Hence, the correct option is (B).

50. It is Prima facie evidence, the banker need not be called in court. As the banker to banks, the Reserve Bank fulfils this role by accounts with different banks or clearing money market transactions between two banks. The function is performed through the Deposit Accounts Department (DAD) at the Centralised Funds Management System (CFMS) to facilitate centralized funds enquiry.

Hence, the correct option is (B).

51. All Scheduled Commercial Banks are at present required to maintain with Reserve Bank of India a Cash Reserve Ratio (CRR) of 3% of the Net Demand and Time Liabilities (NDTL) (excluding liabilities subject to zero CRR prescriptions).

Cash Reserve Ratio is one of the many monetary policy tools that RBI uses to control the money supply in the economy. RBI is the central bank of our country which manages the money supply to various other commercial banks, NBFCs and other lenders, which ultimately supply money to the rest of the country.

Hence, the correct option is (A).

52. The Suspicious Transaction Report (STR) should be furnished within 7 days of arriving at a conclusion that any transaction, whether cash or non-cash or a series of transactions integrally connected are of suspicious nature.

Hence, the correct option is (A).

53. A retail investor, also known as an individual investor, is a non-professional investor who buys and sells securities, mutual funds, or exchange-traded funds (ETFs) through traditional or online brokerage firms or other types of investment accounts.

Hence, the correct option is (B).

54. The following documents are required for the opening bank account of limited companies (both private and public) in the banks. A true copy of the certificate of incorporation attested by a Director or Secretary of the company.

1 - A true copy of the certificate of incorporation attested by a Director or Secretary of the company.

2 - A copy of the updated Memorandum and Articles of Association attested by a Director or Secretary of the company.

3 - A copy of the Board Resolution passed at a meeting of the Board of Directors (not by circulation) duly certified by the Secretary of the Company for opening the account and operation instructions thereon. The resolution should clearly state the name of the bank, persons authorized to open and operate the account and carry on such other transactions as dealing with securities, powers to draw, accept, endorse, etc.

4 - Registered Address proof of the company, as registered with the ministry of corporate affairs

5 - PAN Card of the company or the PAN Card Application Acknowledgement

6 - Power of Attorney granted to its employees, officers, and managers to transact the business on the company's behalf

7 - DIN (Directors Identification Number)

8 - ID Proof of all the working Directors.

Hence, the correct option is (D).

55. The data stored have got characteristics of customer-oriented/integrated and absence of inconsistencies/non-volatile and time-variant for longer storage of say 5 to 10 years in banks. This database system is called Wata Warehouse.

In computing, a data warehouse (DW or DWH), also known as an enterprise data warehouse (EDW), is a system used for reporting and data analysis and is considered a core component of business intelligence. DWs are central repositories of integrated data from one or more disparate sources. They store current and historical data in one single place that is used for creating analytical reports for workers throughout the enterprise.

Hence, the correct option is (B).

56. Liquidity in banking refers to the ability of a bank to meet its financial obligations as they come due. It can come from direct cash holdings in currency or on an account at the Federal Reserve or other central bank. More frequently, it comes from acquiring securities that can be sold quickly with minimal loss.

Hence, the correct option is (D).

57. Product Elimination- The decision to drop a product (for example, in the decline stage of its life cycle) in order to use the costs associated with it to enhance profits or to release resources that could be more effectively used in other ways.

Hence, the correct option is (D).

58. An Indemnity bond is a surety bond used by governments, businesses, and individuals to establish assurance that an agreement will be fulfilled as stated. The indemnity bond outlines a pledge to compensate, financially or otherwise, one party if the second party fails to fulfil a contract or obligation.

Hence, the correct option is (D).

59. Demutualization is a process that changes a mutual or co-operative association into a public company by converting the interests of the members into shareholdings. These holdings can then be traded like the shares of a company. The idea is to change the structure of exchanges that were originally formed as trusts.

Hence, the correct option is (A).

60. Insufficient funds is a banking term for when your account does not have enough money available to cover a payment. For example, say you write a check or sign up for automatic bill pay with your electric company to pay your light bill.

Hence, the correct option is (D).

61. The technical definition of Adjusted Net Bank Credit (ANBC). It is the net bank credit plus investments made by banks in non-SLR bonds held in the held-to-maturity category or credit equivalent amount of off-balance-sheet exposure, whichever is higher. In simple terms, ANBC is the net banking credit after taking into account bill discounting, non-SLR securities and other exemption via long-term bonds.

Hence, the correct option is (D).

62. The basic principles which govern the external and internal relations of the organization. Legislation passed in 2002, the Sarbanes-Oxley Act ("SOX"), requires that corporations whose stock is traded under the provisions of the Securities Exchange Act of 1934 must publish their codes of ethics, if these exist, and also publish any changes to these codes as they are made.

Hence, the correct option is (B).

63. The principal-agent relationship is an arrangement in which one entity legally appoints another to act on its behalf. In a principal-agent relationship, the agent acts on behalf of the principal and should not have a conflict of interest in carrying out the act. The relationship between the principal and the agent is called the "agency," and the law of agency establishes guidelines for such a relationship.

Hence, the correct option is (B).

64. A rights offering (rights issue) is a group of rights offered existing shareholders to purchase additional stock shares, known as subscription warrants, in proportion to their existing holdings. A rights issue is an invitation to existing shareholders to purchase additional new shares in the company. This type of issue gives existing shareholders securities called rights. With the rights, the shareholder can purchase new shares at a discount to the market price on a stated future date.

Hence, the correct option is (C).

65. A digital signature is a mathematical scheme for verifying the authenticity of digital messages or documents. A valid digital signature, where the prerequisites are satisfied, gives a recipient very strong reason to believe that the message was created by a known sender (authentication and that the message was not altered in transit (integrity).

Digital signatures are a standard element of most cryptographic protocol suites and are commonly used for software distribution, financial transactions, contract management software, and in other cases where it is important to detect forgery or tampering.

Hence, the correct option is (D).

66. The CVV Number ("Card Verification Value") on your credit card or debit card is a 3 digit number on VISA, Master Card, and Discover branded credit and debit cards. On your, American Express branded credit or debit card it is a 4 digit numeric code.

Hence, the correct option is (A).

67. The main difference between manual and computerized systems is speed. Accounting software not only processes data and creates reports much faster than manual systems, but also allows faster data entry. Overall computerized accounting will save you a lot of time, as it allows documents such as invoices, purchase orders, and payroll to be collated and printed quickly and accurately.

In manual systems, where accounts are maintained in books, it requires a lot of effort to store the crucial business data - as it requires space. Most importantly, the security of the data gets compromised, as the business owner needs to place his trust in a few individuals in his organization and hope that nothing will go wrong. Computerized accounting allows for a robust system for storing business data, such that it requires lesser efforts and costs to store data, and also allows for automated security levels to be set within the organization, which will give the business owner peace of mind.

Hence, the correct option is (A).

68. Beneficence is defined as an act of charity, mercy, and kindness with a strong connotation of doing good to others including moral obligation. All professionals have the foundational moral imperative of doing right.

The utilitarianism principle basically holds that an action is morally right if it produces the greatest good for the greatest number of people.

Hence, the correct option is (A).

69. The Reserve Bank of India sets Know Your Customer (KYC) norms based on which documentation is collected by Banks for opening an account. The RBI KYC norms layout the following standards for opening Partnership Firm bank account:

- Registration certificate, if registered
- Partnership deed
- Power of Attorney granted to a partner or an employee of the firm to transact business on its behalf
- Any officially valid document identifying the partners and the persons holding the Power of Attorney and their addresses
- Telephone bill in the name of firm/partners

Hence, the correct option is (B).

70. Bancassurance means the distribution of Insurance policies both life and non-life, by banks as corporate agents through their branches. A package of financial services that can fulfil both the banking and insurance needs of the customer at the same time. Bancassurance arrangement benefits both the firms. On the one hand, the bank earns a fee amount (noninterest income) from the insurance company apart from the interest income whereas, on the other hand, the insurance firm increases its market reach and customers. The bank acts as an intermediary, helping insurance firms reach their target customer in order to increase their market share.

Hence, the correct option is (C).

71. Only in case of family pension as family pension will be stopped after the marriage of the family pension holder who can be widow, widower or unmarried daughter as per government rules till 2004, the family pension could only be granted to deceased government employee's spouse and after his or her death to the dependent son or daughter below 25 years of age. In 2004, the rule was changed to stipulate that there will be no age restriction in the case of the divorced or widowed daughter who shall be eligible for family pension even after attaining 25 years of age. An income stipulation was fixed to qualify for getting this pension. The family pension would end once the parents passed away and none of the children qualified for the pension on account of the son or daughter being married or them being above 25 years of age.

Hence, the correct option is (A).

72. The Imperial Bank of India was baptized as State Bank of India followed by the formation of 7 associate banks in 1959. Recognizing the fact that banking plays a crucial role in the economic development of a country, the Government of India nationalized 14 major commercial banks in July 1969. Another six commercial banks were nationalized in April 1980.

Hence, the correct option is (C).

73. The right of set-off is a legal right by a debtor to reduce the amount owed to a creditor by offsetting against it any amounts owed by the creditor to the debtor. For example, a bank can seize the amount in a customer's bank account to offset the amount of an unpaid loan.

Hence, the correct option is (A).

74. As per revised guidelines, loans to individual women beneficiaries up to Rs 1,00,000 per borrower are covered under the weaker section. Individual women beneficiaries up to ₹1 lakh per borrower (For UCBs, existing loans to women will continue to be classified under weaker sections till their maturity/repayment.) Minority communities may be notified by the Government of India from time to time.

Hence, the correct option is (C).

75. The State Bank of India has decided that all top functionaries at their local head office, administrative office, regional business office, and branch managers will devote a minimum of two hours (2.30 pm to 4.30 pm) on the 15th and 25th (the following day in case of holiday/Sunday) of every month to customers for listening to their grievances and suggestions.

Hence, the correct option is (A).

76. There are two depositories that are functional in India – National Securities Depository Ltd (NSDL) and Central Securities Depository Ltd (CDSL). Various depository participants linked to each one of them in India.

NSDL, one of the largest Depositories in the World, established in August 1996 has established a state-of-the-art infrastructure that handles most of the securities held and settled in dematerialized form in the Indian capital market. Although India had a vibrant capital market which is more than a century old, the paper-based settlement of trades caused substantial problems like bad delivery and delayed transfer of title, etc. The enactment of the Depositories Act in August 1996 paved the way for the establishment of NSDL.

CDSL(Central Depository Securities Limited) is another electronic securities depository in India, which began operations in 1999 and is also based in Mumbai, Maharashtra. It is the second-largest securities depository in India and facilitates an account transfer.

Hence, the correct option is (C).

77. Preference shares, more commonly referred to as preferred stock, are shares of a company's stock with dividends that are paid out to shareholders before common stock dividends are issued. Preferred stock shareholders also typically do not hold any voting rights, but common shareholders usually do.

Hence, the correct option is (D).

78. The concept of a Red Flagged Account (RFA) is fraud-prone being introduced in the current framework as an important step in fraud risk control. These signals in a loan account should immediately put the bank on alert regarding a weakness or wrongdoing which may ultimately turn out to be fraudulent.

Hence, the correct option is (C).

79. Due diligence has been used since at least the mid-fifteenth century in the literal sense of "requisite effort." Centuries later, the phrase developed a legal meaning, namely, "the care that a reasonable person takes to avoid harm to other persons or their property" in this sense, it is synonymous with another legal term, ordinary care. More recently, due diligence has extended its reach into business contexts, signifying the research a company performs before engaging in a financial transaction. This meaning may also apply to individuals people are often advised to perform their due diligence before buying a house, signing a loan, or making any important purchase.

Hence, the correct option is (B).

80. The Reserve Bank relaxed the leverage ratio (LR) to 4% for Domestic Systemically Important Banks (DSIBs) and 3.5% for other banks. This has been done to help them boost their lending activities. The reduced leverage ratio will be effective from the quarter commencing October 1, 2019. The leverage ratio, as defined under Basel-III norms, is Tier-I capital as a percentage of the bank's exposures.

Hence, the correct option is (D).

81. Loans to individuals for educational purposes, including vocational courses, not exceeding ₹ 20 lakh will be considered as eligible for priority sector classification. Loans currently classified as priority sectors will continue till maturity.

Priority Sector means those sectors which the Government of India and Reserve Bank of India consider as important for the development of the basic needs of the country and are to be given priority over other sectors. The banks are mandated to encourage the growth of such sectors with adequate and timely credit.

Hence, the correct option is (C).

82. Bank loans up to a limit of ₹ 50 million per borrower for building social infrastructure for activities namely schools, health care facilities, drinking water facilities, and sanitation facilities (including loans for construction/ refurbishment of toilets and improvement in water facilities in the household) in Tier II to Tier VI centre are eligible for classification under priority sector.

Bank credit to Micro Finance Institutions (MFI) extended for on-lending to individuals/ members of SHGs/ JLGs for water and sanitation facilities are also eligible for classification as priority sector loans under 'Social Infrastructure' subject to certain criteria.

Hence, the correct option is (C).

83. There will be a uniform premium of only 2% to be paid by farmers for all Kharif crops and 1.5% for all Rabi crops. In the case of annual commercial and horticultural crops, the premium to be paid by farmers will be only 5%. The premium rates to be paid by farmers are very low and the balance premium will be paid by the Government to provide full insured amount to the farmers against crop loss on account of natural calamities.

Hence, the correct option is (A).

84. A facilitator helps a group of people in a business to reach an outcome or decision for which everyone will take responsibility and be fully committed. A facilitator helps by providing a structure to a process enabling cooperative decision-making. You must note that a facilitator doesn't lead, but rather guides.

Business Correspondents are retail agents who represent banks and are responsible for delivering banking services at locations other than a bank branch/ATM. BCS support banks in providing their limited range of banking services at an affordable cost. Thus, they are pivotal in promoting financial inclusion.

Hence, the correct option is (D).

85. Services- toothpaste a product may be defined as a set of tangible, intangible, and associate attributes capable of being exchanged for a value with the ability to satisfy consumers and business needs. It is anything that can be offered to a market to satisfy the needs or wants of the customer. The products that are marketed include physical goods, services, experiences, events, persons, places, properties, organizations, information, and ideas.

Hence, the correct option is (D).

86. New India Assurance Company Limited, National Insurance Company Limited, The Oriental Insurance Company, United India Insurance, Agricultural Insurance Company of India are the major general insurance companies in India. Bajaj Allianz General Insurance, ICICI Lombard General Insurance, IFFCO-Tokio General Insurance, Reliance General Insurance, Royal Sundaram Alliance Insurance, TATA AIG General Insurance, Cholamandalam General Insurance, HDFC Ergo are the major general insurance private sector companies in India.

Hence, the correct option is (D).

87. The internal rate of return of a project is the discount rate that would yield a net present value of zero, i.e., the rate of interest which makes the present value of the estimated cash inflow equal to the present value of the cash outflow required by the investment.

Hence, the correct option is (D).

88. Tibor is an acronym for the Tokyo Interbank Offered Rate, which is the daily reference rate derived from the interest rates that banks charge to lend funds to other banks in the Japanese interbank market.

Hence, the correct option is (A).

89. In the case of a long-term crop loan, the account will become NPA if the instalment of principal or interest remains overdue for one crop season.

A loan granted for long duration crops will be treated as an NPA if the instalment of the principal or interest thereon remains unpaid for one crop season beyond the due date.

Hence, the correct option is (A).

90. The Annual Financial Inspection (AFI) focuses on statutorily mandated areas of solvency, liquidity, and operational health of the bank. It is based on an internationally adopted CAMEL model modified as CAMELS, i.e. capital adequacy, asset quality, management, earnings, liquidity, and system and control.

Hence, the correct option is (A).

91. Nomination facility is available to account holders operating current accounts, savings bank accounts, and all types of term deposit accounts, safe deposit lockers, or safe custody of articles. Nomination can be made in favour of one person only.

Hence, the correct option is (C).

92. Small and Medium Enterprises or Small and Medium-sized Enterprises (SMEs) are companies whose personnel numbers fall below certain limits. The abbreviation 'SMEs' is used in the European Union and by international organizations such as the World Bank, the United Nations, and the World Trade Organisation.

Therefore, the letter 'M' mean "Medium" in the term SME as used in the financial world

Hence, the correct option is (B).

93. The government has decided to accord special status to Yoga by categorizing its promotion as a charitable activity. The institutions which, as part of genuine charitable activities, undertake activities like publishing books or holding program on yoga or other programs as part of actual carrying out of the objects which are of charitable nature are being put to hardship due to first and second provision to section 2(15) of the Income-tax Act.

Hence, the correct option is (A).

94. (A) Advertising

(B) Personal selling

(C) Public relations

(D) Sales promotion

While these five promotional mix elements-advertising, PR, promotions, direct marketing, and personal selling-have been around for decades, the marketing world is constantly evolving. Digital marketing lets companies target their potential customers more easily, bypassing more traditional marketing channels, and running digital campaigns at a fraction of the cost.

Hence, the correct option is (A).

95. The Swarna Jayanti Swarozgar Yojna (SGSY) has been renamed as National Rural Livelihood Mission (NRLM). With this, the scheme will be made universal, more focussed, and time-bound for poverty alleviation by 2014. The initial scheme Swarnajayanti Gram Swarozgar Yojana (SGSY) was launched in 1999. It was renamed as National Rural Livelihood Mission in 2011.

Hence, the correct option is (C).

96. The Finance Minister believes that wealthier people should pay more. He decided to abolish wealth tax and replace it with 2 per cent surcharge. Wealth tax used to be 1 per cent on net wealth exceeding 30 lakh Rupees and non-resident Indians were exempted from the tax for seven years. Surcharge means additional payment other than tax.

Hence, the correct option is (D).

97. A consortium is an association of two or more individuals, companies, organizations, or governments with the objective of participating in a common activity or pooling their resources for achieving a common goal.

Hence, the correct option is (B).

98. GST will put in place a state-of-the-art indirect tax system from the next fiscal, aiming to create a single tax for goods and services across the country. In the Union Budget 2015-16 presented by the Finance Minister Arun Jaitley proposed to roll out the GST from next fiscal beginning April 2016.

Hence, the correct option is (C).

99. The KYC policy is a mandatory framework for banks and financial institutions used for the customer identification process. Its origin stems from the 2001 Title III of the Patriot Act to provide a range of tools to prevent terrorist activities.

The Company has framed its KYC policy incorporating the following four key elements:
(i) Customer Acceptance Policy.
(ii) Customer Identification Procedures.
(iii) Monitoring of Transactions/On-going Due Diligence.
(iv) Risk Management.

Hence, the correct option is (D).

100. WAN (Wide Area Network) is another important computer network that is spread across a large geographical area. WAN network system could be a connection of a LAN which connects with other LAN's using telephone lines and radio waves.

Hence, the correct option is (B).

101. Priority Sector Lending is an important role given by the (RBI) to the banks for providing a specified portion of the bank lending to few specific sectors like agriculture and allied activities, micro and small enterprises, poor people for housing, students for education, and other low-income groups and weaker sections. This is essentially meant for all-round development of the economy as opposed to focusing only on the financial sector.

These activities are part of the priority sector-

(1) agriculture

(2) micro and small enterprises

(3) renewable energy

(4) social infrastructure

(5) export credit

Hence, the correct option is (A).

102. The Reserve Bank of India, through its notification on 2 June 2016, advised all commercial banks in India to have a cybersecurity policy with the approval of their boards. RBI gave commercial banks a time frame of 4 months to establish such a cybersecurity policy.

Hence, the correct option is (B).

103. Insurance Regulatory and Development Authority of India (IRDAI), is a statutory body formed under an Act of Parliament, (IRDAI Act 1999) for overall supervision and development of the Insurance sector in India. The powers and functions of the Authority are laid down in the IRDAI Act, 1999 and Insurance Act,

1938. The key objectives of the IRDAI include the promotion of competition so as to enhance customer satisfaction through increased consumer choice and fair premiums while ensuring the financial security of the Insurance market.

Hence, the correct option is (C).

104. "Officially Valid Document" (OVD) means the passport, the driving license, proof of possession of Aadhaar number, the voter's identity card issued by the election commission of India, job card issued by NREGA duly signed by an officer of the state government and letter issued by the National Population Register containing details of name and address.

Hence, the correct option is (A).

105. A charge card is a type of electronic payment card that charges no interest but requires the user to pay their balance in full upon receipt of the statement, usually on a monthly basis. Charge cards are offered by a limited number of issuers.

Hence, the correct option is (B).

106. In the case of a short-term crop loan, the account will become NPA if the instalment of principal or interest remains overdue for two crop seasons. A loan granted for short duration crops will be treated as an NPA if the instalment of the principal or interest thereon remains unpaid for two crop seasons beyond the due date.

Hence, the correct option is (B).

107. A very small aperture terminal (VSAT) is a two-way ground station that transmits and receives data from satellites. A VSAT is less than three meters tall and is capable of both narrow and broadband data to satellites in orbit in real-time. The data can then be redirected to other remote terminals or hubs around the planet.

Hence, the correct option is (B).

108. Behind most international money and security transfers is the Society for Worldwide Interbank Financial Telecommunications (SWIFT) system. SWIFT is a vast messaging network used by banks and other financial institutions to quickly, accurately, and securely send and receive information, such as money transfer instructions.

Hence, the correct option is (B).

109. A doubtful asset is an asset that has been non-performing for more than 12 months. Loss assets are loans with losses identified by the bank, auditor, or inspector that need to be fully written off. They typically have an extended period of non-payment, and it can be reasonably assumed that it will not be repaid.

Hence, the correct option is (C).

110. An integrated circuit card is a type of payment or identification card that uses an embedded circuit, such as a computer chip, to store data. Integrated circuit cards are made of plastic or similar material and are most often associated with specific credit cards known as EMV cards.

Hence, the correct option is (D).

111. Drawee's Time for Deliberation (Section 63) The holder must if so required by the drawee of a bill of exchange presented to him for acceptance, allow the drawee 48 hours exclusive of public holidays to consider whether he will accept it. The client on acceptance of such bills binds himself liable to make the payment of the bills at a fixed future date. The supplier of goods may present the accepted bills to his banker and request the bank to discount such bills so that he gets immediate money for the goods sold by him.

Hence, the correct option is (B).

112. The first set of Premises keys shall be with the Branch Manager. If the Branch Manager is exempted from holding the keys by the Head Office /Regional Office, the next Senior Officer should hold the keys. The second set of above internal keys shall be with another Officer if another Officer is available or with the cashier /Joint custodian of the Branch. The first set of all the other internal keys pertaining to other cabinets shall be handled by the Branch Manager /concerned Officer. The second set of keys shall be kept in joint custody in the Branch.

Hence, the correct option is (A).

113. In law, a minor is a person under a certain age, usually the age of majority, which legally demarcates childhood from adulthood. The age of majority depends upon jurisdiction and application, but it is generally 18. Minor may also be used in contexts that are unconnected to the overall age of the majority.

Hence, the correct option is (C).

114. A marketing information system is a continuing and interacting structure of people, equipment, and procedures to gather, sort, analyze, evaluate, and distribute pertinent, timely, and accurate information for use by marketing decision-makers to improve their marketing planning, implementation, and control.

Hence, the correct option is (A).

115. In 1990, the takeoff by the Ministry of Electronics and Information Technology NIC's ICT Network, "NICNET", facilitates the institutional linkages with the Ministries/Departments of the Central Government, State Governments, and District administrations of India.

Hence, the correct option is (B).

116. The drawee of a cheque having sufficient funds of the drawer in his hands properly applicable to the payment of such cheque must pay the cheque when duly required so to do, and, in default of such payment, must compensate the drawer for any loss or damage caused by such default. The bank has to make the payment as there is a sufficient balance in the account to meet the cheque under section 31 of the NI act.

Hence, the correct option is (C).

117. To prevent or mitigate cyber threats, it is recommended that individuals should not set their Simple Passwords. High-profile cyber attacks on companies such as Target and Sears have raised awareness of the growing threat of cybercrime. Recent surveys conducted by the Small Business Authority, Symantec, Kaspersky Lab, and the National Cybersecurity Alliance suggest that many small business owners are still operating under a false sense of cybersecurity.

Hence, the correct option is (A).

118. The certificates will have a standard lot size of ₹25 lakh and multiples thereof. There will be no transfer of credit risk on the underlying as there is no transfer of tangible assets or cash flow. The settlement of funds will be done through the Kuber portal.

Hence, the correct option is (B).

119. SWIFT organization which operates with an objective of creating a unified international transaction processing and transmission to meet the ever-growing telecommunications requirements of the banking industry. SWIFT's messaging services are trusted and used by more than 11,000 financial institutions in more than 200 countries and territories around the world. Providing reliable, secure and efficient messaging services to our community of users, SWIFT is the backbone of global financial communication.

Hence, the correct option is (A).

120. The nominee will be allowed to access the locker after making an application to the bank with the following documents:-

- Copy of hirer's death certificate.
- Photo identification proof of the nominee as per KYC guidelines.
- Acknowledgement as performing.

Hence, the correct option is (D).

Q.1 In case of family pension, the nomination facility is

A. Compulsory

B. Only in exceptional cases

C. Not available

D. Available

Q.2 what are the benefits available under the scheme PPF account?

A. Income tax benefit under sec 80C

B. Balance cannot be attached by court order

C. The account can be extended by five years at a time after the completion of 15 years

D. All the above

Q.3 Who regulates depositories and depository participants?

A. NSDL   **B.** CDSL   **C.** SEBI   **D.** RBI

Q.4 (SLR) Statutory Liquidity Ratio is to be maintained on

A. Total Demand and Time Liabilities

B. Net Demand and Time Liabilities

C. Total Demand and Time Assets

D. Net Demand and Time Assets

Q.5 Whenever RBI does Open Market Operation Transaction actually it wishes to regulate which of the following?

A. Inflation only

B. Liquidity in economy

C. Borrowing powers of the banks

D. The flow of foreign Direct Investments

Q.6 Which among the following are the advantages of managing business ethics in the workplace?

(i) Cultivate strong teamwork and productivity

(ii) Avoid criminal acts

(iii) Lower fines

A. Only (i) and (ii)   **B.** Only (i) and (iii)

C. Only (ii) and (iii)   **D.** (i), (ii) and (iii)

Q.7 In a demutualization process, a stock exchange is transformed from a mutually owned association to

A. Large corporate

B. Shareholders owned company

C. Public sector undertaking

D. Limited liability partnership

Q.8 Retail individual investor' means an investor who applies or bids for securities of or for a value of not more than

A. Rs. 2 Lakh   **B.** Rs. 5 Lakh

C. Rs. 10 Lakh   **D.** Rs. 15 Lakh

Q.9 Insider trading refers to

A. Employee making use of confidential information

B. Passing on confidential information to relatives, friends

C. Trading in the stock market without informing the bank

D. All of the above

Q.10 What are the circumstances when though there is sufficient and adequate funds in the bank account, the cheques are returned unpaid by banks?

A. When payment is stopped

B. When funds are attached by garnishee or are set-off by bank

C. When balance is not clear balance for payments

D. Both (A) and (B)

Q.11 CAMEL model is used by

A. Bankers to evaluated a credit proposal

B. Bankers to manage their risks

C. RBI inspectors to evaluate banks functions

D. Merchant Bankers to evaluate portfolio investment

Q.12 As per SEBI guidelines, in a Book Building process the cap in the price band should not be more than ______ of the floor price.

A. 10%   **B.** 20%   **C.** 30%   **D.** 40%

Q.13 Job discrimination means Employee being denied opportunity based on

A. Race/Religion   **B.** Caste

C. Sex   **D.** All of the above

Q.14 M/s Singh Brothers comprising three partners is availing a CC limit of Rs. 10 lakhs from your branch. Aman Singh, a partner in the firm, expired on 31.01.2018. In order to meet the expenses in connection with his rituals, a cheque of Rs.30000/-, signed by the other two partners, in favor of the eldest son of the deceased partner, was presented for payment on 05.02.2018. The outstanding balance was Rs.585000/- and considering the sufficient available balance, the cheque was paid by you. But subsequently, on the dissolution of the firm, the legal heirs of the deceased partner refused to accept the liability for the entire balance of Rs.615000/- and claimed that they are not liable for the amount of Rs.30000/ paid after the death of a deceased partner. Your manager's operation claims that as one of the legal heirs has obtained that payment, all the legal heirs are also liable. What is the position of your bank?

A. The view of the manager, operation is correct.

B. On the death of the partner, the partnership gets dissolved and the legal heirs are not liable for any debit made after the death. The Bank's action of allowing payment after death is unwarranted even though the partners will be liable for such payments.

C. Neither the Legal heirs of the deceased partner nor the Partners of the dissolved firm are liable for any payment made after the death of the partner.

D. None of the above

Q.15 Which of the following is true about NEFT?

A. NEFT operates in half-hourly batches from 8 am to 7 pm.

B. On weekdays there are 23 batches and on working

Saturdays there are 23 batches.

C. There is no restriction on the minimum and maximum amount that can be remitted through NEFT.

D. All of the above

Q.16 What is the full form of "CORE" in core banking solutions?

A. Customer Online Rupee Exchange

B. Customer Online Real-time Environment

C. Centralized Online Rupee Exchange

D. Centralized Online Real-time Environment

Q.17 As per SEBI guidelines, safety net arrangements can be made available only to all original resident individual allottees limited up to a maximum of ________ per allottee.

A. 1000 shares

B. 5000 shares

C. 6000 shares

D. 7000 shares

Q.18 Retail loans consist of

A. Consumer credit for a specific purpose

B. Credit for general purpose

C. Both (A) and (B)

D. None of the above

Q.19 One of your NRI customers wants to place FCNR deposits in Canadian $ with your bank. You will

A. Accept his request and open an FCNR account

B. Will not accept his request to open an FCNR account in Canadian $

C. Will inform the customer to place an FCNR in any one of the currencies (US$/GBP/JPY/EUR)

D. Both (B) and (C)

Q.20 What would be the sum assured under the scheme in case of Total and irrecoverable loss of sight of one eye or loss of use of one hand or foot?

A. Rs. 1 Lakh

B. Rs. 2 Lakhs

C. Rs. 3 Lakhs

D. Rs. 5 Lakhs

Q.21 Building a sustainable environment includes
(i) Developing a green supply chain
(ii) Omitting hazardous emissions
(iii) Writing a code of ethics

A. Only (i) and (ii)

B. Only (i) and (iii)

C. Only (ii) and (iii)

D. (i), (ii) and (iii)

Q.22 Which of the following does not come in the purview of Retail Banking?

A. Advances to traders

B. Advances to small-scale units

C. Financing of weaker sections of the society

D. Loan syndicate

Q.23 A mutual fund has, apart from its sponsors

A. Trustees

B. Custodian

C. Asset management company

D. All the above

Q.24 Bank employees are expected not to accept bribes while

A. Credit appraisals & Loan disbursements

B. Monitoring and recovery of loans

C. Marketing of bank products and services

D. All of the above

Q.25 Devaluation of currency means

A. Reduction in the value of the currency vis-a-vis major internationally traded currencies.

B. Permitting the currency to seek its worth in the international market.

C. Fixing the value of the currency in conjunction with the movement in the value of the pre-determined currency.

D. Fixing the value of the currency in multilateral consultation with the IMF, the World Bank, and major trading partners.

Q.26 "ASBA" is a term used in which of the following sectors?

A. Aviation

B. Real estate

C. Insurance

D. Capital markets

Q.27 RBI sometimes devaluates its currency primarily to promote

A. Import and reduce export

B. Export and reduce import

C. Both import and export

D. The outflow of foreign exchange

Q.28 What are the functions of IRDA?

A. IRDA has the power to specify the code of conduct for surveyors and loss assessors.

B. IRDA has power to regulate investment of funds by insurance companies.

C. IRDA has power to supervise the functioning of Tariff Advisory Committee.

D. IRDA has duty to regulate, promise and ensure orderly growth of the insurance and reinsurance business of India.

Q.29 Which one of the Non Resident Deposit schemes is not permitted?

A. FCNR a/cs

B. NRNR a/cs

C. NRE a/cs

D. NRO a/cs

Q.30 Which types of threats are there in a computerised system?

A. Errors and omissions in data and software

B. Unauthorised disclosure of confidential information/frauds/computer abuse and mis-utilisation of banks' assets

C. No humidity, flood proof area, free from radio transmissions over data, intercepting during transmissions

D. Both (A) and (B)

Q.31 The type of arrangement under which a bank pays the seller the value of the bills and later collects it from the buyer on the due date is

A. Factoring

B. Forfaiting

C. Bill discounting

D. Bill compounding

Q.32 Bank cannot exercise its right of lien in case
1. where goods have been received for safe custody.
2. where the security has been deposited for a specific purpose.
3. where debt has already fallen due.
4. securities are left by the customer by mistake.

A. 1 to 4 all correct

B. 1, 2, and 3 correct

C. 1, 2, and 4 correct

D. 2, 3, and 4 correct

Q.33 Terminals Connected to a server is known as

A. Clients

B. Nodes

C. Both (A) and (B)

D. CPU

Q.34 Under the Customer Acceptance Policy, which of the following is NOT true?

A. No account is opened in anonymous or fictitious/benami name.

B. No account is opened where the RE is unable to apply appropriate CDD measures, either due to non-cooperation of the customer or non-reliability of the documents/information furnished by the customer.

C. No transaction or account based relationship is undertaken without following the CDD procedure.

D. The mandatory information to be sought for KYC purpose only once while opening an account.

Q.35 Which of the following deals in export insurance?

A. ECGC **B.** SEBI **C.** SIDBI **D.** RBI

Q.36 Guarantee to an importer that the importer of his goods will pay immediately for the goods ordered by him, is known as

A. Letter of credit

B. Laissez-faire

C. Inflation

D. Deflation

Q.37 Which of the following bank is a housing finance regulator?

A. NABARD

B. SIDBI

C. NHB

D. RBI

Q.38 The term 'loan factor' refers to

A. A charge levied by the mutual fund from the unitholders at the time of entry or exit from the mutual fund

B. Charge on staying with the fund

C. Both of the above

D. None of these

Q.39 You receive a cheque in an overdraft account for Rs.27,000.00. The debit balance in the account is Rs.30,000.00 and the OD limit is Rs 55,000.00. What reason you will state while returning?

A. Refer to drawer

B. Effects not cleared

C. Exceeds arrangement

D. Endorsement not correct

Q.40 In case of excess payment of pension the excess payment is to be recovered from the future pension every month is ______%of the pension amount.

A. 50 **B.** 25 **C.** 33.33 **D.** 60

Q.41 The fraud-prone area in a computerized environment is

A. Unauthorized changes to records, manipulations to programs or data bypass of password, amendments as to payment instructions, etc.

B. Unauthorized changes to programs during routine maintenance control checks on specified or selected transactions and transport of data to another computer and returned with manipulations.

C. Authorized amendments to the payment instruction after their entry into the computer.

D. Both (A) and (B)

Q.42 Match the following

List-I	List-II
(i) Payment in Due Course	(A) Insurance
(ii) Karta	(B) Cash Credit
(iii) IRDA	(C) HUF
(iv) Hypothecation of Inventory	(D) Payment Banker

A. i-D,ii-C,iii-A,iv-B

B. i-A,ii-B,iii-C,iv-D

C. i-B,ii-A,iii-D,iv-C

D. i-D,ii-C,iii-B,iv-A

Q.43 Subprime lending' is a term applied to the loans made to

A. Those borrowers who do not have a good credit history

B. Those borrowers who have a good credit history

C. Those borrowers who do not have a good debit history

D. Those borrowers who have a good debit history

Q.44 The aim of balanced funds is to provide

A. Regular income

B. Growth (capital appreciation)

C. Both the above

D. None of these

Q.45 Which committee is related to NPA?

A. Sunil Mehta committee

B. L K Jha Committee

C. Mahalanobis Committee

D. C Rao Committee

Q.46 In the SARFAESI Act 2002, R stands for

A. Reconstruction

B. Random

C. Reflation

D. Re-Asset

Q.47 SEBI is a________.

A. Statutory Body

B. Advisory Body

C. Constitutional Body

D. Non-Statutory Body

Q.48 Bank Rate means the rate of interest

A. Paid by banks to depositors

B. Charged by banks from borrowers

C. Charged on interbank loans

D. Charged by RBI on loans given to commercial banks

Q.49 As part of the Fair Practices Code for the Lenders, in the case of small borrowers seeking loans up to 2 lakhs, the lenders

A. Should convey in writing, the main reason/reasons which, in the opinion of the bank after due consideration, have led to a rejection of the loan applications within the stipulated time

B. Need not convey anything in writing for rejection

C. May, at their own discretion, convey orally the reason for rejection

D. May give reason/reasons for rejection of the loan applications irrespective of application date at the end of the financial year

Q.50 Securitization backed by mortgage relates to

A. Immoveable assets

B. Moveable assets

C. Special vehicles   **D.** All of these

Q.51 As per SEBI guidelines, any entity/person engaged in the marketing and selling of mutual fund products is required to pass a certification test and obtain a registration number from

A. RBI   **B.** SEBI   **C.** AMFI   **D.** None

Q.52 Bank's obligations to customers include

A. Maintain secrecy of the account

B. Honor cheques which fulfill the bank's rules

C. Follow instructions given by the customer

D. Closing customer account without prior information

Q.53 Which among the following is the core method of stabilizing the markets under the market stabilization scheme (MSS)?

A. Issuing T-bills and/or dated securities

B. Purchasing T-bills and/or dated securities

C. Conducting Open Market Operations

D. All of these

Q.54 Expand CRIS

A. Comparative Rating Index for Sovereigns

B. Cumulative Rating Index for Sates

C. Comparative Rating Index for Sates

D. Comparative Rating Index for Societies

Q.55 Which among the following cannot be called an anti-inflationary measure?

A. Raising the Bank Rate

B. Raising the Reserves Ratio requirements

C. Purchase of securities in the market

D. Rationing of the credit

Q.56 What is the validity period of equitable mortgage?

A. 15 years   **B.** 11 years   **C.** 12 years   **D.** 10 years

Q.57 The basic document for sanction of pension, issued by competent authority is called

A. Pension Payment Order (P.P.O)

B. Pension Disbursement Order (P.D.O.)

C. Letter of authority for drawing a pension

D. Pension sanction letter

Q.58 Match the following:

List-I (Committees)	List-II
(i) Classification of Assets	(a) Nayak
(ii) Computerisation in Banks	(b) Tarapore
(iii) Working Capital for SSIs	(c) Narasimham
(iv) Capital Account Convertibility	(d) Rangarajan

A. i-b,ii-d,iii-c,iv-a   **B.** i-d,ii-c,iii-a,iv-b

C. i-b,ii-a,iii-c,iv-d   **D.** i-c,ii-d,iii-a,iv-b

Q.59 _____ is a written document, inspirational in contents and specify clearly what is acceptable or unacceptable behavior at the workplace and beyond when the employees represent their organizations outside.

(i) Business ethics

(ii) Code of conduct

A. Only (i)   **B.** Only (ii)

C. Either (i) or (ii)   **D.** Both (i) and (ii)

Q.60 Review of operations of the established policies, standards and procedures, quality of efficiency of operations, integrity review focused at fraud detection/prevention and monitoring of employees activities is called

A. Audit approaches in computer

B. Audit trails

C. Computer audit

D. Computer operations trails

Q.61 Under a mandate, the mandate holder signs the cheques

A. In his individual capacity

B. As an agent of the account holder

C. As an executor of the customer

D. All of the above

Q.62 The first insurance company was started in India in 1818 at

A. Kolkata   **B.** Chennai

C. Mumbai   **D.** New Delhi

Q.63 Which one of the following statements is true?

A. Business ethics modifies people's behavior

B. Objective of ethics is managing values and conflict resolution

C. Business ethics and corporate social responsibilities are the same

D. Ethics cannot be managed

Q.64 A saving bank customer of Modern Bank issues a cheque of Rs.17000 in favor of M/s Swastic Enterprises or order. The cheque is paid by the bank on presentation through clearing with an endorsement from the payee as 'Svastika Enterprises'. The endorsement is also confirmed by the collecting bank. The drawer claims that the payment has not been made in due course and claims refund of the amount

A. This is a payment on the guarantee by the collecting bank due to which the paying bank's position is safe.

B. The cheque is of a small amount, hence the bank should refund the money.

C. If the customer is valuable, the customer's request should be accepted.

D. The endorsement is irregular due to which the paying bank is not protected under the provisions of Section 85 of the NI Act.

Q.65 Which among the following is an indirect instrument used by RBI to regulate the availability, cost and use of money and credit?

A. CRR

B. Refinance facilities

C. SLR

D. Liquidity Adjustment Facility

Q.66 Which statement(s) is/are correct about the promissory note?

A. The money has to be paid to a certain person

B. It has an unconditional undertaking called promise

C. It is a promise to pay money

D. All of the above

Q.67 What is the main objective of KYC?

A. To provide better customer services

B. To make fast transaction of high value

C. To control on money margin

D. To bring more and more persons under the purview of Income Tax

Q.68 A mandate may not cease to operative in the event of

A. Death of the mandate holder

B. The lunacy of the mandate holder

C. Insolvency of the mandate holder

D. All of the above

Q.69 Match the following:

List-I	List-II
i) Financial intermediaries	a) Mutual funds
ii) ATM's	b) E-Banking
iii) Certificate of Deposits	c) Money Markets
v) Book debts	d) Assignments

A. i-c,ii-d,iii-a,iv-b

B. i-d,ii-c,iii-b,iv-a

C. i-a,ii-b,iii-c,iv-d

D. i-a,ii-c,iii-b,iv-d

Q.70 The distinction between marketing and selling is

A. Marketing relates to producing or creating goods or services needed by the customers while selling the objectives is to sell whatever is available.

B. Marketing is an operational activity whereas selling is a total management concept.

C. Marketing is product focussed while selling customer focussed.

D. Marketing is oriented to the needs of the seller whereas selling is oriented to the needs of the buyer.

Q.71 Kite flying refers to

A. Drawing accommodation bills to arranging funds

B. Discounting of fake bills

C. Hand delivery of bills

D. None of the above

Q.72 In case of discontinuation of the account(PPF), the account can be regularized on payment of a fee of Rs 50 per the defaulted months and also a minimum of Rs._________for each year defaulted.

A. 50

B. 100

C. 500

D. No fine

Q.73 The depositor of a PPF account has been missing for the last 10 years. How can the account be settled?

A. As per sec 107 &108 of the Indian evidence act

B. As per normal claim procedure

C. As per Indian succession act

D. Hindu law in case of Hindus

Q.74 The banking ombudsman is appointed by

A. The central government under the banking regulation act

B. The Reserve bank as required by the RBI act

C. Committee of supreme court judges

D. The Reserve bank in terms of the scheme framed under the banking Regulation Act

Q.75 The committee "various aspects of service rendered by banks to retail and small customers including pensioners" which was formed by the RBI in June 2010 was headed by

A. M. Damodaran

B. Tarapore

C. Ghosh

D. Narayan

Q.76 Functions of marketing management are

A. Scientific analysis of data to understand the needs of customers, planning for long-term marketing, implementation of plans for staffing, budgeting and financing, control and evaluation of goals and targets

B. Planning and distributing goods to customers or services oriented towards the needs of the seller

C. Conversion of customer needs into profitable opportunities and encashment of the same

D. None of the above

Q.77 The banker acts as a Bailee and the customer as Bailor, this relationship is applicable

A. When a bank lends funds to a corporate customer

B. When a bank accepts US$ FCNR deposits from an NRI customer

C. When a customer operates a safe deposit locker

D. When a customer keeps articles in safe custody with a bank

Q.78 The entry-level capital requirement for a new Insurance Company in India is

A. Rs. 1 crore

B. Rs. 10 crores

C. Rs. 100 crores

D. Rs. 200 crores

Q.79 An advocate has two accounts with your branch in his name

1. One in which he transacts his office transactions.

2. One of his client account. A garnishee order is received.

A. The order will attach only the client account and not the official account.

B. The order will not attach the client account and attach the office account only.

C. The order will attach both the accounts.

D. The order will not attach any account, as the accounts belong to an advocate.

Q.80 A negotiable instrument is endorsed as Pay to Rosi only, This is called as

A. Blank endorsement

B. Restrictive endorsement

C. Sans recourse endorsement

D. The endorsement in full

Q.81 The primary legislation that deals with the insurance business in India is

A. Insurance Act, 1938

B. Insurance Regulatory and Development Authority Act, 1999

C. Both the above

D. None of these

Q.82 Which one of the following is not a principle of ethics?

A. Fairness
B. Dignity
C. Goodwill
D. Remaining conscious for profits at all costs

Q.83 What is the meaning of the term "Power of Attorney"?
A. The power of authority given to any person
B. The power of withdrawing the money from anybody's bank account
C. A written document, authorising anybody to do the work on behalf of the other person
D. All of these

Q.84 Some years back, Reverse Mortgage Scheme was begun by some organizations for help of which of the following class of the societies?
A. Senior Citizens
B. Young and un-employed
C. BPL family
D. Army retired persons

Q.85 What is said to be hard currency?
A. Such money, which is paid in exchange of the loan
B. Such money, which is not available easily
C. Such money, which is in the shape of gold
D. Such money, which is easily available.

Q.86 By which of the following institutions, the supply of currency is controlled in India?
A. Finance Ministry
B. Nationalised bank
C. RBI
D. Finance Commission

Q.87 ABC enterprise a partnership firm had availed a loan of Rs.5 lac for purchase of fixed assets. The firm had 3 partners staying at three different places. So, the loan documents were signed by three partners at three different places on January 12, 2015, January 24, 2015 and January 25, 2015. After availing the loan, there was dispute among the partners resulting in default in repayment of the loan & the account became NPA. As there was no recovery, it was decided to file a suit against the firm & its partners to save the account from becoming time barred. On 15th Jan, 2018, the loan officer was instructed to scrutinize & keep the papers ready for filing the suit. The loan officers opined that suit cannot be filed as the documents have already become time barred on 12th Jan, 2018 as there is no repayment in the account. What will be your decision on the validity of the documents for limitation purpose for filing a suit?
A. The loan officer is right, as the limitation begins from January 12, 2015
B. Documents are not valid as these have been executed on different dates at different places
C. The loan officers is wrong, the limitation begins from January 25, 2015 & suit can be filed on any date prior to January 25, 2018
D. Refer the matter to ZO for their advice & further course of action

Q.88 Ram Lal and Sons, HUF, is having a current account in your branch operated by Mr. Ram Lal, the Karta. He has 4 major sons A, B, C & D, the coparceners of the HUF with A being the eldest. On death of Mr. Ram Lal, his younger son 'C' approaches the bank with consent letter from B & D to permit him to operate the HUE Account. What will be your stand in this case?
A. Operations will be stopped and amount paid to legal heirs
B. Eldest among surviving co-parceners 'A' would become Karta automatically and operate the account & C's request will not be accepted
C. HUF would be dissolved & reconstituted with C as the Karta as per the consent letter of B & D
D. None of the above

Q.89 A power to operate the account
A. Necessarily implies overdrawing the account
B. Includes the power to borrow money in accordance with the customer of trade
C. Implies the power to draw, accept, and endorse bills of exchange
D. Does not imply the power to overdraw the account or to draw accept and endorse the bills of exchange

Q.90 One of your customers lost the Fixed Deposit Receipt issued by the bank. To obtain a duplicate FD he needs to furnish
A. A Promissory note
B. A Guarantee
C. A Letter of Credit
D. An Indemnity bond

Q.91 Factoring service means
A. Collection of bills
B. Discounting of bills
C. Maintenance of account books
D. All the above

Q.92 Whistle blower protection Act ,_______________in India, protects people who provide information about wrongdoing.
A. 2009
B. 2010
C. 2005
D. 2011

Q.93 SIDBI provides refinance facilities under ARS. What is the full form of ARS?
A. Automatic Refinance Scheme
B. Allocation and Refinance solutions
C. Automatic Refinance solutions
D. Allocation and Refinance Scheme

Q.94 Index "Residex" is associated with
A. Share prices
B. Mutual fund prices
C. Price inflation index
D. Real estate prices

Q.95 Blue revolution is related to
A. Space research
B. Fisheries
C. Drinking water
D. Sky

Q.96 Bank grant short term financial assistance in modes which includes
A. Cash credit
B. Overdraft
C. Discounting of bills
D. All of these

Q.97 The type of arrangement under which a bank pays the seller the value of the bill and later collects it from the buyer on the due date is called:

A. Bill discounting   **B.** Factoring
C. Forfeiting   **D.** None of these

Q.98 A mandate is

A. An order issued by the competent court to authorize a person to operate any account of the bank

B. An authority, in writing, given by the account holder to another person empowering him to operate his account on his behalf

C. The authority of the board towards the operation of an account

D. All of the above

Q.99 One of your customers dies without leaving a will and the court appoints a person to handle the customer's Property. Such a person is called as

A. An administrator   **B.** An executor
C. A liquidator   **D.** A successor

Q.100 Securitization against moveable assets is known as

A. Moveable securitization
B. Securitization backed by assets
C. Securitization backed by mortgage
D. Pass-through certificates

Q.101 The type of factoring under which the factor collects back from the seller the amount paid by him in case of non-payment of the bills on the due date is called

A. Recourse factoring
B. Non-recourse factoring
C. Both the above
D. None of these

Q.102 Which one of the following is NOT included in a Standard banking code of conduct?

A. Profitability   **B.** Neutrality
C. Reliability   **D.** Integrity

Q.103 Your customer issues a cheque for Rs.10000 in the discharge of his liability towards Mr. Shyam Prasad or order, who endorses the same in favor of Mr. Sita Ram in the blank. This cheque

A. Cannot be endorsed further as the blank endorsement restricts further negotiation

B. Can be negotiated by Mr. Sita Ram without endorsement by him and by mere delivery

C. Can be negotiated further by Mr. Sita ' Ram by a full endorsement by him followed by delivery

D. Can be endorsed by him in blank only

Q.104 Factoring is

A. A means of financing traders a manufacturers by taking over their receivables

B. A means of providing post-shipment finance to exporters
C. A type of agriculture financing
D. None of the above

Q.105 A Cheque written in different language half in English, a part in Hindi and rest in vernacular language. Can the bank pay the same?

A. Yes
B. No
C. Depends on manager discretionary
D. Cheque is wrong

Q.106 In international factoring, the number of factors will be:

A. 1   **B.** 2   **C.** 3   **D.** 4

Q.107 The term "syndicate loan" is in vogue in these days. What is the meaning of the term Syndicate Loan?

A. It is the loan provided by group of companies
B. It is the loan provided by group of banks
C. It is unsecured loan
D. It is a loan provided to group of individuals

Q.108 EXIM is a finance institution established in 1982. Which of the following governs this institution?

A. RBI   **B.** NHB
C. GOI   **D.** Both (A) and (C)

Q.109 Bridge loan refers to

A. loans granted to construction companies for the construction of bridges.

B. loans granted to PWD for construction of bridge over rivers.

C. interim finance allowed by banks to their customer's pending disbursement of term loans by financial institutions.

D. All of these

Q.110 Capital adequacy is worked out based on

A. Total demand and time liabilities
B. Net demand and time assets
C. Risk-weighted assets
D. Risk-weighted liabilities

Q.111 In which of the following circumstances, the bank can exercise its right of set-off to adjust the loan account from deposit in the name of the customer, after giving notice only

A. Death of the customer
B. When the customer has become insolvent
C. When garnishee order has been received by the bank
D. When the loan has become NPA and there is an urgency to recover the amount

Q.112 Forfeiting provides finance against the export receivables to an exporter

A. With recourse to the exporter
B. Without recourse to the exporter
C. Both the above
D. None of these

Q.113 In the banking terminology the word "Sub-prime lending" is used. What do you understand by the term?

A. It means all those sources of finance of bank which are not properly shown in its balance sheet

B. It means all those sources of finance of bank which are properly shown in its balance sheet

C. It means finance granted for unproductive purposes

D. It means lending to more riskier customers

Q.114 A cheque of Rs.65000 issued by Ram Chander, one of your account holders, in favor of Shivaji is stolen by one Radhey Shyam who forges Shivaji's signatures and endorses it in favor of Ganeshi Lal, who obtains the payment from the bank. In this situation what would be a bank

A. The bank will be liable for the forgery

B. The bank will be liable only if the drawer proves that the instrument is forged

C. The bank will not be liable if Ganeshi Lal agrees to refund the amount

D. Bank will get protection available to it under Section 85(1) NI Act and will not be liable for the payment made

Q.115 Business Ethics is helpful in

A. Dealing with a dilemma

B. Guards reputation

C. Helps in avoiding future risk

D. All the above

Q.116 Forfaiting provides to the exporter against receivables

A. 100 percent financing

B. 50 percent financing

C. 150 percent financing

D. 200 percent financing

Q.117 The advantage of leasing is

A. It is cent percent of finance. It is better than a term loan where the borrower has to contribute a margin

B. The leased assets, as well as leased obligations, do not reflect in the balance sheet of the lessee, and a such it does not disturb the Debt equity ratio

C. Leasing allows the lessee, the use of the asset acquired at today's cost by making payment in future out of future earnings

D. All of the above

Q.118 The approved assets against which currency notes are issued by RBI comprise of

A. Gold coin and bullion

B. Foreign securities and rupee securities of Government of India, of any maturity

C. Bills of exchange and promissory notes payable in India are eligible for purchase by RBI

D. All of the above

Q.119 In a demand draft the word "order" is changed to "bearer" by the holder of the dd. It is called as

A. Endorsement

B. Material alteration

C. Crossing

D. None of the above

Q.120 A non-resident person under the Non-Resident Rules in India means

A. A person is away from India for more than 182 days or more for taking up employment/vocation

B. For any other purposes, it would indicate his stay outside India for uncertain period

C. A body incorporated/registered outside India or controlled by a person resident outside India

D. Both (A) and (B)

// Smart Answer Sheet //

Correct — Indicates percentage of students who answered questions correctly.

Skipped — Indicates percentage of students who skipped questions.

Q.	Ans.	Correct / Skipped
1	D	28.96 % / 14.17 %
2	D	66.81 % / 24.1 %
3	C	49.89 % / 21.15 %
4	B	49.89 % / 25.37 %
5	B	35.52 % / 25.58 %
6	D	36.58 % / 24.73 %
7	B	48.41 % / 25.8 %
8	A	29.39 % / 25.37 %
9	D	43.55 % / 25.58 %
10	D	63.64 % / 24.31 %
11	C	32.35 % / 23.46 %
12	B	30.87 % / 25.58 %
13	D	73.36 % / 19.45 %
14	B	45.24 % / 26.22 %
15	D	47.36 % / 22.62 %
16	D	61.1 % / 22.62 %

Q.	Ans.	Correct / Skipped
17	A	43.55 % / 26.01 %
18	C	60.68 % / 25.58 %
19	A	32.35 % / 10.36 %
20	A	37.0 % / 18.18 %
21	B	14.16 % / 19.24 %
22	D	44.4 % / 25.37 %
23	D	55.6 % / 15.65 %
24	D	64.69 % / 24.95 %
25	A	43.55 % / 26.01 %
26	D	54.33 % / 26.01 %
27	B	35.31 % / 18.6 %
28	D	49.47 % / 26.01 %
29	B	53.91 % / 19.45 %
30	D	62.58 % / 23.89 %
31	C	38.27 % / 23.46 %
32	C	37.42 % / 22.2 %

Q.	Ans.	Correct / Skipped
33	C	53.28 % / 17.12 %
34	D	39.32 % / 24.95 %
35	A	63.42 % / 22.42 %
36	A	63.64 % / 22.62 %
37	D	14.8 % / 26.0 %
38	A	21.35 % / 25.58 %
39	B	10.15 % / 26.21 %
40	C	33.19 % / 26.43 %
41	D	64.69 % / 20.51 %
42	A	63.21 % / 25.8 %
43	A	40.8 % / 21.78 %
44	C	59.83 % / 26.22 %
45	A	35.73 % / 20.72 %
46	A	65.96 % / 25.37 %
47	A	61.52 % / 23.47 %
48	D	52.22 % / 25.37 %

Q.	Ans.	Correct / Skipped
49	A	48.41 % / 26.22 %
50	A	50.74 % / 24.74 %
51	C	53.28 % / 21.77 %
52	D	22.41 % / 21.14 %
53	A	8.25 % / 26.21 %
54	A	31.29 % / 24.95 %
55	C	31.29 % / 23.68 %
56	C	40.17 % / 25.58 %
57	A	54.12 % / 26.43 %
58	D	35.1 % / 25.15 %
59	B	34.88 % / 23.68 %
60	C	17.34 % / 20.93 %
61	B	22.41 % / 25.79 %
62	A	53.07 % / 24.73 %
63	B	37.21 % / 24.1 %
64	D	45.45 % / 26.85 %

Q.	Ans.	Correct / Skipped
65	D	35.73 % / 24.52 %
66	D	64.27 % / 24.31 %
67	D	33.62 % / 26.21 %
68	C	11.42 % / 26.0 %
69	C	56.24 % / 26.0 %
70	A	38.48 % / 26.0 %
71	A	45.03 % / 16.92 %
72	C	30.02 % / 20.93 %
73	A	43.97 % / 26.43 %
74	D	42.49 % / 24.53 %
75	A	25.58 % / 26.64 %
76	A	53.28 % / 24.52 %
77	D	48.63 % / 26.21 %
78	C	54.12 % / 25.37 %
79	B	29.6 % / 17.33 %
80	B	47.99 % / 20.93 %

Q.	Ans.	Correct		Q.	Ans.	Correct		Q.	Ans.	Correct		Q.	Ans.	Correct		Q.	Ans.	Correct
		Skipped				Skipped				Skipped				Skipped				Skipped
81	C	44.4 %		89	D	20.51 %		97	A	34.88 %		105	A	45.24 %		113	D	29.39 %
		19.45 %				26.64 %				26.22 %				26.01 %				18.6 %
82	D	59.83 %		90	D	66.38 %		98	B	29.6 %		106	B	42.07 %		114	D	50.32 %
		24.53 %				25.37 %				24.95 %				26.01 %				26.0 %
83	C	33.62 %		91	D	48.84 %		99	A	26.22 %		107	B	36.58 %		115	D	63.42 %
		26.21 %				25.79 %				23.67 %				21.98 %				24.32 %
84	A	57.72 %		92	D	23.68 %		100	B	31.5 %		108	C	14.38 %		116	A	49.68 %
		24.31 %				26.21 %				22.83 %				25.58 %				26.01 %
85	B	29.81 %		93	A	31.71 %		101	A	44.19 %		109	C	58.99 %		117	B	15.64 %
		26.64 %				20.09 %				26.0 %				20.5 %				18.19 %
86	C	66.17 %		94	D	36.58 %		102	A	36.79 %		110	C	31.71 %		118	D	56.24 %
		24.53 %				26.0 %				26.0 %				24.74 %				24.52 %
87	C	38.27 %		95	B	58.99 %		103	B	21.99 %		111	D	52.01 %		119	B	49.26 %
		27.48 %				23.89 %				25.79 %				17.76 %				18.39 %
88	B	47.36 %		96	D	58.35 %		104	A	48.84 %		112	C	29.6 %		120	D	56.45 %
		26.64 %				24.1 %				24.52 %				25.37 %				21.14 %

Performance Analysis	
Avg. Score (%)	41.0%
Toppers Score (%)	97.0%
Your Score	

//Hints and Solutions//

1. Pensioners drawing pension through Public Sector Banks may avail nomination facilities available in the Bank. If the pensioner has already an account, savings or current, in his/her individual name with that branch of the bank, the pensioner is not required to open a separate account for this purpose.

Hence, the correct option is (D).

2. Income tax exemptions are applicable on the principal amount invested in a PPF as account. The entire value of an investment can be claimed for tax waiver under section 80C of the Income Tax Act of 1961. However, it should be kept in mind that the total principal that can be invested in one financial year cannot exceed Rs.1.5 Lakh.

The total interest accrued on PPF investment is also exempt from any tax calculations.

Therefore, the entire amount redeemed from a PPF account upon completion of maturity is not subject to taxation. This policy makes the public provident fund scheme attractive to many investors in India.

Mandatory lock-in of 15 years is imposed on the principal amount invested in such plans. In case of emergencies related to specific end-uses, partial withdrawal can be made. However, this amount can only be extracted after the completion of 5 years of activation of the account. Up to 50% of the total balance can be withdrawn in one transaction each financial year succeeding in the 4th year.

Hence, the correct option is (D).

3. The (SEBI) Securities and Exchange Board of India is responsible for the registration, regulation and inspection of the depository. A depository participant is also answerable to the SEBI. It can be operational only after registration with SEBI post recommendation by NSDL or CDSL.

Hence, the correct option is (C).

4. Every bank must have a particular portion of their Net Demand and Time Liabilities (NDTL) in the form of cash, gold, or other liquid assets by the end of the day. The ratio of these liquid assets to the demand and time liabilities is called the Statutory Liquidity Ratio (SLR). The Reserve Bank of India (RBI) has the authority to increase this ratio by up to 40%. An increase in the ratio constricts the ability of the bank to inject money into the economy.

Hence, the correct option is (B).

5. Liquidity means how quickly you can get your hands on your cash. In simpler terms, liquidity is to get your money whenever you need it.

Description: Liquidity might be your emergency savings account or the cash lying with you that you can access in case of any unforeseen happening or any financial setback.

Hence, the correct option is (B).

6. Ethics programs align employee behaviours with those top priority ethical values preferred by leaders of the organization.

Employees feel a strong alignment between their values and those of the organization. They react with strong motivation and performance.

Ethics programs help avoid criminal acts "of omission" and can lower fines. Ethics programs tend to detect ethical issues and violations early on so they can be reported or addressed.

The recent Federal Sentencing Guidelines specify major penalties for various types of major ethics violations. However, the guidelines potentially lowers fines if an organization has clearly made an effort to operate ethically.

Hence, the correct option is (D).

7. This process of transition from a "mutually-owned" association to a company "owned by shareholders", in other words transforming the legal structure from a mutual form to a business corporation form and privatizing the corporations so constituted, is referred to as demutualization.

Hence, the correct option is (B).

8. Sebi law defines a retail individual investor as an investor who applies or bids for securities of or for a value of not more than Rs 2,00,000 in an IPO and buys or holds shares worth less than Rs 2,00,000 in a stock.

Hence, the correct option is (A).

9. Insider trading is defined as a malpractice wherein trade of a company's securities is undertaken by people who by virtue of their work have access to the otherwise non-public information which can be crucial for making investment decisions.

Insider trading involves trading in a public company's stock by someone who has non-public, material information about that stock for any reason. Insider trading can be either illegal or legal depending on when the insider makes the trade.

Hence, the correct option is (D).

10. A stopped payment is usually requested if the cheque has been declared missing or lost. But many times the drawer, to escape his debt or liability has used it as an instrument of deception. The 1988 amendment in Section 138 of the Negotiable Instruments Act is also silent about Stopped Payment.

A garnishee order is a common form of enforcing a judgment debt against a creditor to recover money. Put simply, the court directs a third party that owes money to the judgment debtor to instead pay the judgment creditor.

Hence, the correct option is (D).

11. The Annual Financial Inspection (AFI) focuses on statutorily mandated areas of solvency, liquidity, and operational health of the bank. It is based on the internationally adopted CAMEL model modified as CAMELS, i.e., capital adequacy, asset quality, management, earnings, liquidity, and system and control. While the compliance to the inspection findings is followed up in the usual course, the top management of the Reserve Bank addresses supervisory letters to the top management of the banks highlighting the major areas of supervisory concern that need immediate rectification, holds supervisory discussions, and draws up an action plan that can be monitored. All these are followed

up vigorously. Indian commercial banks are rated as per the supervisory rating model approved by the BFS which is based on the 'CAMELS' concept.

Hence, the correct option is (C).

12. The spread between the floor and the cap of the price band shall not be more than 20%. The price band can be revised. If revised, the bidding period shall be extended for a further period of three days, subject to the total bidding period not exceeding ten days.

Hence, the correct option is (B).

13. Employment discrimination happens when an employee or job candidate is treated unfavorably because of age, disability, genetic information, national origin, pregnancy, race or skin color, religion, or sex.

Hence, the correct option is (D).

14. With the death of a partner, a partnership gets dissolved and the estate of the expired partner or the legal heirs do not remain liable for any debts after the death. So the action of the bank, in this case, to allow withdrawal of Rs. 30030/- was not warranted, for which the legal heirs are not liable. But other partners will continue to be liable.

Hence, the correct option is (B).

15. NEFT operates in half-hourly batches from 8 am to 7 pm.

On weekdays there are 23 batches and on working Saturdays there are 23 batches.

There is no restriction on the minimum and maximum amount that can be remitted through NEFT.

NEFT is a nation-wide payment system facilitating one-to-one funds transfer. Currently, fund transfer transactions are settled in batches under NEFT, which operates in 23 half-hourly batches from 8 am to 7 pm on working days.

There is no limit imposed by the RBI for funds transfer through NEFT system. However, banks may place amount limits based on their own risk perception with the approval of its Board.

Hence, the correct option is (D).

16. In fact, CORE is an acronym for "Centralized Online Real-time Exchange", thus the bank's branches can access applications from centralized data centers.

Hence, the correct option is (D).

17. Resident individual allottees limited up to a maximum of 1000 shares per allottee and the offer is kept open for a period of 6 months from the last date of dispatch of securities. The details regarding Safety Net are covered under Clause 8.18 of the DIP Guidelines.

Hence, the correct option is (A).

18. Retail loans include a vast range of different loans. Personal loans such as car loans, mortgages, signature loans, and credit cards all fall into the category of retail loans, but business loans can also fall into the category of retail loans.

A retail credit facility is a method of financing essentially, a type of loan or line of credit—used by retailers and real estate companies. Retail credit facilities can be business-to-business, as in a company obtaining financing from a bank.

Hence, the correct option is (C).

19. You (NRI) can open an FCNR account with two or more NRI joint account holders. You have the option to select multiple currencies - Pound Sterling, US Dollar, Yen, and Euro. With an FCNR account, you can easily repatriate the principal as well as the interest earned to the country of residence/origin.

Hence, the correct option is (A).

20. You get paid a sum insured of ₹2 lakh in case of death, in case of loss of total and irrecoverable loss of both eyes or both hands or feet or loss of sight of one eye and loss of use of hand or foot and ₹1 lakh for a total loss of sight of one eye or loss of use of one hand or foot.

Hence, the correct option is (A).

21. The main objectives of sustainable design are to reduce, or completely avoid, depletion of critical resources like energy, water, land, and raw materials; prevent environmental degradation caused by facilities and infrastructure throughout their life cycle; and create built environments that are livable, comfortable, safe, and productive.

While going green looks at only the environmental aspect of it, being sustainable is equivalent to taking into account the social, economical and environmental impact of that particular product or organisation.

Hence, the correct option is (B).

22. Loan syndication is the process of involving a group of lenders in funding various portions of a loan for a single borrower. Loan syndication most often occurs when a borrower requires an amount too large for a single lender to provide or when the loan is outside the scope of a lender's risk exposure levels.

Hence, the correct option is (D).

23. In India, mutual funds function as a trust created under the Indian Trust Act, 1882. There are three layers of mutual funds in India. (i) Sponsors (ii) Trustee and (iii) Asset Management Company. Sponsors work as Promoters of the company. They take responsibility for starting a mutual fund business. Sponsors contribute initial capital (40% of the net worth of AMC) and appoint Trustees and Board of Trustees. Board of Trustees act as guardians of investors and ensure that money invested by investors is used according to the objective of the scheme. Asset Management Company is the public face of the fund management business. Sponsors and Trustees together form AMC and appoint Fund Manager. A fund manager with the help of the fund management team makes all investment decisions.

Hence, the correct option is (D).

24. Assessing the creditworthiness of a borrower by a lender before granting the credit is termed credit appraisal. The process includes the collection of related information of customers and

projects or business to undertake, assessing the risk involved before providing any loans.

This indicates that banks take a keen interest in loan repayment to ensure that they undergo minimal losses. The study has given the following recommendations; the policymakers in the banking institutions should use credit score cards as a tool for monitoring loans and recovering such loans.

Marketing of bank products refers to the various ways in which a bank can help a customer, such as operating accounts, making transfers, paying standing orders, and selling foreign currency. Banking is the business activity of banks and similar institutions.

Hence, the correct option is (D).

25. Devaluation of currency means reduction in the value of the currency vis-a-vis major internationally traded currencies.

In modern monetary policy, a devaluation is an official lowering of the value of a country's currency within a fixed-exchange-rate system, in which a monetary authority formally sets a lower exchange rate of the national currency in relation to a foreign reference currency or currency basket.

Hence, the correct option is (A).

26. A capital market is a financial market in which long-term debt or equity-backed securities are bought and sold. Capital markets channel the wealth of savers to those who can put it to long-term productive use, such as companies or governments making long-term investments.

Hence, the correct option is (D).

27. First, depreciation (devaluation) of the currency increases the volume of exports and reduces the volume of imports, both of which have a favourable effect on the balance of trade, that is, they will lower the trade deficit or increase the trade surplus.

How to Decrease Imports/Increase Exports

1. Taxes and quotas. Governments decrease excessive import activity by imposing tariffs.
2. Subsidies. Governments provide subsidies to domestic businesses in order to reduce their business costs.
3. Trade agreements.
4. Currency devaluation.

Hence, the correct option is (B).

28. IRDA has a duty to regulate, promise, and ensure orderly growth of the insurance and reinsurance business of India.

Insurance Regulatory and Development Authority (IRDA) Act, 1999 spells out the Mission of IRDAI as: " to protect the interests of the policyholders, to regulate, promote and ensure orderly growth of the insurance industry and for matters connected therewith or incidental thereto.

Functions and Duties of IRDAI

Section 14 of the IRDA Act, 1999 lays down the duties, powers, and functions of IRDA.

- Registering and regulating insurance companies

- Protecting policyholders' interests
- Licensing and establishing norms for insurance intermediaries
- Promoting professional organizations in insurance
- Regulating and overseeing premium rates and terms of non-life insurance covers
- Specifying financial reporting norms of insurance companies
- Regulating investment of policyholders' funds by insurance companies
- Ensuring the maintenance of solvency margin by insurance companies
- Ensuring insurance coverage in rural areas and of vulnerable sections of society

Hence, the correct option is (D).

29. A Non-Resident Non-Repatriable account could be opened and maintained by any person resident outside India (other than individuals or entities of Pakistan/Bangladesh) including an NRI who is a citizen of India or a foreign citizen of Indian origin residing outside India.

Scheme of NRNR accounts is discontinued from 1-4-2002, the accounts were non-convertible/non-repatriable and were maintained in Indian rupees in the form of savings, current and recurring or fixed deposit accounts.

Hence, the correct option is (B).

30. Types of computer security threats-

- Computer Viruses. Perhaps the most well-known computer security threat, a computer virus is a program written to alter the way a computer operates, without the permission or knowledge of the user.
- Spyware Threats.
- Hackers and Predators.
- Phishing.

Herein, the term "threat" is defined as any kind of software potentially or directly capable of inflicting damage to a computer or network and compromising the user's information or rights (that is, malicious and other unwanted software).

Hence, the correct option is (D).

31. The terms 'invoice discounting' or 'bills discounting' or 'purchase of bills' are all same. Invoice discounting is a source of working capital finance for the seller of goods on credit. Bill discounting is an arrangement whereby the seller recovers an amount of sales bill from the financial intermediaries before it is due. Such intermediaries charge a fee for the service. From the other side, it is a business vertical for all types of financial intermediaries such as banks, financial institutions, NBFCs, etc.

Hence, the correct option is (C).

32. The right of lien can be exercised on goods or other securities standing in the name of the borrower and not jointly with others. For example, in case the securities are held in the joint names of two or more persons the banker cannot exercise his right of general lien in respect of a debt due from a single person.

A security deposit serves as a means to fix or replace something in a rental unit that was damaged, lost, or stolen by the renter. Security deposits typically must be paid prior to moving in and state laws dictate how security deposits are applied once needed.

Hence, the correct option is (C).

33. A physical network node is an electronic device that is attached to a network and is capable of creating, receiving, or transmitting information over a communication channel. A passive distribution point such as a distribution frame or patch panel is consequently not a node.

A terminal server is a server or network device that enables connections to multiple client systems to connect to a LAN network without using a modem or a network interface. Microsoft introduced this concept by releasing terminal services as a part of the Windows Server operating system.

Hence, the correct option is (C).

34. The mandatory information to be sought for KYC purposes only once while opening an account.

Commercial Bank policy for acceptance of customers takes into consideration all factors related to the customer, his activity, his related accounts, and any other relevant indicators.

Hence, the correct option is (D).

35. The ECGC Limited is a company wholly owned by the Government of India based in Mumbai, Maharashtra. It provides export credit insurance support to Indian exporters and is controlled by the Ministry of Commerce. The government of India had initially set up Export Risks Insurance Corporation in July 1957.

Hence, the correct option is (A).

36. Guarantee to an exporter that the importer of his goods will pay immediately for the goods ordered by him, is known as Letter of Credit (L/C). A Letter of Credit, also known as LC or Documentary Credit, is a commonly used instrument for effecting payment between a buyer and a seller.

Hence, the correct option is (A).

37. RBI to replace regulations for housing finance companies with the new regulator. The Reserve Bank of India (RBI) has proposed modifications in the existing regulations pertaining to the housing finance companies, as the apex bank is now the regulator of these financial entities.

Hence, the correct option is (D).

38. The term 'loan factor' refers to a charge levied by the mutual fund from the unitholders at the time of entry or exit from the mutual fund.

Loan Factor means, with respect to each Loan, the amount set forth as a percentage in the Loan Terms Schedule with respect to such Loan, which fully amortizes the Loan over the Repayment Period applicable to such Loan in equal periodic installments at the Basic Rate.

Hence, the correct option is (A).

39. There were incoming funds to the cheque issuer's account but they did not clear in time to fund this cheque. Exceeds Arrangement: The cheque amount may have exceeded the transfer limit on the issuer's account.

Overdraft is a financial instrument to provide an extension of credit when the savings or the current account balance reaches zero. Most of the banks offer an overdraft limit depending on the customer's existing relationship with the bank. Bank also charges the interest and fees on exceeding the overdraft limit of the accounts.

Hence, the correct option is (B).

40. In case of excess payment of pension the excess payment is to be recovered from the future pension every month is 33.33 %of the pension amount. For recovering the overpayment made to pensioner from his future pension payment
in installments 1/3rd of net (pension + relief) payable each month may be recovered unless the pensioner concerned gives consent in writing to pay a higher installment amount.

Hence, the correct option is (C).

41. Unauthorized changes to records, manipulations to programs or data bypass of password, amendments as to payment instructions, etc

Unauthorized changes to programs during routine maintenance control checks on specified or selected transactions and transport of data to another computer and returned with manipulations.

Computer Systems are at the center of the information systems security policy. The computation power, provided by these systems, allows the organizations more flexibility and processing capability than ever before. The complex array of computer capabilities offers both operational advantages and at the same time, raises security concerns also. The following controls, among others, will require to be implemented to protect the integrity of the computer systems which include, among others, mainframes, minicomputers, microcomputers, laptops, notebooks, palmtops, servers, workstations, and personal computers in use in the organization.

Hence, the correct option is (D).

42. The banker who is liable to pay the value of a cheque of a customer as per the contract, when the amount is due from him to the customer is called "Paying Banker" or "Drawee Bank." The payment to be made by him has arisen due to the contractual obligation. He is also called drawee bank as the cheque is drawn on him.

"IRDA" or "IRDAI" means the Insurance Regulatory and Development Authority which was renamed as Insurance Regulatory and Development Authority of India in the year 2014; m) "Lapsed Policy" means a policy which has been terminated for non-payment of premiums where a premium is not paid within the grace period.

As your mother would only be a member of the HUF and she would not qualify as a coparcener, she can't become the karta. By definition, the karta of a HUF would compulsorily need to be a coparcener. A coparcener has various rights at birth itself in the HUF property that may not all be available to a member.

Cash Credit (CC) Hypo is one of the most favorite modes of financing. CC HYPO is sometimes allowed against hypothecation of goods. In a manufacturing company, whose Stock of Raw Materials and manufacturing of goods constantly fluctuate, it is difficult for the bank to control such changes.

Hence, the correct option is (A).

43. The term subprime ending became known widely after the (2008/09) Global economic crisis. The term basically describes those loans given by banks to individuals who might not be able to pay back the entire loan or would not pay the loan back as per the repayment schedule. This kind of lending is strictly prohibited as it is a large sum it can fracture the entire economic system.

Hence, the correct option is (A).

44. Most people still prefer the regular monthly income method as it helps them manage their finances better. Aside from pension plans which offer monthly income after a certain age, there is another option for regular monthly income.

Capital growth is the appreciation in the value of an asset over a period of time. It is calculated by comparing the current value, sometimes known as the market value of an asset or investment, to the amount paid when you originally bought it.

Hence, the correct option is (C).

45. Sunil Mehta panel incorporates 'Sashakt India AMC' for large NPAs. The Sunil Mehta committee comprises representatives of all major banks, including the State Bank of India (SBI).

The committee led by Punjab National Bank Chairman Sunil Mehta has submitted its draft report titled 'Sashakt' to the Finance Ministry with a strategy to tackle stress in the banking sector. However, there is no proposal or recommendation to create a bad bank.

Hence, the correct option is (A).

46. The Securitisation and Reconstruction of Financial Assets and Enforcement of Securities Interest Act, 2002 (also known as the SARFAESI Act) is an Indian law. It allows banks and other financial institutions to auction residential or commercial properties (of Defaulter) to recover loans.

Hence, the correct option is (A).

47. The Securities and Exchange Board of India (SEBI) is the regulator of the securities and commodity market in India owned by the Government of India. It was established in 1992 and given Statutory Powers on 12 April 1992 through the SEBI Act, 1992.

Hence, the correct option is (A).

48. A bank rate is the interest rate at which a nation's central bank lends money to domestic banks, often in the form of very short-term loans. Managing the bank rate is a method by which central banks affect economic activity.

Repo rate refers to the rate at which commercial banks borrow money by selling their securities to the Central bank of our country i.e Reserve Bank of India (RBI) to maintain liquidity, in case of shortage of funds or due to some statutory measures. It is one of the main tools of RBI to keep inflation under control.

Hence, the correct option is (D).

49. Post disbursement supervision by lenders, particularly in respect of loans up to Rs.2 lakhs, should be constructive with a view to taking care of any" lender-related" genuine difficulty that the borrower may face.

In the case of small borrowers seeking loans up to Rs. 2 lakhs the lenders should convey in writing, the main reason/reasons which, in the opinion of the bank after due consideration, have led to the rejection of the loan applications within the stipulated time.

Hence, the correct option is (A).

50. For homeowners, the securitization of mortgages means that their mortgage loan does not belong to a single lender. The loan is part of a pool owned by investors. A mortgage service company is responsible for collecting mortgage payments and sending them along to the pool.

An immovable asset or immovable property is a piece of property tied to the land, meaning we can not physically move it somewhere else. It can be as estate, building, premises, etc. From the company's point of view, immovable assets are part of tangible assets.

Hence, the correct option is (A).

51. The Association of Mutual Funds in India (AMFI) is an industry standards organization in India in the mutual fund sector. It was formed in 1995. Most mutual funds firms in India are its members. The organization aims to develop the mutual funds market in India, by improving ethical and professional standards.

Hence, the correct option is (C).

52. A bank can end its relationship with a customer at any time, just as a customer can move to another bank at any time. A customer may move because a competitor offers a better deal or because the relationship with the bank is unsatisfactory or has broken down. A bank may decide to close a customer's account because of how that person has been operating it, or because of regulatory requirements, or because the bank also feels the relationship has broken down. Banks are under no obligation to continue doing business with a person or company, but they should not close an account without good reason.

Obligations of Bankers towards Customers

- Obligation to Pay Cheques. It is a statutory obligation of the bank, having sufficient funds for the customer to pay cheques duly drawn and presented.
- 2 Secrecy.
- Banker's Lien.
- Mandate.
- Power of Attorney.
- Circumstances Leading to Closure of Accounts.
- Loans and Advances.

Hence, the correct option is (D).

53. Dated securities are long-term instruments issued by the government for borrowing. Short-term instruments are treasury bills that have a maturity of less than one year (91 days, 182 days (now not issued), and 364 days). For treasury bills, there are no interest payments but the bill is obtained at a discount.

Hence, the correct option is (A).

54. A particular nation's rating score is independent of the performance of other nations. But in the comparative rating index of sovereigns (CRIS) introduced by India, the performance of one nation is compared with all other nations. Perhaps it was the first sovereign rating index by any country in the world.

Hence, the correct option is (A).

55. Purchase of securities in the market called an anti-inflationary measure.

One of the most common and easiest ways of buying and selling stocks, mutual funds, and bonds is through a brokerage house. Although most banks don't sell stocks, they do offer mutual funds and bonds. There are many ways to buy and sell securities; each comes with its own advantages, challenges, and risks.

Hence, the correct option is (C).

56. In equitable mortgage deed, need not be a registered document and the time limit is not three years but extended up to 12 years and therefore, the revision petitioner has to subsist right over the property, being a mortgagee and the decree obtained by the second respondent is subject to the claim of the revision petitioner herein, hence, the Execution Application was filed before the Court below.

Hence, the correct option is (C).

57. Pension Payment Order (P.P.O)-

Such a number is called Pension Payment Order (PPO) and is allotted by the EPFO to every employee who retires from any organization. After retirement, The Employees' Provident Fund Organisation (EPFO) sends a letter to every retiring employee carrying details of PPO, provident fund, and disbursement of pension.

Hence, the correct option is (A).

58. A Committee was set up in 1983 under the chairmanship of Dr. C. Rangarajan. The banking industry has since come a long way in computerizing their front and back-office operations as per the guidelines of the Rangarajan Committee.

Considering the contribution of the SSI sector to the overall industrial production, exports, and employment and also recognizing the need to give a fillip to this sector, a special package of measures was devised by RBI(during April 1993) to ensure adequate and timely credit to this sector. While doing so the recommendations of the PR Nayak committee were taken into account.

The Committee on Capital Account Convertibility (CAC) or Tarapore Committee was constituted by the Reserve Bank of India for suggesting a roadmap on full convertibility of Rupee on Capital Account. The committee submitted its report in May 1997.

Internationally income from Non-Performing Assets (NPAs) is not recognized on accrual basis but is booked as income only when it is actually received. In line with the international practices and in terms of recommendations made by Mr.Narasimham committee on financial system, RBI has introduced prudential norms for income recognition and asset classifications for Indian banks and financial institutions, to ensure proper provisioning and transparency in the published accounts.

Hence, the correct option is (D).

59. Code of conduct is a written document, inspirational in contents and specify clearly what is acceptable or unacceptable behavior at the workplace and beyond when the employees represent their organizations outside.

A code of ethics, or professional code of ethics, is usually a set of general guidelines or values. A code of conduct policy is typically more specific, giving guidelines for how to respond in certain situations. A code of conduct example would be a rule expressly prohibiting accepting or offering bribes.

Hence, the correct option is (B).

60. Computer auditing is a systematic and logical process that follows a risk-based approach to determine whether the information systems of an entity, including its detailed information technology processes, controls, and activities, will achieve its IT objectives and will thereby ultimately enable the organization to achieve their organizational goals.

Hence, the correct option is (C).

61. The mandate holder can carry out day-to-day operations of the account on behalf of the NRI. These include drawing cheques to make local payments, make and renew fixed deposits, and invest in avenues open for NRIs.

A mandate holder operates the bank account on behalf of the NRI. He/She does not have any rights over the account. A nominee, on the other hand, is the person who will be eligible to claim the balance in the bank account when the account holder expires. The nominee is appointed by the account holder.

Hence, the correct option is (B).

62. In 1818, the first insurance company in India was established in Calcutta (modern-day Kolkata), The Oriental Life Insurance Company.

Hence, the correct option is (A).

63. "The role of management in establishing an ethical culture." The culture of an organization evolves from the values and ethical standards that should guide all actions and decisions. Today's blog addresses "How to Deal with Ethical Dilemmas in the Workplace." Ethical conflicts that remain unresolved can lead to frustration for employees, managers, and external stakeholders.

Hence, the correct option is (B).

64. Section 85(1), 85(2), 128 of negotiable instrument acts provide statutory protection to paying bankers for making payments of order cheque, bearer cheque, or crossed cheque in that order.

Where a cheque payable to order purports to be endorsed by or on behalf of the payee, the drawee is discharged by payment in due course"

Hence, the correct option is (D).

65. The Liquidity Adjustment Facility (LAF) is an indirect instrument for monetary control. It controls the flow of money through repo rates and reverses repo rates. The repo rate is actually the rate at which commercial banks and other institutes obtain short-term loans from the Central Bank.

Hence, the correct option is (D).

66. A promissory note is a financial instrument that contains a written promise by one party (the note's issuer or maker) to pay another party (the note's payee) a definite sum of money, either on-demand or at a specified future date.

Some key features of promissory notes are as follows, It must be in writing It must contain an unconditional promise to pay. The sum payable must be certain. The promissory notes must be signed by the maker. It must be payable to a certain person, cannot be made payable to the bearer. It should be properly stamped.

Hence, the correct option is (D).

67. The objective of KYC guidelines is to prevent banks from being used, by criminal elements for money laundering activities. It also enables banks to understand their customers and their financial dealings to serve them better and manage their risks prudently.

Aadhaar based e-KYC (electronic Know Your Customer) is an online service provided by UIDAI for verification of identity and address of Aadhaar holders. Income Tax Department leverages this Aadhaar based e-KYC for instant e-PAN allotment.

Hence, the correct option is (D).

68. Insolvency and bankruptcy code (Amendment) act, 2019 seeks to address critical gaps and inconsistencies in insolvency resolution timelines, payments received by operational creditors under a resolution plan, and manner of voting by an authorized representative on behalf of the class of financial creditors.

Hence, the correct option is (C).

69. Automated teller machines(ATMs) are electronic banking outlets that allow people to complete transactions without going into a branch of their bank. Some are simple cash dispensers while others allow a variety of transactions such as check deposits, balance transfers, and bill payments.

A mutual fund is simply a financial intermediary that allows a group of investors to pool their money together with a predetermined investment objective. The mutual fund will have a fund manager who is responsible for investing the pooled money into specific securities.

A certificate of deposit (CD) is a product offered by banks and credit unions that provides an interest rate premium in exchange for the customer agreeing to leave a lump-sum deposit untouched for a predetermined period of time.

Debt assignment is a transfer of debt, and all the associated rights and obligations, from a creditor to a third party (often a debt collector).

Hence, the correct option is (C).

70. The distinction between marketing and selling is marketing relates to producing or creating goods or services needed by the customers while selling the objectives is to sell whatever is available.

Difference Between Selling and Marketing. Selling is an action that converts the product into cash, but marketing is the process of meeting and satisfying the customer's needs. Marketing consists of all those activities that are associated with product planning, pricing, promoting, and distributing the product or service Selling focuses on the seller's needs whereas marketing concentrates on the needs of the buyer.

Hence, the correct option is (A).

71. Kite flying is when you use one or more credit cards to withdraw cash at an ATM as a cash advance and pay dues on another credit card. But, this term has now been extended to credit cards as well.

The accommodation bill is drawn to cater to the fund requirements of both the parties. A bill, draft, or note made, drawn, accepted, or endorsed by one person for another without consideration to enable that other to raise money or obtain credit thereby.

Hence, the correct option is (A).

72. In case of discontinuation of the account(PPF), the account can be regularized on payment of a fee of Rs 50 per the defaulted months and also a minimum of Rs. 500 for each year defaulted.

The Public Provident Fund (PPF) is a long-term investment where one has to invest a minimum of Rs 500 a year (maximum allowed is Rs 1.5 lakh in a financial year) to keep the account active during its 15-year term. There are people who are not able to put money into their PPF account every year or some who may just forget to do so.

Hence, the correct option is (C).

73. As per sec 107 &108 of the Indian evidence act.

Summary In case of a PPF account holder fails to contribute the minimum amount in any financial year, the account is treated as discontinued. If one wants to revive a discontinued PPF account, it can be done any time before its maturity date, which is mentioned on the PPF passbook.

Hence, the correct option is (A).

74. The Banking Ombudsman is a senior official appointed by the Reserve Bank of India to redress customer complaints against deficiency in certain banking services covered under the grounds of complaint specified under Clause 8 of the Banking Ombudsman Scheme 2006 (As amended up to July 1, 2017).

Hence, the correct option is (D).

75. The committee "various aspects of service rendered by banks to retail and small customers including pensioners" which was formed by the RBI in June 2010 was headed by M. Damodaran.

The Reserve Bank of India has decided to constitute a Committee to look into banking services rendered to retail and small customers, including pensioners, and also to look into the system of grievance redressal mechanism prevalent in banks, its structure, and efficacy and suggest measures for expeditious resolution of complaints.

Hence, the correct option is (A).

76. Scientific analysis of data to understand the needs of customers, planning for long-term marketing, implementation of plans for staffing, budgeting and financing, control and evaluation of goals and targets.

Marketing Management has the responsibility to perform many functions in the field of marketing such as planning, organizing, directing, motivating, coordinating, and controlling. All these functions aim to achieve marketing goals.

Hence, the correct option is (A).

77. Articles like shares, securities, etc., can be kept in safe custody with the Bank on prescribed charges wherever such facility is offered. Large/small boxes must be locked by the customer(s) and particulars must be written/painted thereon. The lock should be covered by stout cloth and sealed with the customer's seal.

Hence, the correct option is (D).

78. At least, one-third of the directors on the board should be independent directors. The minimum capital requirement for insurance companies is Rs 100 crore. There are two kinds of capital involved –– minimum capital requirement and solvency capital requirement.

Hence, the correct option is (C).

79. A court order instructing a garnishee (a bank) that funds held on behalf of a debtor (the judgment debtor) should not be released until directed by the court. The order may also instruct the bank to pay a given sum to the judgment creditor (the person to whom a debt is owed by the judgment debtor) from these funds. It is an order of the court to attach money or goods belonging to the judgment debtor in the hands of a third person. It is a remedy available to any judgment creditor; this order may be made by the court to holders of funds (3rd party) that no payments are to make until the court authorizes them.

Hence, the correct option is (B).

80. A restrictive endorsement is an endorsement signed on the back of a check, note, or bill of exchange which restricts to whom the paper may be transferred. In addition to the holder's signature, it includes a restriction on how the paper may be used by the transferee. Only the payee can write a restrictive endorsement.

Hence, the correct option is (B).

81. The Insurance Act, 1938 is the principal Act governing the Insurance sector in India. It provides the powers to IRDAI to frame regulations which lay down the regulatory framework for the supervision of the entities operating in the sector.

Hence, the correct option is (C).

82. The core ethical principles of beneficence (do good), nonmaleficence (do not harm), autonomy (control by the individual), and justice (fairness) stated by Beauchamp and Childress are important to a code of ethics.

Hence, the correct option is (D).

83. A power of attorney (POA) is a legal document giving one person (the agent or attorney-in-fact) the power to act for another person (the principal). The agent can have broad legal authority or limited authority to make legal decisions about the principal's property, finances, or medical care.

Hence, the correct option is (C).

84. In a word, a reverse mortgage is a loan. A homeowner who is 62 or older and has considerable home equity can borrow against the value of their home and receive funds as a lump sum, fixed monthly payment, or line of credit. Unlike a forward mortgage the type used to buy a home-a, a reverse mortgage doesn't require the homeowner to make any loan payments.

Hence, the correct option is (A).

85. Hard currency refers to money that is issued by a nation that is seen as politically and economically stable. Hard currencies are widely accepted around the world as a form of payment for goods and services and may be preferred over the domestic currency.

Hence, the correct option is (B).

86. It regulates the money supply and credit in the country. The RBI carries out India's monetary policy and exercises supervision and control over banks and non-banking finance companies in India. RBI was set up in 1935 under the Reserve Bank of India Act,1934.

Hence, the correct option is (C).

87. The document signed by the last partner on 25.01.2015. Hence the limitation period will start from 25.01.2015 & will remain to live up to 25.01.2018.

Hence, the correct option is (C).

88. One the death of a kurta, the next senior-most member automatically becomes the new Korto of the HUF but at times, statutory authorities may require a declaration from the members forming part of the HUF declaring the eldest coparcener as the new Korto of the HUF. Further, a declaration from the members forming part of the HUF along with the death certificate of the old Korto may be mandated by banks in order to give effect to the change of name of Korto in the HUF's bank account. Further, in order to transmit securities in the account of the new kurta, a joint application coupled with a set of prescribed documents should be filed with the depository participant.

Hence, the correct option is (B).

89. A power to operate the account does not imply the power to overdraw the account or to draw accept and endorse the bills of exchange.

Authority to operate is when you give another person the authority to use and transact on your account on your behalf. An example of when you would do this is when you're away for an extended amount of time e.g. living overseas.

Hence, the correct option is (D).

90. To apply for a duplicate fixed deposit receipt, submit a statement to your bank, clearly mentioning the amount and date of receipt, and explaining the manner in which the receipt was lost. If the bank is satisfied with your statement, it will issue a duplicate copy.

An indemnity bond is a bond that is intended to provide financial reimbursement to the holder for any actual or claimed loss caused by the issuer's conduct or another person's conduct.

Hence, the correct option is (D).

91. Factoring is a financial transaction and a type of debtor finance in which a business sells its accounts receivable (i.e., invoices) to a third party (called a factor) at a discount. A business will sometimes factor in its receivable assets to meet its present and immediate cash needs.

Hence, the correct option is (D).

92. Whistle-Blowers Protection Act, 2011 (renamed as Whistle Blowers Protection Act, 2014 by the second schedule of the Repealing and Amending Act, 2015) is an Act of the Parliament of India which provides a mechanism to investigate alleged corruption and misuse of power by public servants and also protect anyone who exposes alleged wrongdoing in government bodies, projects, and offices. The wrongdoing might take the form of fraud, corruption, or mismanagement. The Act will also ensure punishment for false or frivolous complaints.

Hence, the correct option is (D).

93. Small Industries Development Bank of India (SIDBI) provides refinance facilities under Automatic Refinance Scheme (ARS).

Hence, the correct option is (A).

94. NHB RESIDEX is built to ensure ease and clarity in decision-making within the sectors of real estate and real estate finance. It aims to provide guidance to stakeholders, not only in terms of a macroeconomic index but also in the form of quarterly updated prices at a neighbourhood level. In doing so, NHB RESIDEX aspires to bring in greater transparency into India's real estate markets by providing more structure, science, and discipline to property valuation. The idea is to establish greater trust among stakeholders and encourage wider and more competitive participation in the housing market. NHB RESIDEX will also serve as an effective tool to monitor the health and behaviour of housing markets in India.

Hence, the correct option is (D).

95. The term "blue revolution" refers to the remarkable emergence of aquaculture as an important and highly productive agricultural activity. Aquaculture refers to all forms of active culturing of aquatic animals and plants, occurring in marine, brackish, or freshwaters.

The Blue Revolution, with its multi-dimensional activities, focuses mainly on increasing fisheries production and productivity from aquaculture and fisheries resources, both inland and marine.

Hence, the correct option is (B).

96. Modes of short-term financial assistance. Banks grant short-term financial assistance by way of cash credit, overdraft, and bill discounting. Cash credit is an arrangement whereby the bank allows the borrower to draw amounts up to a specified limit.

Hence, the correct option is (D).

97. The terms 'invoice discounting' or 'bills discounting' or purchase of bills' are all same. Invoice discounting is a source of working capital finance for the seller of goods on credit. Bill discounting is an arrangement whereby the seller recovers an amount of sales bill from the financial intermediaries before it is due. Such intermediaries charge a fee for the service. From the other side, it is a business vertical for all types of financial intermediaries such as banks, financial institutions, NBFCs, etc.

Hence, the correct option is (A).

98. Universal agents have a broad mandate to act on behalf of their clients. Often these agents have been power of attorney for a client, which gives them considerable authority to represent a client in legal proceedings. They may also be authorized to make financial transactions on behalf of their clients.

An agent is a person who acts in the name of and on behalf of another, having been given and assumed some degree of authority to do so.

Hence, the correct option is (B).

99. An Administrator provides office support to either an individual or team and is vital for the smooth running of a business. Their duties may include fielding telephone calls, receiving and directing visitors, word processing, creating spreadsheets and presentations, and filing.

Hence, the correct option is (A).

100. Asset-backed securities (ABS) are financial securities backed by assets such as credit card receivables, home equity loans, and auto loans. Pooling securities into an ABS is a process called securitization. ABS appeals to investors looking to invest in something other than corporate debt.

Hence, the correct option is (B).

101. The type of factoring under which the factor collects back from the seller/supplier the amount paid by him, in case of non-payment of the bills on the due date is called 'Recourse factoring'. The term 'Without recourse' means that the seller has no further interest in the transaction.

Hence, the correct option is (A).

102. Profitability is the primary goal of all business ventures. Profitability is measured with income and expenses. Income is money generated from the activities of the business. For example, if crops and livestock are produced and sold, income is generated.

Hence, the correct option is (A).

103. The act of a person who is a holder of a negotiable instrument in signing his or her name on the back of that instrument, thereby transferring title or ownership is an endorsement. An endorsement may be in favor of another individual or legal entity. An endorsement provides a transfer of the property to that other individual or legal entity. The person to whom the instrument is endorsed is called the endorsee. The person making the endorsement is the endorser. Let us discuss the Endorsement of Instruments here in detail.

Hence, the correct option is (B).

104. Factoring is a means of financing traders manufacturers by taking over their receivables.

Factoring is a financial transaction and a type of debtor finance in which a business sells its accounts receivable to a third party at a discount. A business will sometimes factor in its receivable assets to meet its present and immediate cash needs.

Hence, the correct option is (A).

105. The Reserve Bank of India (RBI) governor, Raghuram Rajan, recently stressed that use of regional languages while engaging with banking customers can go a long way in penetrating banking services. He was speaking at the occasion of presenting the Rajbhasha awards for the financial year 2013-14 to banks. Rajan emphasized that it is the responsibility of the government and the banking sector to provide banking facilities to those who have money but have no access to formal banking channels in a language that they would understand. He added that in these efforts, Hindi and other Indian languages can act as a bridge between the banker and the customer and also pointed out that financial literacy should also be provided in regional languages because customers can connect better when they can speak in their native tongue. Rajan also mentioned the fact that a lot of people fall prey to Ponzi schemes because of the lack of financial literacy.

Hence, the correct option is (A).

106. International factoring usually has two factors viz. export factor and import factor. The export factor looks at financing the exporter and collection of account receivables. The import factor evaluates the importer in respect of collecting the dues in time and assessment of chances of default by the importer.

Hence, the correct option is (B).

107. A syndicated loan, also known as a syndicated bank facility, is financing offered by a group of lenders referred to as a syndicate who work together to provide funds for a single borrower. The loan can involve a fixed amount of funds, a credit line, or a combination of the two.

Hence, the correct option is (B).

108. The Export-Import Bank of India (EXIM Bank) is a specialized financial institution, wholly owned by the Government of India (GOI), for financing, facilitating, and promoting foreign trade in India. It was set up in 1982 by an Act of the Parliament "THE

EXPORT-IMPORT BANK OF INDIA ACT, 1981" at Mumbai, Maharashtra.

Hence, the correct option is (C).

109. A bridge loan is a short-term loan used until a person or company secures permanent financing or removes an existing obligation. Bridge loans are short-term, up to one year, have relatively high-interest rates, and are usually backed by some form of collateral, such as real estate or inventory.

Interim finance allowed by banks to their customer's pending disbursement of term loans by financial institutions.

Hence, the correct option is (C).

110. The capital adequacy ratio is calculated by dividing a bank's capital by its risk-weighted assets. The capital used to calculate the capital adequacy ratio is divided into two tiers

Hence, the correct option is (C).

111. The Reserve Bank is likely to announce within a fortnight the guidelines to operationalize the NPA ordinance so as to expedite the recovery of bad loans that have crossed Rs 8 lakh crore.

The framework would include the creation of a separate cell to identify issues pertaining to non-performing assets (NPAs) or bad loans and have a clause providing a definitive time-frame for the resolution process, sources said.

Hence, the correct option is (D).

112. The forfeiting agency discounts trade receivables of the exporter, without any recourse to him, in the unlikely event of the buyer not paying for the transaction. By converting the exporter's credit sales into cash sales, the forfeiter Protects the exporter from all the risks associated with selling overseas on credit.

Hence, the correct option is (C).

113. It means lending to riskier customers used to describe a mortgage that has a high risk of not being paid back: subprime mortgages/loans/lending This credit crunch was sparked by fears that banks gave out too many subprime mortgages.

Hence, the correct option is (D).

114. Where a cheque payable to order purports to be endorsed by or on behalf of the payee the banker is discharged by payment in due course. He can debit the account of the customer with the amount even though the endorsement turns out subsequently to have been forged, or the agent of the payee without authority endorsed it on behalf of the payee.

Hence, the correct option is (D).

115. Having a code of ethics helps your company define and maintain standards of acceptable behavior. A good ethical framework can help guide your company through times of increased stress, such as rapid growth or organizational change, and decreases your firm's susceptibility to misconduct.

Hence, the correct option is (D).

116. Forfaiting is a method of trade finance that allows exporters to obtain cash by selling their medium and long-term foreign accounts receivable at a discount on a "without recourse" basis.

Forfaiting eliminates virtually all risk to the exporter, with 100 percent financing of the contract value.

Hence, the correct option is (A).

117. Leasing allows the lessee, the use of the asset acquired at today's cost by making payment in future out of future earnings. Perhaps the greatest benefit of leasing a car is the lower out-of-pocket costs when acquiring and maintaining the car. Leases require little or no down payment, and there are no upfront sales tax charges. Additionally, monthly payments are usually lower, and you get the pleasure of owning a new car every few years.

Hence, the correct option is (B).

118. The assets of the Issue Department, against which currency notes are issued under Section 33 of the RBI Act, consist of gold coin and bullion, foreign securities, rupee coin, Government of India rupee securities of any maturity and bills of exchange and promissory notes payable in India which are eligible for purchase by the Bank. The original Act prescribed a proportional reserve of gold and sterling (later foreign) securities against note issue, whereby, not less than 40 percent of the total assets was to consist of gold coin and bullion and sterling (later foreign) securities, stipulating further that gold coin and gold bullion were not, at any time, to be less than Rs. 40 crore. The proportional reserve system was substituted by a minimum reserve system in 1956 through the Reserve Bank of India (Amendment) Act, 1956. The minimum reserve system stipulated the foreign exchange reserves in absolute terms at Rs. 400 crore and gold coins at Rs. 115 crore, making the total minimum asset backing of Rs. 515 crore.

Hence, the correct option is (D).

119. The term 'material alteration' indicates alteration or change in the material parts of the instrument. It may be defined as any change, which alters the very nature of the instrument. Thus, it is the alteration, which changes and destroys the legal identity of the original instrument and causes it to speak a different language in legal effect from that which it originally spoke.

Hence, the correct option is (B).

120. The Goods and Services Tax Law has defined a 'non-resident taxable person' as any person who occasionally undertakes transactions involving the supply of goods or services, or both, whether as principal or agent or in any other capacity, but who has no fixed place of business or residence in India.

From the FEMA angle, a person resident in India means a person residing in India for more than one hundred and eighty-two days during the course of the preceding financial year (April-March) and who has come to or stays in India either for taking up employment, carrying on business or vocation in India or for any other.

Hence, the correct option is (D).

// Notes //